Making Content Comprehensible for English Language Learners

Related Titles

The Crosscultural, Language, and Academic Development Handbook:
A Complete K–12 Reference Guide
Lynne T. Díaz-Rico and Kathryn Z. Weed
ISBN: 0-205-15048-9

Sheltered Content Instruction: Teaching English-Language Learners
with Diverse Abilities
Jana Echevarria and Anne Graves
ISBN: 0-205-16874-4

Language and Cognitive Development in Second Language Learning:
Educational Implications for Children and Adults
Virginia Gonzalez (Editor)
ISBN: 0-205-26170-1

Making Content Comprehensible for English Language Learners

The SIOP Model

Jana Echevarria

California State University, Long Beach

MaryEllen Vogt

California State University, Long Beach

Deborah J. Short

Center for Applied Linguistics, Washington, D.C.

Allyn and Bacon

Boston ▪ London ▪ Toronto ▪ Sydney ▪ Tokyo ▪ Singapore

Series editor: *Arnis E. Burvikovs*
Series editorial assistant: *Bridget Keane*
Marketing manager: *Stephen Smith*
Manufacturing buyer: *Suzanne Lareau*

Library of Congress Cataloging-in-Publication Data

Echevarria, Jana (date)
    Making content comprehensible for English language learners: the SIOP model / Jana Echevarria, MaryEllen Vogt, Deborah J. Short.
        p.   cm.
    Includes bibliographical references (p.) and index.
    ISBN 0-205-29017-5
    1. English language—Study and teaching—Foreign speakers.   2. Language arts—Correlation with content subjects.   I. Vogt, MaryEllen.   II. Short, Deborah. III. Title.

PE1128.A2 E24   1999
428'.0071—dc21   99-048623

Printed in the United States of America
10   9   03   02

For my grandmother, a teacher, and my mother, my first teacher,
for their examples of strength and faith.   J.E.

To my mother, a teacher, and my grandmother, a poet, whose love
of the English language inspired me to follow in their footsteps.
                                                    M.E.V.

To my mother and grandmother, for their tradition of strength
and determination and for their support and encouragement over
the years.   D.J.S.

CONTENTS

PREFACE AND ACKNOWLEDGMENTS

In our many years of teaching English language learners and of preparing teachers to work effectively with them, we found that one critical element was missing: a well-articulated model of sheltered instruction. Few educators agreed on what constituted an effective sheltered lesson, and in our observations of classes across the country we found great variability in the implementation of what was called a sheltered lesson (also called specially designed academic instruction in English, or SDAIE).

The genesis of this book was five years ago when we began reviewing the literature and examining district-produced guidelines for English language learners to find agreement on a definition of sheltered instruction, or SDAIE. A preliminary observation protocol was drafted and we began field testing it with sheltered teachers. Through this process of classroom observation, the instrument was refined and changed, and eventually it evolved into the Sheltered Instruction Observation Protocol (SIOP). (See Appendix A.) The SIOP operationalizes the sheltered model. A research project through the Center for Research on Education, Diversity, & Excellence (CREDE) provided an opportunity to work closely with a group of teachers on the east coast and a group on the west coast to engage in an intensive refinement process and to use the sheltered model in a sustained professional development effort.

The three authors of this book come from different and complementary professional fields. Jana Echevarria's research and publications have focused on issues in the education of English language learners (ELLs), and on ELLs with special education needs, as well as on professional development for regular and special education teachers. MaryEllen Vogt has expertise in reading and language development, with research interests in assessment, intervention for older readers, and effecting teacher change. Deborah Short is a researcher and former sheltered instruction teacher with expertise in second language development, methods for integrating language and content instruction, materials development, and teacher change.

The strength of our differences is that we approach the issue of educating English language learners from different perspectives. In writing the book, each author provided a slightly different lens through which to view and discuss instructional situations. But our varied experiences have led us to the same conclusion: Educators need a resource for planning and implementing high-quality sheltered lessons.

In this book, we illustrate the sheltered model in the most accessible format possible. Using vignettes based on real classroom lessons, we describe each of the 30 components. It is our desire that this book will provide educators with a resource to improve significantly the level of instruction for English language learners.

Acknowledgments

First and foremost we would like to thank Chris Montone who assisted in the development of an earlier version of the SIOP, as well as the many teachers who have provided us with valuable feedback over the past several years. We have had the privilege of working closely with a number of teachers who collaborated with us in refining and clarifying the model: Angie Alvarez, Angela Bennett, Martin Castillo, Jennifer Cesta, Carey Crimmel, Barbara Formoso, Randi Gibson, Enid Good, Danielle Guryansky, Satinder Hawkins, Vernon Johnson, Lew Kerns, Maggie Kerns, Juli Kendall, Rebekkah Kline, Jennifer Kumnick, Robin Liten-Tejada, Charles Norman, Michele Pa'u, Melissa Sutkus, and Janice Tichauer. We would also like to acknowledge the assistance of colleagues who have made this book possible: Rajia Blank, Beverly Boyson, Annette Holmes, Richard Kato, Christina Moreno, Ndeke Nyrenda, and Keith Vogt. Rebecca Dennis, Cathleen McCargo, and Christopher Montone have helped coordinate our research in schools over the past three years, and Jerome Shaw organized a demonstration project of our model at a new site.

This work was supported under the Education Research and Development Program, PR/Award No. R306A60001, The Center for Research on Education, Diversity, & Excellence (CREDE), as administered by the Office of Educational Research and Improvement (OERI), National Institute on the Education of At-Risk Students (NIEARS), U.S. Department of Education (USDOE). The contents, findings, and opinions expressed here are those of the authors and do not necessarily represent the positions or policies of OERI, NIEARS, or the USDOE.

Finally, we express appreciation to our families, whose support has enabled us to pursue our professional interests.

1 Introducing Sheltered Instruction

Javier put his head in his hands and sighed. He watched Ms. Barnett standing at the board and tried to understand what she was telling him. He looked at the clock; she'd been talking for 12 minutes now. She wrote some numbers on the board and he noticed his classmates getting out their books. Copying their actions, he too opened his social studies book to the page matching the first number on the board. He looked at the words on the page and began to sound them out, one by one, softly under his breath. He knew some words but not others. The sentences didn't make much sense. Why was this class so tough? He could understand the teacher much better in science. Mrs. Ontero let them do things. They would all crowd around a table and watch her as she did an experiment and then he got to work with his friends, Maria, Huynh, and Carlos, trying out the same experiment. He even liked the science book; it had lots of pictures and drawings. Mrs. Ontero always made them look at the pictures first and they talked about what they saw. The words on the pages weren't so strange either. Even the big ones matched the words Mrs. Ontero had them write down in their personal science dictionaries. If he forgot what a word meant in the textbook, he would look it up in his science dictionary. Or he could ask someone at his table. Mrs. Ontero didn't mind if he asked for help. This social studies class just wasn't the same. He had to keep quiet, he had to read, he couldn't use a dictionary, they didn't do things. . . .

Javier is experiencing different teaching styles in his seventh-grade classes. He has been in the United States for 14 months now and gets along with his classmates in English pretty well. They talk about CDs and TV shows, jeans and sneakers, soccer and basketball. But schoolwork is hard. Only science class and PE make sense to him. Social studies, health, math, language arts—they're all confusing. He had a class in English as a second language (ESL) last year, but not now. He wonders why Mrs. Ontero's science class is easier for him to understand than the others.

This book addresses the reasons why the science teacher is more effective than her colleagues in promoting Javier's learning. It introduces a research-based model of sheltered instruction (SI) and demonstrates through classroom vignettes how the model can be implemented well. Sheltered instruction is an approach for teaching content to English language learners (ELLs) in strategic ways that make the subject matter concepts comprehensible while promoting the students' English language development. It also may be referred to as SDAIE (specially designed academic instruction in English). Sheltering techniques are used increasingly in schools across the United States, particularly as teachers prepare students to meet high academic standards. However, the use of these techniques is inconsistent from class to class, discipline to discipline, school to school, and district to district. The model of sheltered instruction presented here is intended to mitigate this variability and provide guidance as to what constitutes the best practices for SI, grounded in two decades of classroom-based research, the experiences of competent teachers, and findings from the professional literature.

The goal of this book is to help prepare skillful teachers to teach content effectively to English language learners while they develop the students' language ability. The chapters revolve around the Sheltered Instruction Observation Protocol (SIOP), seen in Appendix A, a training and evaluation instrument that codifies and exemplifies the model. The SIOP may be used as part of a program for preservice and inservice professional development, as a lesson planner for sheltered content lessons, as a training resource for faculty, and as an observation and evaluation measure for site-based administrators and researchers who evaluate teachers. The book is intended for teachers of linguistically and culturally diverse students in K–12 settings, university faculty who prepare such teachers, site-based administrators, and others who provide technical assistance or professional development to K–12 schools.

Background

Each year, the United States becomes more ethnically and linguistically diverse, with over 90% of recent immigrants coming from non-English speaking countries. From the 1985–1986 school year through 1994–1995, the number of limited English proficient (LEP) students in public schools grew 109% while total enrollment increased by only 9.5% (Olsen, 1997). Thus, the proportion of language minority students in the schools is growing even more rapidly than the actual numbers. In 1994–1995, over 3.1 million school-age children were identified as LEP, approximately 7.3% of the K–12 public school student population. It is projected that by the year 2000, Hispanics will constitute the largest minority group of pre-K–12 students in the United States; by 2050, they will represent 30% of that school population (reported in Waggoner, 1999).

While the number of LEP students has grown exponentially across the United States, their level of academic achievement has lagged significantly behind that of their language majority peers. One congressionally mandated study reported that LEP students receive lower grades, are judged by their teachers to have lower academic abilities, and score below their classmates on standardized tests of reading and mathematics (Moss & Puma, 1995). Furthermore, these students have high dropout rates and are more frequently placed in lower ability groups and academic tracks than language majority students (Bennici & Strang, 1995; Cummins, 1994).

These findings reflect growing evidence that most schools are not meeting the challenge of educating linguistically and culturally diverse students well. This

is quite problematic because federal and state governments are calling for *all* students to meet high standards and are adjusting national and state assessments as well as state graduation requirements to reflect these new levels of achievement. In order for students whose first language is not English to succeed in school and become productive citizens in our society, they need to receive better educational opportunities in U.S. schools.

All English language learners in schools today are not alike. They enter U.S. schools with a wide range of language proficiencies (in English and in their native languages) and of subject matter knowledge. In addition to the limited English proficiency and the approximately 180 native languages among the students, we also find diversity in their educational backgrounds, their expectations of schooling, their socioeconomic status, their age of arrival, and their personal experiences while coming to and living in the United States. All these factors impinge on the type of programs and instructional experiences the students should receive in order to succeed in school.

At one end of the spectrum among immigrant students, we find some ELLs who had strong academic backgrounds before they came to the United States and entered our schools. Some of them are above equivalent grade levels in the school's curricula, in math and science for example. They are literate in their native language and may have already begun study of a second language. For these students, much of what they need is English language development so that, as they become more proficient in English, they can transfer the knowledge they learned in their native country's schools to the courses they are taking in the United States.

A few subjects, such as U.S. history, may need special attention because these students may not have studied them before.

At the other end, some immigrant students arrive at our schoolhouse doors with very limited formal schooling—perhaps due to war in their native countries or the remote, rural location of their home. These students are not literate in their native language (i.e., they cannot read or write); and they have not had schooling experiences such as sitting at desks all day, changing teachers per subject, or taking a district- or countrywide test. They have significant gaps in their educational backgrounds, lack knowledge in specific subject areas, and often need time to become accustomed to school routines and expectations.

We also have students who have grown up in the United States but speak a language other than English at home. At one end of the range of students in this group are those students who are literate in their home language, such as Chinese, Arabic, or Spanish, and just need to add English to their knowledge base in school. At the other end are those who are not literate in any language. They have mastered neither English nor the home language and may be caught in a state of semi-literacy that is hard to escape.

Given the variability in these students' backgrounds, they often need different pathways for academic success. To meet this challenge, fundamental shifts need to occur in teacher development, program design, curricula and materials, and instructional and assessment practices. This book will address, in particular, strategies for improved teacher development and instructional practice.

Teacher Preparation and School Reform

Students have difficulty in school for a number of reasons; one may be the mismatch between student needs and teacher preparation. Most teacher preparation colleges do not provide undergraduates with strategies for teaching linguistically and culturally diverse students (Crawford, 1993; Zeichner, 1993). According to the 1993–1994 Schools and Staffing Survey (NCES, 1997), although teachers in regions with larger percentages of limited English proficient students were more likely to have received *some* preparation geared to the needs of these learners, many teachers remain unprepared, not getting training through their undergraduate or graduate work or through inservice opportunities.

Furthermore, the supply of teachers is too small for the demand. The National Commission on Teaching and America's Future (NCTAF, 1996) and McDonnell and Hill (1993) have reported significant shortages of teachers qualified to teach students with limited English proficiency and of bilingual teachers trained to teach in another language. To compensate, principals hire less qualified teachers, use substitutes, cancel courses, increase class size, or ask teachers to teach outside their field of preparation. It is not uncommon to find untrained instructional aides acting as the English language teachers for these students. Thus, many ELLs receive much of their instruction from content area teachers or aides who have not had appropriate professional development to address their second language development needs.

Another reason students may have difficulty is the mismatch among program design, instructional goals, and student needs. Traditionally, when schools have hired ESL or bilingual teachers, they have been placed in charge of the English language learners and were often isolated from regular school programs. Depending on school policy and resource availability, ELLs were schooled in English as a second language or bilingual classes and were not a concern of the regular content classroom teacher until they were ready for exit from the language support program. In theory, the ELLs would be exited when they were proficient in English and able to perform subject area course work in English-medium classrooms. In practice, though, teachers and students could not wait until students were proficient in academic English—the language needed to understand content and do school assignments successfully—before they began to study the subject matter in English.

Research has shown that it may take students from 4 to 10 years of study, depending on the background factors described earlier, before they are proficient in academic English (Cummins, 1981; Collier, 1995). That amount of time, in most cases, is too long to wait. Moreover, in areas where the number of years that students are permitted access to language support services (e.g., bilingual education or ESL) are quite limited, such as in California after the passage of Proposition 227, students are moved into regular classrooms more rapidly and those teachers need appropriate training.

The advent of educational reform that began in the mid-1980s and has taken dramatic steps forward since the passage of Goals 2000: Educate America Act (PL 103-227) in 1994 has significantly raised the stakes for English language learners as most states have restructured their state level accountability measures. In many states, there are new standards for core subject areas, such as English language arts, mathematics, science, and social studies, and all students are expected to pass end-of-grade (or in high school, end-of-course) tests in order to be promoted and graduate. These tests, moreover, have been designed for native English speakers who have spent their entire educational careers in U.S. schools. Most states permit ELLs to be exempted from the tests for 1 to 3 years, although a few states allow no exemption—that is, no time for students to learn English before being required to take the assessments. The result of these accountability changes is that a student who enters a high school with no English proficiency will nonetheless be expected to pass tests in mathematics, biology, and other courses after 3 years of U.S. schooling (at best), and without the benefit, in many cases, of teachers trained to make content instruction comprehensible for English language learners.

Changes in Instructional Practice

The ESL profession has always been sensitive to student needs and the evolution of ESL methodologies has been a dynamic process over the past five decades. Teachers have realized that students would benefit from new instructional approaches and accordingly have adjusted both pedagogical practice and the content of the curriculum. But ESL and bilingual teachers alone cannot provide the necessary educational opportunities these learners need.

In the first half of the twentieth century, most language teaching relied on the direct method of instruction or a grammar translation approach. Yet by the 1950s, direct method and grammar translation languished and audiolingual methods surfaced. In the 1970s and after, the audiolingual method was displaced by the communicative method for ESL teaching, preparing students to use functional language in meaningful, relevant ways. As districts implemented communicative curricula, students were given opportunities to discuss material of high interest and topicality, which in turn motivated them to learn and participate in class. Students were encouraged to experiment with language and assume greater responsibility for their learning.

The communicative approach has engendered the content-based ESL approach. Viewing the grade-level curricula as relevant, meaningful content for ELLs, educators have developed content-based ESL curricula and accompanying instructional strategies to help better prepare the students for their transition to mainstream classes. Content-based ESL classes, in which all the students are ELLs, are taught by language educators whose main goal is English language skill development but whose secondary goal is preparing the students for the regular, English-medium classroom (Cantoni-Harvey, 1987; Crandall, 1993; Mohan, 1986; Short, 1994). The content-based language approach transforms an ESL class into a forum for subject area knowledge generation, application, and reinforcement, by addressing key topics found in grade-level curricula. The sophistication of the material presented necessarily varies according to the language proficiency of the students in class, but nonetheless this material is considered relevant and meaningful by the students.

In content-based ESL, content from multiple subject areas is often presented through thematic instruction. For example, in a primary grade classroom, one theme might be "Life on a Farm." While students learn such language-related elements as names of animals, adjectives, the present continuous tense, and question formation, they also solve addition and subtraction problems, read poems and sing songs about farm animals, discuss the food chain, and draw picture stories, thus exploring objectives from mathematics, language arts, music, science, and art. For the high school classroom, a theme such as "urbanization" might be selected, and lessons could include objectives drawn from environmental science, geography, world history, economics, and algebra. Students with less proficiency might take field trips around a local city and create maps, transportation routes and schedules, and plans for new businesses. Advanced students might learn to use reference materials and computers to conduct research on the development of cities and their respective population growth in their native countries. They might study comparative language structures to compare the cities studied or persuasive language to debate advantages and disadvantages to urbanization.

In general, content-based ESL teachers seek to develop the students' English language proficiency by incorporating information from the subject areas that students are likely to study or from courses they may have missed if they are fairly new to the school system. Whatever subject matter is included, for effective content-based ESL instruction to occur, teachers need to provide practice in academic skills and tasks common to mainstream classes (Adamson, 1990; Mohan, 1990; Chamot & O'Malley, 1994; Short, 1994).

Content-based ESL instruction, however, has not been sufficient to help all ELLs succeed academically. The growth in numbers of students learning English as an additional language and the shortage of qualified ESL and bilingual teachers has quickly extended the need to teach content to these students outside ESL classrooms. The ESL profession began to develop the sheltered content instruction approach in conjunction with content teachers and this process was accelerated by the educational reform movement. Through sheltered instruction, which is described in more detail in the next section, ELLs would participate in a content course with grade-level objectives delivered through modified instruction that made the information comprehensible to the students. The classes may be variously named ESL Pre-Algebra, Sheltered Chemistry, or the like, and a series of courses may constitute a program called Content-ESL, Sheltered Instruction, or SDAIE, yet the goal remains the same: to teach content to students learning English through a developmental language approach.

Content-based ESL and sheltered instruction are favored methods for ELLs today, as reflected in the national standards for English as a second language developed by the professional association, Teachers of English to Speakers of Other Languages. Three of the nine standards in the *ESL Standards for Pre-K–12 Students* (TESOL, 1997) fall under the goal of students being able to use English to achieve academically in all content areas. Students should be able to (1) interact in the classroom; (2) obtain, process, construct, and provide subject matter information in spoken and written form; and (3) use appropriate learning strategies to construct and apply academic knowledge. It is particularly important, therefore, that more teachers be prepared to teach ELLs in appropriate ways so that the students can learn English and the subject matter required for school.

The Sheltered Instruction Approach

This book focuses specifically on sheltered instruction, an approach that can extend the time students have for getting language support services while giving them a jump-start on the content subjects they will need for graduation. The SI approach must *not* be viewed as simply a set of additional or replacement instructional techniques that teachers implement in their classroom. Indeed, the sheltered approach draws from and complements methods and strategies advocated for both second language and mainstream classrooms. This fact is beneficial to English language learners because the more familiar they are with academic tasks and routine classroom activities, the easier it will be for them to focus on the new content once they are in a regular, English-medium classroom. To really make a difference for these students, sheltered instruction must be part of a broader school-based initiative that takes into account the total schooling they need.

For English language learners to succeed, they must master not only English vocabulary and grammar, but also the way English is used in core content classes. This "school English" or "academic English" includes semantic and syntactic knowledge along with functional language use. Using English, students, for example, must be able to read and understand expository prose such as that found in textbooks, write persuasively, argue points of view, and take notes from teacher lectures. They must also articulate their thinking skills in English—make hypotheses and predictions, express analyses, draw conclusions, and so forth. In their various content classes, ELLs must pull together their emerging knowledge of the English language with the content knowledge they are studying in order to complete the academic tasks associated with the content area. They must, however, also learn *how* to do these tasks—generate the format of an outline, negotiate roles in cooperative learning groups, interpret charts and maps, and such. The combination of these three knowledge bases—knowledge of English, knowledge of the content topic, and knowledge of how the tasks are to be accomplished—constitutes the major components of academic literacy (Short, 1998).

Another consideration for school success is the explicit socialization of students to the often implicit cultural expectations of the classroom such as turn-taking, participation rules, and established routines. As Erickson and Shultz (1991) have discussed, student comfort with the social participation structure of an academic task, for instance, can vary according to culturally learned assumptions about appropriateness in communication and in social relationships, individual personality, and power relations in the classroom social system and in society at large. Therefore, many English language learners could benefit from being socialized into culturally appropriate classroom behaviors and interactional styles. As Bartolome (1994) states, teachers need to engage in culturally responsive teaching so that their instruction is sensitive to and builds on culturally different ways of learning, behaving, and using language.

The SI classroom that integrates language and content and infuses sociocultural awareness is an excellent place to scaffold instruction for students learning English. According to Vygotsky (1978) and others, students' language learning is promoted through social interaction and contextualized communication, which can be readily generated in all subject areas. Teachers guide students to construct meaning from texts and classroom discourse and to understand complex content concepts by scaffolding instruction.

When scaffolding, teachers pay careful attention to students' capacity for working in English, beginning instruction at the current level of student understanding, and moving students to higher levels of understanding through tailored support. One way they do so is by adjusting their speech (e.g., paraphrase, give examples, provide analogies, elaborate on student responses) to facilitate student comprehension and participation in discussions where otherwise the discourse might be beyond their language proficiency level (Bruner, 1978). Another way to scaffold is by adjusting instructional tasks so that they are incrementally challenging (e.g., preteach vocabulary before a reading assignment, have students write an outline before drafting an essay) and students learn the skills necessary to complete tasks on their own (Applebee & Langer, 1983). Through these strategies, teachers can socialize students to the academic language setting. Without such teacher assistance, however, ELLs may fail to succeed in content area courses.

Sheltered instruction plays a major role in a variety of educational program designs. It may be part of an ESL program, a late-exit bilingual program, a two-way bilingual immersion program, a newcomer program, or a foreign language immersion program. For students studying content-based ESL or bilingual courses, SI often provides the bridge to the mainstream and the amount of SI provided should increase as students move toward transition out of these programs. Any program in which students are learning content through a non-native language should use the sheltered instruction approach.

In some schools, sheltered instruction is provided to classes composed entirely of English language learners. In others, a heterogeneous mix of native and non-native English speakers may be present. Bilingual, ESL, and content teachers may be the instructors for these classes (Sheppard, 1995). Depending on school system regulations, a sheltered pre-algebra course, for example, might be delivered by an ESL teacher or a mathematics teacher. Ideally, all content teachers would be trained in areas such as second language acquisition and ESL methodology although, as mentioned earlier, often that is not the case. At the high school level, sheltered content courses are generally delivered by content teachers so that students may receive the core content, not elective, credit required for graduation.

Research has shown, however, that a great deal of variability exists in the design of SI courses and the delivery of SI lessons, even among trained teachers (August & Hakuta, 1997; Berman et al., 1995; Kauffman et al., 1994; Sheppard, 1995; Short, 1998) and within the same schools. Some schools, for instance, offer only sheltered instruction courses in one subject area, such as social studies, but not in other areas ELLs must study. It is our experience as well, after two decades of observing SI teachers in class, that one SI classroom does not look like the next in terms of the teacher's instructional language; the tasks the students have to accomplish; the degree of interaction that occurs between teacher and student, student and student, and student and text; the amount of class time devoted to language development issues versus assessing content knowledge; the learning strategies taught to and used by the students; the availability of appropriate materials; and more.

This lack of consistency across SI classes is somewhat predictable. Sheltered curricula for all content areas are few in number and vary widely from school district to school district. Commercial publishers offer a relatively small amount of instructional and pedagogical resources aimed for the SI course. Moreover, much of the literature on SI to date has focused on identifying a wide variety of instructional strategies and techniques that teachers might use to make content comprehensible. Teachers have been encouraged to pick and choose those techniques they enjoy or believe work best with their students and very few teachers are specially prepared to be SI teachers through undergraduate or graduate work. Even those programs that include SI topics on the syllabi of an ESL or bilingual methods course, for example, lack a model for teachers to follow. As a result, teachers do not have sufficient preparation at colleges and universities to implement sheltered instruction effectively. School districts, through inservice workshops may try to address SI techniques on occasion, but the common, traditional models of teacher training—one-shot or short-term workshops or conferences—have been shown to be ineffective (González & Darling-Hammond, 1997; NCTAF, 1997; U.S. Department of Education, 1997), and there is little systematic and sustained forms of professional development available for SI teachers.

A Model for Sheltered Instruction

The development of an SI model is one key to improving the academic success of English language learners: Preservice teachers need it to develop a strong foundation in sheltered instruction, practicing teachers need it to strengthen their lesson planning and delivery and to provide students with more consistent instruction, site-based supervisors need it to train and evaluate teachers. The model described in this book is the product of several research studies conducted by the authors over the past decade. It is grounded in the professional literature and in the experiences and best practice of the researchers and participating teachers who worked collaboratively on developing the observation instrument that codifies it. The theoretical underpinning of the model is that language acquisition is enhanced through meaningful use and interaction. Through the study of content, students interact in English with meaningful material that is relevant to their schooling. Because language processes, such as listening, speaking, reading, and writing, develop interdependently, SI lessons incorporate activities that integrate those skills.

In model SI courses, language and content objectives are systematically woven into the curriculum of one particular subject area, such as fourth-grade language arts, U.S. history, algebra, or life science. Teachers generally present the regular, grade-level subject curriculum to the students through modified instruction in English, although some special curricula may be designed for students with significant gaps in their educational backgrounds or very low literacy skills. Teachers must develop the students' academic language proficiency consistently and regularly as part of the lessons and units they plan and deliver (Crandall, 1993; Echevarria & Graves, 1998; Short, 1991). The SI model we have developed shares many strategies found in high-quality, nonsheltered teaching for native English speakers, but it is characterized by careful attention to the English language learners' distinctive second language development needs.

Accomplished SI teachers modulate the level of English used with and among students and make the content comprehensible through techniques such as the use of visual aids, modeling, demonstrations, graphic organizers, vocabulary previews, predictions, adapted texts, cooperative learning, peer tutoring, multicultural content, and native language support. They strive to create a nonthreatening environment where students feel comfortable taking risks with language. They also make specific connections between the content being taught and students' experiences and prior knowledge and focus on expanding the students' vocabulary base. In effective SI lessons, there is a high level of student engagement and interaction with the teacher, with each other, and with text that leads to elaborated discourse and higher-order thinking. Students also are explicitly taught functional language skills such as how to negotiate meaning, ask for clarification, confirm information, argue, persuade, and disagree. Through instructional conversations and meaningful activities, students practice and apply their new language and content knowledge.

Depending on the students' proficiency levels, SI teachers also offer multiple pathways for students to demonstrate their understanding of the content. For example, teachers may plan pictorial, hands-on, or performance-based assessments for individual students, group tasks or projects, informal class discussions, oral reports, written assignments, portfolios, and more common measures such as paper-and-pencil tests and quizzes to check on student comprehension of the subject matter and language growth. Besides increasing students' declarative knowledge (i.e., factual information), teachers highlight and model procedural knowledge (i.e., how an academic task, such as organizing a science laboratory report, may be accomplished) along with study skills and learning strategies (e.g., note-taking).

The sheltered instruction model is also distinguished by use of supplementary materials that support the academic text. These may include related reading texts (e.g., trade books), graphs and other illustrations, models and other realia, audiovisual and computer-based resources, adapted text, and the like. The purpose of these materials is to enhance student understanding of key topics, issues, and details in the content concepts being taught through alternate means than teacher lecture or dense textbook prose. Supplementary materials can also aid teachers in providing information to students with mixed proficiency levels of English. Some students in a mixed class may be able to use the textbook while others may need an adapted text.

The SI model has been designed for flexibility and tested in a wide range of classroom situations: those with all ELLs and those with a mix of native and non-native English speakers; those with students who have strong academic backgrounds and those with students who have had limited formal schooling; those with students who are recent arrivals and those who have been in U.S. schools for several years; those with students at beginning levels of English proficiency and those with students at advanced levels. In a preliminary study of student writing (using pre- and postmeasures), students who participated in classes taught by teachers trained in the SI model significantly improved their writing skills more than students in classes with non-SI-trained teachers.

It is important to recognize that the SI model does not require teachers to throw away their favored techniques, or add copious new elements to a lesson. Rather, the sheltered instruction model brings together *what* to teach by providing an approach for *how* to teach it. As Figure 1.1 shows, the model offers a framework for selecting and organizing techniques and strategies and facilitates the integration of district- or state-level standards for ESL and for specific content areas.

FIGURE 1.1 What Students Need to Learn: Language and Content

Planning Sheet

ESL Standards (What to Teach)	How to Teach What Students Need SIOP	Content Area Standards (What to Teach)
Listening in English	Preparation	Standard
Speaking in English	Building Background	Benchmark
Reading in English	Comprehensible Input	Performance Task
Writing in English	Strategies	Scoring Guide
	Interaction	
	Practice/Application	
	Lesson Delivery	
	Review/Assessment	

Adapted from Juli Kendall (1998).

Sheltered Instruction Observation Protocol

The first version of the Sheltered Instruction Observation Protocol was drafted five years ago in order to exemplify the model of sheltered instruction we were developing. The preliminary instrument was field-tested with sheltered teachers and refined according to teacher feedback and observations in the classrooms. This early draft, like subsequent ones, pulled together findings and recommendations from the research literature with our professional experiences and those of our collaborating teachers on effective classroom-based practices from the areas of ESL, bilingual education, reading, language and literacy acquisition, discourse studies, special education, and classroom management.

In 1996, the National Center for Research on Education, Diversity & Excellence (CREDE) was funded by the Office of Educational Research and Improvement, U.S. Department of Education, and included a study on sheltered instruction in its research program. The purpose of the research project was to develop an explicit model of sheltered instruction that could be implemented by teachers of students with limited English proficiency in order to improve their academic success. The project built on preliminary versions of the SIOP as a small cohort of teachers worked with the researchers to refine the SIOP further: distinguishing between effective strategies for beginners, intermediate, and advanced English language learners; determining "critical" versus "unique" sheltered teaching strategies; and making the SIOP more user-friendly.

Over the course of the next three years, and with an expanded team of teachers from districts on both the East and West Coasts, the SIOP continued to be refined, strengthened, and used for professional development with research project teachers. A sub-study conducted in 1997 confirmed the SIOP to be a valid and reliable measure of the SI model. The SIOP is used both as an observation instrument for researchers and teachers to match the implementation of lesson delivery to the model of instruction and, as will be explained in more detail in the chapters that follow, as a tool for planning and delivering lessons.

Specifically, the SIOP provides concrete examples of the features of sheltered instruction that can enhance and expand teachers' instructional practice. The protocol is composed of 30 items grouped into three main sections: Preparation, Instruction, and Review/Assessment. The six items under *Preparation* examine the lesson planning process, including the language and content objectives, the use of supplementary materials, and the meaningfulness of the activities. *Instruction* is subdivided into six smaller categories: Building Background, Comprehensible Input, Strategies, Interaction, Practice/Application, and Lesson Delivery. The 20 items in these six categories emphasize the instructional practices that are critical for ELLs, such as making connections with students' background experiences and prior learning, adjusting teacher speech, emphasizing vocabulary development, using multimodal techniques, promoting higher-order thinking skills, grouping students appropriately for language and content development, and providing hands-on materials. As part of the *Review/Assessment* section, four items consider whether the teacher reviewed the key vocabulary and content concepts, assessed student learning, and provided feedback to students on their output.

Each individual item is scored using a five-point Likert scale with scores ranging from "0" to "4." For example, under Preparation item 4 (use of supplementary materials), a teacher would receive a score of "4" if he used supplementary materials (e.g., graphic organizers, visual aids, trade books) to a high degree throughout the lesson, making the lesson clear and meaningful for the ELLs. Another teacher would receive a score of "2" if she only made some use of supplementary materials. A third might receive a "0" if no supplementary materials were used at all. NA (not applicable) is also available if a lesson does not warrant the presence of a particular item. It is not expected that each item would be present in every daily lesson, but it is expected that effective SI teachers would address each item several times over the course of a week.

Overview of the Chapters

This first chapter has introduced you to the pressing educational needs of English language learners and the sheltered instruction model. In Chapters 2 through 9 of this book, we explain the model in detail, drawing from educational theory, research, and practice to describe each category and item on the SIOP. Accompanying each item description are instructional vignettes drawn from classroom lessons of SI teachers and an evaluation of the teachers' performance vis-à-vis the SIOP item under discussion. The illustrated classroom scenes reflect a different grade level and content area in each chapter and are linked to core curriculum objectives. All the classrooms include English language learners. In Chapter 10, we provide a discussion on scoring and interpreting the SIOP, explaining how the instrument can be used holistically to measure teacher fidelity to the model and strategically to explore teacher change in one or more targeted categories. A full lesson from one research classroom is described and scored, revealing areas of strength and areas for improvement that can guide the teacher in future efforts.

As you read each scenario in the chapters that follow, reflect on how effectively the teacher is meeting the linguistic and academic needs of English language learners, especially as related to the item being described. If you were observing this teacher, how would you evaluate his or her teaching effectiveness along the five-point scale? Is the teacher clearly adjusting his or her instruction to meet and move the students' linguistic and cognitive abilities forward, thus earning a "4" for the SIOP indicator? Or, is he or she attempting to modify the instruction but with marginal success, thus earning a "2"? Or, is it clear that he or she has not modified the teaching practices at all to accommodate the needs of ELLs, thus earning a "0"? Then, compare your assessment of the teachers' ability to use sheltered instruction effectively with our evaluations at the conclusion of each vignette.

Using the SIOP: Getting Started

As you begin using the SIOP as a guide to teaching high-quality sheltered instruction, you may want to assess your areas of strength and areas that you want to begin practicing. There are some elements of sheltered instruction that are particularly critical to include when teaching English language learners, while other aspects of the model may be implemented as experience in SI is gained. Therefore, you may wish to begin using the SIOP by focusing on one set of indicators at a time. For example, comprehensible input (see Chapter 4) is critical for ELLs. If you are unfamiliar with comprehensible input techniques, you may want to practice implementing them as a first step. Another important element of sheltered instruction that increases its effectiveness is setting language and content objectives (see Chapter 2) and the way those objectives influence sheltered lessons (see Chapters 8 and 9). Accordingly, those new to SI may want to start with writing and teaching to language and content objectives early in the process of using SI. As proficiency in SI is attained, other elements of the model should be added to one's teaching repertoire.

It is important for coaches and supervisors (e.g., administrators and university field-experience supervisors) to understand that learning to implement the SI model is a process and not all elements will be observed to a high degree in the beginning stages. We encourage supervisors to use a collaborative approach with teachers who are implementing sheltered instruction, including conferencing about observations, setting goals for implementing other features of the model, reflecting on progress in using SI, and so forth.

Summary

Students who are learning English as an additional language are the fastest-growing segment of the school-age population in the United States and almost all candidates in teacher education programs will have linguistically and culturally diverse students in their classes during their teaching careers. However, most of these future teachers—as well as most practicing teachers—are not prepared to instruct these learners. Given school reform efforts and increased state accountability measures, this lack of teacher preparation puts ELLs at risk of educational failure.

This book describes and illustrates a research-based, professional development model of sheltered instruction, an effective approach for teaching both language and content to ELLs, that can increase English language learners' chances of success in school. The model has already been used in a long-term, collaborative, professional development program to train and coach middle school teachers in implementing effective SI in their classes in several large urban districts on the East and West coasts and in the South. The model is operationalized in the Sheltered Instruction Observation Protocol.

The model does not mandate cookie-cutter instruction, but it provides a framework for well-prepared and well-delivered sheltered lessons for any subject area. As SI teachers design their lessons, they have room for creativity and the *art* of teaching. Nonetheless, critical instructional features must be attended to in order for teachers to respond appropriately to the unique academic and language development needs of these students. As you read through this book, you will have the opportunity to explore ways to enhance, expand, and improve your own instructional practice through use of the SI model.

Discussion Questions

1. How would you characterize the type(s) of instruction offered to English language learners in your school or schools you know: traditional ESL, content-based ESL, sheltered content, bilingual content, traditional content? Provide evidence of your characterization in terms of curricula and instruction. Are the ELLs successful when they enter regular, mainstream content classes? Explain.

2. Many sheltered teachers, whether they had special training in a subject area or in second language acquisition, fail to take advantage of the language learning opportunities for students in sheltered content classes. Why do you think this is so? Offer two concrete suggestions for these teachers to enhance their students' language development.

3. Would sheltered classes look different if they were part of a bilingual program rather than an ESL one? Explain your response.

4. What do you think are some necessary conditions for offering sheltered classes to English language learners in your school, or one you are familiar with?

2 Indicators of Lesson Preparation

In this and subsequent chapters, we offer an explanation of each category and indicator on the Sheltered Instruction Observation Protocol (SIOP). At the end of each description, you will find three teaching vignettes for the respective indicator. As you read each scenario, reflect on how effectively the teacher is meeting the needs of English language learners (ELLs), especially as related to the indicator that is described. At the conclusion of each vignette, we offer you our assessment of the teacher's attempts to shelter content instruction and invite you to compare your appraisal to ours.

This chapter introduces the first section of the SIOP: Preparation. Within this section are subsections 1–6: Content Objectives, Language Objectives, Content Concepts, Supplementary Materials, Adaptation of Content, and Meaningful Activities.

Background

As we all know, lesson planning is critical to both a student's and a teacher's success. For maximum learning to occur, planning must produce lessons that enable students to make connections between their own knowledge and experiences, and the new information being taught (Rummelhart, 1995). With careful planning, we make learning meaningful and relevant by including appropriate motivating materials and activities that foster real-life application of concepts studied.

Traditionally, to meet the needs of students who struggled with grade-level reading materials, texts were rewritten according to readability formulae (Gray & Leary, 1935; Ruddell, 1997). The adapted texts included controlled vocabulary and a limited number of concepts, resulting in the omission of critical pieces of information. We have learned that if students' exposure to content concepts is limited by vocabulary-controlled materials, the amount of information they learn over time is considerably less than that of their peers who use grade-level texts. The result is that the "rich get richer and the poor get poorer" (Stanovich, 1986). That is, instead of closing the gap between native English speakers and ELLs, the learning gap is increased and eventually it becomes nearly impossible to close. Therefore, it is imperative that we plan lessons that are not negatively biased for students acquiring English and that include age-appropriate content and materials.

FIGURE 2.1 Preparation Section of the SIOP

4	3	2	1	0	NA
1. Clearly defined **content objectives** for students		**Content objectives** for students implied		No clearly defined **content objectives**	
2. Clearly defined **language objectives** for students		**Language objectives** for students implied		No clearly defined **language objectives** for students	
3. **Content concepts** appropriate for age and educational background level of students		**Content concepts** somewhat appropriate for age and educational background level of students		**Content concepts** inappropriate for age and educational background level of students	
4. **Supplementary materials** used to a high degree, making the lesson clear and meaningful (e.g., graphs, models, visuals)		Some use of **supplementary materials**		No use of **supplementary materials**	NA
5. **Adaptation of content** (e.g., text, assignment) to all levels of student proficiency		Some **adaptation of content** to all levels of student proficiency		No significant **adaptation of content** to all levels of student proficiency	
6. **Meaningful activities** that integrate lesson concepts (e.g., surveys, letter writing, simulations, constructing models) with language practice opportunities for reading, writing, listening, and/or speaking		**Meaningful activities** that integrate lesson concepts, but provide little opportunity for language practice with opportunities for reading, writing, listening, and/or speaking		No **meaningful activities** that integrate language practice	NA

FIGURE 2.2   Unit: The Gold Rush (4th grade)

The classrooms described in the teaching vignettes in this chapter are all in a suburban elementary school with heterogeneously mixed students. English language learners represent approximately 30% of the student population and the children speak a variety of languages. In the fourth-grade classrooms of teachers Ms. Chen, Mrs. Hensen, and Mr. Hargroves, the majority of the ELLs are at the intermediate stage of English fluency.

As part of the fourth-grade social studies curriculum, Ms. Chen, Mrs. Hensen, and Mr. Hargroves have planned a unit on the California Gold Rush. The school district requires the use of the adopted social studies series although teachers are encouraged to supplement the text with primary source materials, literature, and realia. The content topics for the Gold Rush unit include: westward expansion, routes and trails to the West, the people who sought their fortunes, hardships, settlements, the discovery of gold, the life of miners, methods for extracting gold, the impact of the Gold Rush, and so forth.

Each of the teachers has created several lessons for this unit. The first teaching vignettes illustrated here are from a two-day lesson plan (approximately 45 minutes per day) on routes and trails to the West. Specifically, the content of this lesson covers the Oregon Trail, the Overland Trail, and the route around Cape Horn.

The second set of vignettes is from another two-day lesson on how gold was extracted from California's mines and streams, and includes the topics of gold panning, the rocker, and mining.

To demonstrate how three teachers planned instruction for their English language learners, we look at how each designed lessons on the Gold Rush (see Figure 2.2).

Content Objectives

In effective instruction, concrete content objectives that identify what students should know and be able to do should guide teaching and learning. Optimally, these objectives support school-district and state-content standards and learning outcomes. Frequently, in texts and teachers' guides, content objectives are complex and comprehensive, and teachers may or may not present them to students. For English language learners, however, content objectives for each lesson need to be stated simply, orally and in writing, and they need to be tied to specific grade-level content standards (Echevarria & Graves, 1998). An effective lesson plan focuses on products and learning directly related to these objectives. In some cases, students with major gaps in their educational backgrounds may be in special classes, which pull objectives from earlier grades in order to provide the foundational knowledge the students need to perform on-grade-level work successfully. Also, it may be necessary to limit content objectives to only one or two per lesson to reduce the complexity of the learning task.

Most of us learned about the importance of writing and teaching to content objectives early in our professional preparation. However, with all of the other things we must remember to include in each lesson, it is often easy to overlook sharing the objectives, orally and in writing, with students. One of the sheltered teachers who has been using the SIOP during field-testing shared her growing awareness of the importance of clearly stated content objectives for ELLs:

> The objectives are still going on in my class. They're on the board everyday and the students are getting used to seeing them, reading them out loud, and evaluating whether or not we achieved them at the end of each class. I still have questions about the wording and what's a good objective . . . but that will come with time and more discussion and study. I just wanted to say that defining the objectives each day definitely brings more focus to my planning and thinking, and it helps bring order to my classroom procedures. So far, it has not been too burdensome and the habit is definitely forming.

Teaching Scenarios

During their planning, Ms. Chen, Mrs. Hensen, and Mr. Hargroves approached the task of writing and delivering content objectives in different ways.

Example 1   A review of Ms. Chen's lesson plan book indicated the following content objectives for her first lessons on the Gold Rush: "The learner will be able to (1) identify the three main routes to the West on a map, and (2) articulate at least one distinct fact about each of the three trails."

At the beginning of the second day's lesson, Ms. Chen introduced the topic by saying, "Yesterday, we learned that some explorers and adventurers decided that it would be easiest and fastest to travel to the West by boat. They went around Cape Horn [*points to wall map*]. Others decided to go a different way. They chose to go across the country by land."

Ms. Chen then referred to the written objectives on the board and added, "Today, we're going to learn about two more of the land routes to the West called the Overland Trail and the Oregon Trail [*points to the objectives on the board*]. You will learn where these trails were and what they were like. You will show that you know where the routes were by coloring them on your map of the United States. You will also be able to tell a friend one important fact about each trail."

SIOP Evaluation: On the SIOP, Ms. Chen received a "4" for the Content Objectives indicator. She clearly, explicitly, and simply stated the content objectives for the lesson. She reinforced the objectives by relating them to what was taught the previous day. She also wrote the objectives on the board and referred students to them as she presented them orally.

FIGURE 2.3   SIOP Evaluation for Ms. Chen: Content Objectives

④	3	2	1	0	NA
1. Clearly defined **content objectives** for students		**Content objectives** for students implied		No clearly defined **content objectives**	

Example 2   A review of Mr. Hargroves's lesson plan book indicated the following content objective for his first lesson on the Gold Rush: "The learner will be able to compare and contrast the three major routes to California."

Mr. Hargroves began his lesson by stating, "Today, you'll learn about the Overland Trail. Eventually, you need to compare and contrast the Overland Trail, the route around Cape Horn, and the Oregon Trail." He then added, "We'll also be working on maps and I want you to color the Overland Trail a different color from the color you used for the Cape Horn route. When you learn about the Oregon Trail, you'll complete the map with a third color. By the time you're finished, you should have all three routes drawn on the map using different colors."

SIOP Evaluation: On the SIOP, Mr. Hargroves received a "2" for the Content Objectives indicator. He had written a content objective and he had orally stated what it was he wanted his students to learn. However, his English language learners might have had difficulty understanding what they were to learn and do. He did not state his objectives in simple terms and some students may have inferred that the purpose for the lesson was the coloring activity rather than learning where the trails and routes were. Further, the content objectives were not written on the board or shown on an overhead projector for the students to see.

FIGURE 2.4   SIOP Evaluation for Mr. Hargroves: Content Objectives

4	3	②	1	0	NA
1. Clearly defined **content objectives** for students		**Content objectives** for students implied		No clearly defined **content objectives**	

Example 3   A review of Mrs. Hensen's lesson plan book revealed no content objectives for the Gold Rush lessons on the routes and trails. She began her lesson with a brief lecture on the Overland Trail, after which she distributed a map of the United States. She then directed the students to independently read the paragraphs describing the route around Cape Horn and the Overland Trail. When they were finished reading, students were told to color both trails onto their maps.

SIOP Evaluation: Mrs. Hensen received a "0" on the SIOP for the Content Objectives indicator. She did not define any content objectives for the students, but just began the lesson with her brief lecture followed by the other assignments. Some students may have been able to infer the purpose of the map work but English language learners may have been unaware of the purpose for these assignments.

FIGURE 2.5   SIOP Evaluation for Mrs. Hensen: Content Objectives

4	3	②	1	0	NA
1. Clearly defined **content objectives** for students		**Content objectives** for students implied		No clearly defined **content objectives**	

Language Objectives

While carefully planning and delivering content objectives, sheltered instruction teachers should also incorporate in their lesson plans techniques that support students' language development (Short, 1999). As with content objectives, language objectives should be stated clearly and simply, and students should be informed of them, both orally and in writing.

A wide variety of language objectives can be planned according to the goals and activities in the lesson. In some cases, language objectives may focus on developing students' vocabulary. Other lessons may lend themselves to reading comprehension skills practice or the writing process, helping students to brainstorm, outline, draft, revise, edit, and complete a text. Students also benefit from objectives that highlight functional language use such as how to request information, justify opinions, negotiate meaning, provide detailed explanations, and so forth. Higher-order thinking skills, such as articulating predictions or hypotheses, stating conclusions, summarizing information, and making comparisons, can be tied to language objectives too. Sometimes specific grammar points can be taught as well; for example, learning about capitalization when studying famous historical events and persons, or teaching language structure to help ELLs develop new vocabulary.

To illustrate, in a science lesson on photosynthesis, you might introduce the meaning of the morpheme "photo" along with other words that carry the meaning of "light" such as "photography," "photogenic," and "photo-finish." It is important to draw students' attention to opportunities for identifying English words through analogy, recognizing similarities in English structure.

Remember, as you teach and assess these language objectives in your lessons, you can plan for multilevel responses from the students according to their proficiency in English. For example, you might use group response techniques (e.g., thumbs-up/thumbs-down) for students who are in the early stages of English language development. For students who are more proficient English speakers, incorporate activities that involve partner work and small group assignments so that ELLs can practice their English in a less-threatening setting. When possible, accept approximations and multiple word responses rather than complete sentences because this supports English development. However, it is also appropriate to require ELLs, depending on their level of proficiency, to give answers in one or two complete sentences. This develops language skills because it requires students to move beyond what may be their comfort zone in using English.

English language development is also nurtured in classrooms where language structure is taught in order to help ELLs develop new vocabulary.

Teaching Scenarios

The three teachers' lessons on routes and trails to the West continue.

Example 1   A review of Ms. Chen's lesson plans revealed the following language objectives: "The learner will be able to (1) articulate why names are given to particular places, (2) generate names of local streets and landmarks, (3) tell why the three routes were given their names, and (4) explain how the structure of some words gives clues to their meanings."

Prior to reading the text, Ms. Chen referred to the words she had previously written on the board: Route around Cape Horn, Oregon Trail, and Overland Trail. She also read the written language objective from the board, "You will be able tell why the routes were named the way they were, and how places receive their names. You will also learn how the structure of some words gives clues to their meanings." She told students to think about the names of the places they were going to be reading about and to be ready to talk about why places have particular names. On the board she wrote the question, "Why are places given particular names?"

Following a shared reading of the text, Ms. Chen asked the students to examine the map of the United States on the wall and try to determine why the three main trails to the West were named as they were. The children volunteered appropriate ideas for the first two. Ms. Chen then wrote, "Over + land = Overland." One child said, "I get it! They went over the land!" The teacher reinforced this by pointing out the "over the land" route on the wall map. She then wrote "Route around Cape Horn" on the board and asked students to think about the name's meaning while directing them to look at the map. One child said, "Look, the land looks kind of like a horn. And, they had to sail around it!"

After validating his response, Ms. Chen asked students to call out some of the names of streets on which they lived. They offered First Street, River Avenue, Main Street, and Mill Creek Road, among others. Ms. Chen then suggested that trails, routes, streets, avenues, highways, and so forth are often named after geographical landmarks. She explained that we can learn about places and surrounding areas by examining their names. To check students' understandings, she asked each student to tell another child why the three routes to the West were given their respective names.

SIOP Evaluation: Ms. Chen received a "4" on the SIOP for the Language Objectives indicator. First, she read the primary language objective from the board. She scaffolded the students' understandings of the names of the routes and trails by having them examine the names of familiar street names, and then she led them through an analysis of the names of the historical routes, such as "over + land." She pointed out the compound word and supported students' approximations. Her language objectives were clearly stated in her lesson plan, she told them to her students, and she wrote them on the board.

FIGURE 2.6   SIOP Evaluation for Ms. Chen: Language Objectives

④	3	2	1	0	NA
2. Clearly defined **language objectives** for students		**Language objectives** for students implied		No clearly defined **language objectives** for students	

Example 2   A review of Mrs. Hensen's plan book indicated no specific language objectives for this lesson. She began the Gold Rush lesson on routes and trails by assigning a section of the text to be read independently. When students finished reading, Mrs. Hensen directed them to work with two other children. She wrote the names of the three trails on the board as well as a list of terms the students encountered in their reading. She asked each triad to divide up the routes and directed the students to retrace them on their maps.

One child in each group was to trace the route around Cape Horn and to identify, from the board, the key vocabulary associated with that route. Then, this child was to tell the other two students how to color their maps, using the map in the text and the key language on the board as a guide. The second child in each group traced the Overland Trail, and it was his or her job to explain the route to the other two students who then completed their maps. The third child in each group repeated the process with the Oregon Trail. Mrs. Hensen circulated throughout the room while the children completed the mapping activity, assisting as necessary.

SIOP Evaluation: Mrs. Hensen received a "2" for the Language Objectives indicator. Although she had no stated language objectives, she did write key vocabulary on the board. She scaffolded the mapping activity by having the children work in triads and by having each group member explain the mapping and key words to the others. This activity was appropriate for beginning ELLs because each child only explained one route and the explanation was not "public." She also had her students practice listening and speaking as they gave explanations orally in their groups. It would have been more effective had Mrs. Hensen explained her language objectives to the children, emphasizing the importance of listening carefully and of giving clear directions. Even though one purpose of the lesson was to build listening and speaking skills, the children were not informed of these objectives either orally or in writing.

FIGURE 2.7   SIOP Evaluation for Mrs. Hensen: Language Objectives

4	3	②2	1	0	NA
2. Clearly defined **language objectives** for students		**Language objectives** for students implied		No clearly defined **language objectives** for students	

Example 3   A review of Mr. Hargroves's lesson plan revealed no specific language objectives. Throughout his lesson, he had the students working independently on both the reading assignment and the map activity. His directions were given orally and, although he used the names of the routes and trails, he did not write any of them on the board. He used the wall map to illustrate the location of the three trails. Because the children were working independently, they had no opportunity to use language skills or key vocabulary.

SIOP Evaluation: Mr. Hargroves received a "0" for the Language Objectives indicator. He did not include any language objectives in his lesson plan and he did not suggest any to the students. He did not discuss the meanings of the names or terms used in his demonstration and explanations, nor did he encourage his students to orally use the terminology and concepts during discussion. Further, Mr. Hargroves expected students to read the textbook without any type of support. All his instruction was conveyed orally and the students worked independently throughout the lesson.

FIGURE 2.8 SIOP Evaluation for Mr. Hargroves: Language Objectives

4	3	2	1	⓪	NA
2. Clearly defined **language objectives** for students		**Language objectives** for students implied		No clearly defined **language objectives** for students	

Content Concepts

While planning, carefully consider the content concepts you wish to teach and use district curriculum guidelines and grade-level content standards to guide you. In sheltered classrooms, this entails ensuring that although materials may be adapted to meet the needs of English language learners, the content is not diminished. When planning lessons around content concepts, consider the following: (1) the students' first language (L1) literacy, (2) their second language (L2) proficiency, (3) their reading ability, (4) the cultural and age appropriateness of the L2 materials, and (5) the difficulty level of the material to be read (Gunderson, 1991, p. 21).

Additionally, reflect on the amount of background experience needed to learn and apply the content concepts and include ways to activate students' prior knowledge related to them. For example, fourth-grade students typically learn about magnetism, yet some ELLs may not have the requisite background knowledge to understand this concept. Rather than defuse the content, use what prior knowledge students do have and then include explicit background information that builds a foundation for their understanding of magnetism.

Providing adequate background requires teachers to perform a *task analysis*—a process in which you carefully analyze the requisite knowledge a student must possess in order to understand what is being taught. The purpose is to lessen the gap between what a student knows and what he or she must learn. This can be accomplished by modifying the lesson to include substantial background building, or through a small group mini-lesson that precedes the regular whole class lesson (Vogt, 1995). This mini-lesson provides a "jump-start" by reviewing key background concepts, introducing vocabulary, leading a picture or text "walk" through the reading material, engaging in simulations or role-plays, or hands-on experiential activities. The jump-start mini-lesson develops context and access for children who may lack appropriate background knowledge or experience with the grade-level content concepts. In heterogeneous classes in which ELLs study with native English speakers, peer tutors can be used to teach some of the requisite background information as well.

You are the one to decide when to modify content concepts by providing extensive background building for the whole class, or by teaching a brief jump-start lesson to a small group. If you have a large number of English language learners who are in the early stages of language development, you may need to include extensive background building. If you have a small group of ELLs who have intermediate language proficiency, the jump-start mini-lesson may provide sufficient scaffolding and access to the content concepts.

Remember that it is usually inappropriate to teach students curriculum intended for younger children simply because of their limited English proficiency. It is your responsibility to determine students' background knowledge and provide the necessary scaffolding to enable everyone to learn the age-appropriate concepts and information. Occasionally, this requires teaching lower grade-level curriculum to fill gaps in students' background knowledge.

Teaching Scenarios

Examples 1, 2, and 3   Each of the previous scenarios indicates that the three fourth-grade teachers, Ms. Chen, Mrs. Hensen, and Mr. Hargroves, were teaching a unit on the Gold Rush. This unit is appropriate because in the state where these teachers teach, California history is the required social studies curriculum for the fourth grade. The teachers did not dilute the content and concepts for their English language learners.

SIOP Evaluation: The three teachers, Ms. Chen, Mrs. Hensen, and Mr. Hargroves, all received a "4" on the SIOP for the Content Concepts indicator. The content they taught was appropriate for the grade level they were teaching and for the district's content standards.

FIGURE 2.9 SIOP Evaluation for Ms. Chen, Mrs. Hensen, and Mr. Hargroves: Content Concepts

④	3	2	1	0	NA
3. **Content concepts** appropriate for age and educational background level of students		**Content concepts** somewhat appropriate for age and educational background level of students		**Content concepts** inappropriate for age and educational background level of students	

Supplementary Materials

Information that is embedded in context allows English language learners to understand and complete more cognitively demanding tasks. Effective sheltered instruction involves the use of many supplementary materials that support the core curriculum and contextualize learning. This is especially important for students who do not have grade-level academic backgrounds and/or who have language and learning difficulties. Since lectures and pencil-and-paper activities centered around a text are often difficult for these students, remember to plan for supplementary materials that will enhance meaning and clarify confusing concepts, making lessons more relevant.

A variety of supplementary materials also supports different learning styles and multiple ways of knowing (multiple intelligences) because information and concepts are presented in a multifaceted manner. Students can see, hear, feel, perform, create, and participate in order to make connections and construct personal, relevant meanings. Supplementary materials provide a real-life context and enable students to bridge prior experiences with new learning.

Examples of supplementary materials that can be used to create context and support content concepts include the following:

- **Hands-on manipulatives:** These can include anything from Cuisinaire rods for math to microscopes for science to globes for social studies.
- **Realia:** These are real-life objects that enable students to make connections to their own lives. Examples include bank deposit slips and check registers for a unit on banking, or nutrition labels on food products for a health unit.
- **Pictures:** Photographs and illustrations depict nearly any object, process, or topic, and magazines, commercial photos, and hand drawings can provide visual support for a wide variety of content and vocabulary concepts.
- **Visuals:** These can include overhead transparencies, models, graphs, charts, timelines, maps, props, and bulletin board displays. Students with diverse abilities often have difficulty processing an inordinate amount of auditory information and are advantaged with visual clues.
- **Multimedia:** A wide variety of multimedia materials are available to enhance teaching and learning. These range from simple tape recordings to videos to interactive CD-ROMs to an increasing number of resources available on the World Wide Web.
- **Demonstrations:** Vygotsky (1978) states that students' learning is enhanced when teachers or other individuals provide scaffolding for less-experienced students. You can scaffold ELLs by carefully planning demonstrations that model how to follow steps or directions needed to complete tasks, and that include supplementary materials. Teachers can also demonstrate and/or model language, like how to give an oral presentation. Students can then practice these steps in groups or alone, with you or other experienced individuals nearby to assist as needed.

- **Related literature:** A wide variety of fiction and nonfiction can be included to support content teaching. The literature enables readers to create what Rosenblatt (1991) refers to as an "aesthetic response." This type of literature response is characterized by personal feelings about what is read. Aesthetic responses to literature promote more reading of literature, and hopefully, a deeper understanding of the concepts that are depicted—what Rosenblatt refers to as a *transactional experience.*
- **Adapted text:** A type of supplementary reading material that can be very effective for English language learners, as well as struggling readers, is adapted text. Without significantly diminishing the content concepts, a piece of text (usually from a grade-level textbook) is adapted to reduce the readability demands. Complicated, lengthy sentences with specialized terminology are rewritten in abbreviated form with definitions given for difficult vocabulary, if possible, in context. Please note that we are not advocating "dumbing down" the textbook, an approach that in the past yielded easy-to-read materials with virtually no content concepts left intact. Rather, we suggest that the major concepts be retained and just the readability level of the text be reduced. (For more discussion about adapted text, see the Adaptation of Content section later in this chapter.)
- **Graphic organizers:** Organizers that help students make relationships among key concepts and vocabulary can also supplement instruction (see Adaptation of Content, p. 31, for a full discussion of graphic organizers).

Teaching Scenarios

Examples of lessons from the three previously introduced fourth-grade teachers follow for the Supplementary Materials indicator.

Example 1   Ms. Chen's lesson plan revealed a long list of supplementary materials, including pans, washtub, water, pyrite, rocker, sand, pick, library books on the Gold Rush, worksheets, and butcher paper.

She began her lesson on the various methods used to extract gold by having the children brainstorm all the places they could imagine where gold can be found. She listed the students' ideas on the board: mountains, rocks, rivers, ground, dirt, and lakes. After Ms. Chen asked how miners might get gold from each of the listed spots, the students offered several possibilities.

In small groups, the students then read a brief section of the textbook together, with members volunteering to read a paragraph at a time. Ms. Chen asked each group to jot down any vocabulary from the reading related to extracting gold, in particular panning, rockers, and mining.

Following the reading, Ms. Chen introduced the process of panning for gold. She brought to the front table a large plastic dishpan, an old pie pan, a container of sand, and a pitcher of water. She poured the water into the dishpan, added the sand, and from her pocket she took several small chunks of iron pyrite ("fool's gold"), which she dropped into the sandy water. She then invited volunteers to try to "pan," encouraging them to "shake" the pan by gently moving it back and forth.

Ms. Chen then asked for volunteers to try the "rocker"—a model of the primitive plywood device intended to sort gold from rocks, dirt, and debris. Several children rocked the wooden device back and forth and the class discussed which of the two methods, panning or rocking, might be the most effective in extracting gold.

Last, Ms. Chen showed the class a pick that resembled what the miners might have used. She also showed several pictures of miners deep in caves, picking at the stone walls searching for a gold strain.

Following the experiment, the students were referred back to the pictures and explanations in the textbook for help in understanding the use of the three methods. Each group was given a resource book from the library on the topic of the Gold Rush. Students were asked to find additional information about gold panning, the rocker, and mining, and to complete, as a group, a graphic organizer. It was divided into nine boxes; each vertical column was labeled with "Panning," "Rocker," and "Mining." The three horizontal sections were labeled with "Describe the process," "Where the process was used," and "Tools needed." Students were asked to use the resource books and the textbook to fill in the three columns. The groups then reported to the entire class and Ms. Chen clarified responses by referring back to the models, photos, and illustrations.

SIOP Evaluation: Ms. Chen received a "4" for the Supplementary Materials indicator. She incorporated in her lesson plan the use of realia, visuals, and related nonfiction literature to support and enhance her instruction.

FIGURE 2.10   SIOP Evaluation for Ms. Chen: Supplementary Materials

④	3	2	1	0	NA
4. **Supplementary materials** used to a high degree, making the lesson clear and meaningful (e.g., graphs, models, visuals)		Some use of **supplementary materials**		No use of **supplementary materials**	

Example 2   In her lesson plan, Mrs. Hensen listed the textbook and a poster as resources for her lesson on panning gold. She introduced the lesson by having the students turn to page 143 in their history textbooks. This chapter is in the middle of the unit on the Gold Rush and Mrs. Hensen began by reading the chapter aloud. On page 144 were illustrations of a pan and a rocker, and she drew attention to these as she continued to read. Additionally, she held up a large, poster-sized picture of a miner, which was an enlarged version of a picture in the textbook. As Mrs. Hensen wrote vocabulary on the board (pan, rocker, fool's gold, nugget), she

motioned to the poster of the miner and had students find examples of the words in the picture.

SIOP Evaluation: On the SIOP, Mrs. Hensen received a "1" for the Supplementary Materials indicator. She attempted to help her students understand the panning process by showing them the pictures in the text. She used the poster-sized picture of the miner replicated from the textbook to reinforce some vocabulary but did not plan for the use of any other supplementary materials to enhance the lesson.

FIGURE 2.11 SIOP Evaluation for Mrs. Hensen: Supplementary Materials

4	3	2	①	0	NA
4. **Supplementary materials** used to a high degree, making the lesson clear and meaningful (e.g., graphs, models, visuals)		Some use of **supplementary materials**		No use of **supplementary materials**	

Example 3 In Mr. Hargroves's plan book, he listed the textbook as the resource for this lesson. Recall that during the previous lesson on the routes and trails, Mr. Hargroves had students read the chapter independently. He discovered the text was too difficult, so he changed his approach for this lesson. He presented a lecture on gold panning and the use of the rocker, and referred students to the pictures in the textbook. One student had visited Sutter's Fort in Sacramento and had actually panned for gold. This child enthusiastically shared his information with the other children. The students were then asked to write an essay on how gold was found during the Gold Rush. Mr. Hargroves collected these and told the students they would receive a writing grade for their efforts.

SIOP Evaluation: Mr. Hargroves received a "0" for the Supplementary Materials indicator. He made no attempt to demonstrate, model, or show visuals or other resources to support learning other than the illustrations in the students' textbooks. Because Mr. Hargroves delivered the content orally, some ELLs may have had difficulty making connections between the lecture and the illustrations in their books.

FIGURE 2.12 SIOP Evaluation for Mr. Hargroves: Supplementary Materials

4	3	2	1	⓪	NA
4. **Supplementary materials** used to a high degree, making the lesson clear and meaningful (e.g., graphs, models, visuals)		Some use of **supplementary materials**		No use of **supplementary materials**	

Adaptation of Content

In many schools, teachers are required to teach from textbooks that are too difficult for English language learners to read. We have previously mentioned the problem of "watering down" text to the point where all students can read it; content concepts are frequently lost when the text is adapted in this way. We also know ELLs cannot be expected to learn all content information through listening to lectures.

Therefore, we must find ways to make the text and other resource materials accessible for all students, adapting them so that the content concepts are left intact (Short, 1991). Several ways of doing this have been recommended for students who have reading difficulties (Readance, Bean, & Baldwin, 1991; Ruddell, 1997; Vacca & Vacca, 1998; Vogt, 1992), and they work equally well for English language learners. These approaches can be used throughout a lesson, as a prereading instructional strategy, as an aid during reading, and as a postreading method for organizing newly learned information.

Suggestions for adapting content to make it more accessible include the following:

- **Graphic organizers:** These are schematic diagrams that provide conceptual clarity for information that is difficult to grasp. They help students identify key content concepts and make relationships among them (Muth & Alvermann, 1999). Graphic organizers also provide students with visual clues they can use to supplement written or spoken words that may be hard to understand. When used prior to reading, students can use the organizers as a guide and as a supplement to build background for difficult or dense text. When used concurrently with reading, they focus students' attention and help them make connections (e.g., Venn diagram), take notes, and understand the text structure (e.g., a timeline informs students the text will be organized chronologically). When used after reading, graphic organizers can be used to record personal understandings and responses (Macon, Buell, & Vogt, 1991; Buehl, 1995). Graphic organizers include story or text structure charts, Venn diagrams, story or text maps, timelines, discussion webs, word webs, clusters, thinking maps, and so forth.
- **Outlines:** Teacher-prepared outlines equip students with a form for note-taking while reading dense portions of text, thus providing scaffolded support. These are especially helpful if major concepts, such as the Roman numeral level of the outline, are already filled in. The students can then add other information to the outline as they read. For some students, an outline that is entirely completed may be helpful to use as a guide to reading and understanding the text.
- **Leveled study guides:** These are study guides designed specifically for diverse students' needs. All students are expected to master the key concepts in the text; however, depending on students' language and literacy development, the leveled study guides are written differently. For some students who can easily read the text material, the study guides extend and enrich the

subject material and they include challenging questions or tasks. For other students, leveled study guides lead them through the material with definitions and "hints" for unlocking the meaning, and they include less challenging questions and tasks. For some ELLs and struggling readers, the study guides may include brief summaries of the text along with more manageable questions and tasks. Questions, tasks, and statements on the leveled study guides can be marked with asterisks as follows (from most manageable to most challenging):

* All students are to respond to these questions/statements/tasks

** Group 1 students are required to complete these questions/statements/tasks

*** Group 2 students are required to complete these questions/statements/tasks

Of course, the option to try the more challenging questions or statements should be open to all students.

- **Highlighted text:** A few literature anthologies or content textbooks may be reserved for students acquiring English and/or for those with delayed literacy development. Overriding ideas, key concepts, important vocabulary, and summary statements are highlighted (by the teacher or other knowledgeable person) prior to the students using the books. Students are encouraged to first read only the highlighted sections. As confidence and reading ability improve, more of the unmarked text is attempted. The purpose of highlighted text is to reduce the reading demands of the text, while still maintaining key concepts and information.

- **Taped text:** Key portions (such as the highlighted text just mentioned), or the entire text is recorded and students are encouraged to listen to the tape while they follow along in the book. For some students, multiple exposures to the taped text may result in a more thorough understanding. Ideally, tapes should be available for both home and school learning center use.

- **Adapted text:** As mentioned earlier in this chapter, text adaptation involves rewriting selected sections of text that contain key concepts and information. Although time consuming, rewriting text is an effective modification of curricular materials because information is organized in small sequential steps, avoiding long, dense passages. Short, simpler sentences are rewritten from long, complex ones. An example of a complex sentence from a science text follows: "Electrons have negative electric charges and orbit around the core, nucleus, of an atom." A simple adaptation of this sentence is, "Electrons have negative charges. They orbit around the core. The core of the atom is called the nucleus."

Ideally, rewritten paragraphs should include a topic sentence with several supporting details. Maintaining a consistent format promotes easier reading for information-seeking purposes. All sentences included in the rewritten text should be direct and relevant to the subject. In the following example, a paragraph of original text is taken from an anthology theme in a reading series (Cooper, Pikulski, Au, Calderon, Comas, Lipson, Mims, Page, Valencia, & Vogt, 1999). This passage was excerpted from a piece of nonfiction literature, *Into the Mummy's Tomb*, written by Nicholas Reeves.

Original text: "Tutankhamen's mummy bore a magnificent mask of burnished gold, which covered its face and shoulders. Its headcloth was inlaid with blue glass. The vulture and cobra on its forehead, ready to spit fire at the pharaoh's enemies, were of solid gold" (p. 237).

We have rewritten the original text as follows:

Adapted text: "King Tutankhamen's mummy wore a grand mask, made of very shiny gold. It covered the face and shoulders of the body. The part of the mask over the forehead looked like a gold headcloth. Blue glass was set into the headcloth. Shapes of a vulture (a type of bird) and a cobra (a type of snake) were above the eyes on the mask. They were solid gold. The artist made them look like they could attack the pharaoh's (King Tut's) enemies."

Obviously, adapting text like this takes time and is not easy to do. Note here that the adapted version is slightly longer than the original, which often happens when definitions are included. If you have a large number of ELLs in your classroom, adapted text can be very beneficial, and it is worth the time and effort to provide students with more accessible material. Be sure to have a colleague read the adapted text to make sure it clarifies rather than confuses the content.

- **Jigsaw text reading:** Originally designed as a cooperative learning activity for all students, Jigsaw works well with English language learners when there is a difficult-to-read text. One or two members from each cooperative learning group come together to form a new group of "experts." Assign each new "expert" group one section of the text to be read. This group either reads the text orally taking turns, or in partners they read to each other, or they can read the text silently. Following the reading, each "expert" group reviews and discusses what was read, determining the essential information and key vocabulary. You need to check carefully with each "expert" group to make sure all members understand the material they have read.

After you feel sure that the "experts" know their assigned information, they return to their original groups and teach fellow group members what they learned. This process scaffolds the learning of ELLs because in both groups they are working with others who have English proficiency and perhaps more background information on the topic. Text can be read with other students, reducing the demands of lengthy sections. Depending on English proficiency, ELLs may join an "expert" group individually or with a partner. It is important that you select the "expert" groups rather than letting the students choose their own group members.

- **Marginal notes:** As with highlighted text, you may wish to reserve a few textbooks for English language learners and struggling readers. Print marginal notes directly in the margin of the textbook pages or duplicate notes on a handout that students can put alongside a page they are reading. The marginal notes, or handout, should include hints for understanding the content, key concepts, and/or key vocabulary and definitions. The notes, whether in the textbook's margin or on a handout, are similar to the ones often found in teachers' guides.

  Most marginal notes either deal specifically with content (e.g., "Cell division includes two phases: mitosis and meiosis"), or with hints for reading a passage (e.g., "This paragraph explains why General George Armstrong Custer believed he could win the Battle of Little Big Horn. As you read it, think about whether his reasons make sense."). Marginal notes reduce ambiguity as well as the reading difficulty of the text, making it more accessible and less intimidating.

  You may be thinking that marginal notes create an unnecessary burden for the teacher. Please note that once you have completed a set for one textbook, whether in the margins or on handouts, teaching assistants (parent volunteers, other adults, or capable students) can copy them in other student texts. Obviously, this type of scaffolding only works when you have extra textbooks you can write in or when you can assign specific books to particular students.

Teaching Scenarios

How do the fourth-grade teachers plan for content adaptations to accommodate their English language learners? Let's take a look at their classrooms.

Example 1   Recall that Ms. Chen demonstrated the various methods for extracting gold. She assigned the graphic organizer for comparing the methods of extracting gold and students completed these in groups. Together, students read the supplementary library articles dealing with the three processes, and compared the new information with what they gleaned from the textbook. The library resources were at a variety of interest and readability levels, and all included colorful illustrations.

SIOP Evaluation: Ms. Chen received a "4" for the Adaptation of Content indicator. Following the demonstration and "hands-on" experience (trying the rocker), students read the text with a partner or small group, reducing the reading demands. Then students worked with group members to complete the nine-box graphic organizer, checking their responses with the information from the text and resource books. Last, all groups reported to the whole class, reinforcing once again what had been learned.

  Throughout Ms. Chen's lesson plans, she included specific adaptations and methods that provide scaffolded support for students. Her careful attention to planning for her English language learners' linguistic and learning needs is reflected in the lessons she taught.

FIGURE 2.13 SIOP Evaluation for Ms. Chen: Adaptation of Content

④	3	2	1	0	NA
5. **Adaptation of content** (e.g., text, assignment) to all levels of student proficiency		Some **adaptation of content** to all levels of student proficiency		No significant **adaptation of content** to all levels of student proficiency	

Example 2 Following the lesson on the various methods for finding gold, Mrs. Hensen prepared a study guide to help her students read an article on the settling of Columbia, an 1860s Gold Rush town in the California Sierra Mountains. The article, taken from an old newspaper, contained some archaic expressions as well as references to the events of the day. Predicting the article would be quite difficult for her English language learners, Mrs. Hensen summarized some of the key points in it, defined some unusual terminology, and included questions in the study guide to direct the students' reading. All students, including those acquiring English, were expected to read the article and complete the study guide questions independently.

SIOP Evaluation: On the SIOP, Mrs. Hensen received a "3" for the Adaptation of Content indicator. The study guide she prepared most likely helped students focus on the key concepts and vocabulary in the article. However, because the same study guide was used by all students regardless of their language and literacy proficiencies and because they were required to read the article independently, some ELLs still may have had difficulty completing the reading. A leveled study guide along with partner or small group reading would have better scaffolded ELLs as they completed the assignment.

Mrs. Hensen's lesson plans listed the primary source newspaper article as well as the study guide as resource materials. She included the key concepts and vocabulary she wanted her students to learn, indicating that she had thought ahead about what might cause difficulty in the text for some of her students.

FIGURE 2.14 SIOP Evaluation for Mrs. Hensen: Adaptation of Content

4	③	2	1	0	NA
5. **Adaptation of content** (e.g., text, assignment) to all levels of student proficiency		Some **adaptation of content** to all levels of student proficiency		No significant **adaptation of content** to all levels of student proficiency	

Example 3 As you may recall, Mr. Hargroves believed the textbook to be too difficult for his students to read independently. Therefore, he presented a lecture on the methods for extracting gold. He encouraged students to discuss their

experiences with gold panning prior to assigning them an essay to write about the various gold extraction methods.

SIOP Evaluation: Mr. Hargroves received a "1" for the Adaptation of Content indicator. He realized the text was too difficult, so he lectured on the Gold Rush topic. However, without any supplementary support other than the pictures in the textbook, ELLs may have had difficulty learning key concepts just by listening. Further, Mr. Hargroves did not paraphrase or clarify important points during his lecture nor did he explain or define key language or vocabulary. His lesson plans made no mention of other ways to adapt the content of the text.

FIGURE 2.15   SIOP Evaluation for Mr. Hargroves: Content Adaptation

4	3	2	①	0	NA
5. **Adaptation of content** (e.g., text, assignment) to all levels of student proficiency		Some **adaptation of content** to all levels of student proficiency		No significant **adaptation of content** to all levels of student proficiency	

Meaningful Activities

To the extent possible, lesson activities should be planned to promote language development in all skills while ELLs are mastering content objectives. Students are more successful when they are able to make connections between what they know and what they are learning by relating classroom experiences to their own lives. These meaningful experiences are often described as "authentic," because they represent a reality for students. That is, classroom experiences mirror that which actually occurs in the learner's world. Authentic, meaningful experiences are especially important for ELLs because they are learning to attach labels and terms to things already familiar to them. Their learning becomes situated rather than abstract when they are provided with the opportunity to actually experience what they are learning about.

Too often, however, English language learners are relegated to activities that are not meaningful and are unrelated to the content and activities pursued by the other English-proficient students in their classes. It is essential that content standards that apply to students with English proficiency also apply to ELLs, and that the planned activities reflect and support these standards.

For example, a class of middle school students is studying insects, butterflies in particular. While the rest of the class learns the scientific names and habitats of varied kinds of butterflies, the teacher has the ELLs color and cut out pictures of butterflies to make a butterfly mobile. This activity is neither authentic nor is it meaningful for these adolescent students. In this example, the teacher obviously has not provided meaningful activities that support the grade-level science content standards.

Teaching Scenarios

In this section of the SIOP, we are looking at the extent to which the three fourth-grade teachers incorporated meaningful learning experiences into their Gold Rush lessons.

Example 1 Recall that in the first lesson example, Ms. Chen asked students to think about the names of streets they lived on. The purpose of this was to make meaningful the names of geographic locations, such as familiar street names, as well as routes to California. She had students locate the three routes on a U.S. map with the help of peers.

In the second lesson example, Ms. Chen asked her students to brainstorm various ways they might extract gold from rocks and streams. She also incorporated realia, models, and demonstrations. The lesson was hands-on, with her students involved in attempting to pan for gold (pyrite). Students then compared library resources to learn more about the various methods for finding gold, and then they shared this information with each other. A review of Ms. Chen's lesson plan revealed her thoughtful preparation as she planned meaningful activities for all students, including ELLs.

SIOP Evaluation: Ms. Chen received a "4" for the Meaningful Activities indicator. For the students, gold panning became real as they eagerly searched for their own gold. All students participated in the activities and read, discussed, and wrote about their experiences. Ms. Chen's models and demonstrations were meaningful and helped the children connect what they were learning to what they already knew.

FIGURE 2.16   SIOP Evaluation for Ms. Chen: Meaningful Activities

④	3	2	1	0	NA
6. **Meaningful activities** that integrate lesson concepts (e.g., surveys, letter writing, simulations, constructing models) with language practice opportunities for reading, writing, listening, and/or speaking		**Meaningful activities** that integrate lesson concepts, but provide little opportunity for language practice with opportunities for reading, writing, listening, and/or speaking		No **meaningful activities** that integrate lesson concepts with language practice	

Example 2 Mrs. Hensen attempted to make her lessons meaningful by using (1) the maps of the trails; (2) the poster of the miner and the discussion of his clothing and mining tools; (3) the primary source material, which was a reproduction of a newspaper written during the Gold Rush days; and (4) the study guide. Further, she had the children working in groups and as partners to assist and support each other. Mrs. Hensen's lesson plans included all these, as well as the provisions for flexible groups, partner work, and whole-class instruction.

SIOP Evaluation: Mrs. Hensen received a "4" for the Meaningful Activities indicator. She attempted to bring interesting and meaningful activities into her teaching, and she tried to assist students in making connections between their own lives and what they were learning. For example, she found the copy of the old newspaper, and she created a study guide to help students more effectively read it.

FIGURE 2.17   SIOP Evaluation for Mrs. Hensen: Meaningful Activities

④	3	2	1	0	NA
6. **Meaningful activities** that integrate lesson concepts (e.g., surveys, letter writing, simulations, constructing models) with language practice opportunities for reading, writing, listening, and/or speaking		**Meaningful activities** that integrate lesson concepts, but provide little opportunity for language practice with opportunities for reading, writing, listening, and/or speaking		No **meaningful activities** that integrate lesson concepts with language practice	

Example 3   Mr. Hargroves's lesson plans included the mapping activity, the independent reading, and his lecture. Locating the trails by coloring the map was meaningful for students if they understood what they were doing; however, if they were unable to access the text, the mapping activity may have been irrelevant. Likewise, Mr. Hargroves assigned a writing assignment based on the information he conveyed through lecture. If students did not understand the lecture, it is unlikely they were able to write a meaningful essay about what they learned.

SIOP Evaluation: Mr. Hargroves received a "1" for the Meaningful Activities indicator. He attempted to have students demonstrate their understanding of the locations of the three trails; however, he included no other activities, assignments,

FIGURE 2.18   SIOP Evaluation for Mr. Hargroves: Meaningful Activities

4	3	2	①	0	NA
6. **Meaningful activities** that integrate lesson concepts (e.g., surveys, letter writing, simulations, constructing models) with language practice opportunities for reading, writing, listening, and/or speaking		**Meaningful activities** that integrate lesson concepts, but provide little opportunity for language practice with opportunities for reading, writing, listening, and/or speaking		No **meaningful activities** that integrate lesson concepts with language practice	

or tasks that were particularly relevant or meaningful. His lessons were quite teacher-centered with lecture and independent seat-work the predominant activities. He did not teach note-taking skills and he expected students to complete the writing assignment based only on the information they could gather from the lecture.

Summary

Separating "preparation" from "instruction" is difficult because they are closely linked. Hopefully, thoughtful planning leads to effective teaching—but a great plan does not always guarantee a great lesson for ELLs. English language learners require sensitive teachers who realize that curriculum must be grade-level appropriate, based on content standards and learning outcomes. If children lack background knowledge and experience about content concepts, effective SI teachers provide it through explicit instruction, and they can enhance student learning with appropriate supplementary materials. They provide scaffolded support by adapting dense and difficult text. They situate lessons in meaningful real-life activities and experiences that involve students in reading, writing, and discussing important concepts and ideas.

These principles of effective sheltered instruction should be reflected in teachers' lesson plans. As we explore the other indicators on the Sheltered Instruction Observation Protocol, and see how teachers apply many other important principles in their classrooms, remember that the first step in the instructional process is comprehensive and thoughtful lesson design.

Discussion Questions

1. What are some advantages to writing both content objectives and language objectives for students to see? How might written objectives affect teacher and student performance in the classroom?
2. Think of a lesson you have recently taught or one you might teach. What would be an appropriate content objective and language objective for that lesson?
3. What are some ways that curriculum intended for younger learners can be used effectively as a supplement for teaching grade-level content concepts? Give examples.
4. Many teachers in sheltered settings rely on paper-and-pencil tasks or lectures for teaching concepts. Think of a curricular area (e.g., science, language arts, math, social studies) and discuss some meaningful activities that could be used to teach a concept in that area. What makes each of these activities "meaningful"?

3 Indicators of Instruction: Building Background

FIGURE 3.1 Instruction Section of the SIOP: Building Background

4	3	2	1	0	NA
7. **Concepts explicitly linked** to students' background experiences		**Concepts loosely linked** to students' background experiences		**Concepts not explicitly linked** to students' background experiences	

4	3	2	1	0	NA
8. **Links explicitly made** between past learning and new concepts		**Few links made** between past learning and new concepts		**No links made** between past learning and new concepts	

4	3	2	1	0	NA
9. **Key vocabulary emphasized** (e.g., introduced, written, repeated, and highlighted for students to see)		**Key vocabulary** introduced, but not emphasized		**Key vocabulary** not emphasized	

This section of the Sheltered Instruction Observation Protocol (SIOP), Instruction, includes six subsections that represent the features that ordinarily constitute the major portion of the lesson. These subsections address the following:

1. How the teacher builds background and uses it to increase student understanding of the content.
2. Ways the teacher makes verbal communication more comprehensible (comprehensible input).
3. The kinds of strategies the teacher uses to guide students to greater understanding.

4. The extent to which students have opportunities to interact in a quality way with the teacher and other students.
5. The amount and quality of practice the students are given to apply new concepts and information.
6. How well the teacher maintains a focus to the lesson that reflects the language and content objectives of the lesson, keeping students engaged throughout.

In our work in classrooms, we have seen teachers with good intentions go through the motions of a lesson. They have a lesson plan and follow the plan, but fail to connect with the students. The features of the SIOP are designed, in part, to make sure teachers of English language learners (ELLs) pay attention to some very important aspects of teaching that can be overlooked. Effective teaching takes students from where they are and leads them to a higher level of understanding (Krashen, 1984; Vygotsky, 1978). Students learning English must have ample opportunity to use the target language (English); to hear and see comprehensible English; and to read, write and speak the new language within the context of subject matter learning. But there is a caveat to this: *the language must be meaningful.* It is not only the amount of exposure to English that affects learning, but the quality as well (Wong-Fillmore & Valadez, 1986). As we will discuss in the next few chapters of this book, effective sheltered teachers present information in a way that students can understand, bearing in mind their language development needs and the gaps in their educational experiences. New information is tied to students' background and experiences, and strategies are used to scaffold students' acquisition of knowledge and skills (see Chapter 5 for a detailed discussion). All students benefit from scaffolded instruction, but it is a necessity for English language learners.

Each subsection of the SIOP's Instruction section is discussed in a separate chapter (3 through 8). This chapter focuses on the *Building Background* subsection.

Background

During the past two decades, researchers have investigated how highly proficient readers and writers process new information (Carrell, 1987; Dole, Duffy, Roehler & Pearson, 1991). It is a widely accepted notion among experts that a reader's "schema"—knowledge of the world—provides a basis for understanding, learning, and remembering facts and ideas found in stories and texts. Individuals with knowledge of a topic have better recall and are better able to elaborate on aspects of the topic than those who have limited knowledge of the topic (Chiesi, Splich, & Voss, 1979).

The importance of background experiences are expressed in the following ways:

Schemata are the reader's concepts, beliefs, expectations, processes—virtually everything from past experiences—that are used in making sense of things and actions. In reading, schemata are used in making sense of text; the printed work evoking the reader's associated experiences, and past and potential relationships. (John McNeil)

When reading, the learner forms meaning by reviewing past experiences that given images and sounds evoke. (Edmund Huey)

Children from culturally diverse backgrounds may struggle with comprehending a text or concept presented in class because their schemata do not match those of the culture for which the text was written (Jimenez, Garcia, & Pearson, 1996; Anderson, 1984). In the United States, most school reading material, such as content area texts, relies on the assumption that students' prior knowledge is knowledge that is common to all children. Many English language learners emigrate from other countries and bring an array of experiences that are quite different from those of the majority culture in the United States, and many have gaps in their education. Even for those students born in the United States, culture has strong effects on reading comprehension. As a teacher reads "The man walked briskly down the dark alley, glancing from side to side," do all children get a sense of fear or danger? Anderson (1994) questions whether we can assume that "when reading the same story, children from every subculture will have the same experience with the setting, ascribe the same goals and motives to characters, imagine the same sequence of actions, make predictions with the same emotional reactions, or expect the same outcomes" (pp. 480–481).

An actual example of cultural mismatch of schemata occurred in a middle school's self-contained special education class with a small group of students for whom English was their second language. The teacher was participating in a project using instructional conversations, an approach that, among other features, explicitly links students' background to text (Echevarria, 1995a). The teacher read a passage from a grade-level novel about a young man who was reading a magazine (his favorite subscription) while riding a public bus home. He left the magazine on the bus and as he exited, he spoke a quick Russian greeting to some passengers whom he had overheard speaking Russian. The story states that the young man, Mike, had learned a few phrases from his brother-in-law who is Russian. After Mike got off the bus, he heard the bus make its next stop with quite a commotion. He turned to see the Russians running toward him with guns! After taking a circuitous route home, he got to his second-floor apartment, breathing a sigh of relief. He had no idea why the Russians were so angry with him, but he was relieved that he had lost them. A half-hour later he heard a noise outside, looked out the window and saw the Russians coming into his building.

The teacher paused and asked the students about how the Russians could possibly have found where Mike lived when the story made it clear that he had lost them. The teacher expected that the students would remember that Mike had left the magazine, which had his address label on it, on the bus. However, one student volunteered that the Russians found Mike by asking his brother-in-law. The teacher admitted that she found the answer to be "out in left field" and would ordinarily have tactfully asked someone else for the answer. But the nature of instructional conversations is to discuss ideas, drawing out students' thoughts and linking them to the text. So the teacher asked the student to elaborate. He explained that in their community, which was 99% Latino with a small population of Samoans, if he needed to know where a certain Samoan person lived, he'd simply ask someone from the Samoan neighborhood.

The teacher admitted that she had learned an important lesson: the students' schemata were different from hers yet just as valid. Moreover, she nearly dismissed his excellent contribution because she was looking for a specific answer that matched her schemata. In reality, none of the students in her group would have had any idea about magazine subscriptions and address labels. In the students' experience, if one wanted a magazine, one merely walked to the store and bought it.

The example clearly demonstrates that the student and teacher had very different ideas and assumptions about the characters and events in the story and a different "magazine" schema. Some of the differences can be attributed to cultural variation and a difference in home environments.

Teachers of English language learners need to be aware that what may appear to be poor comprehension and memory skills, may in fact be a lack of, or failure to activate, the background knowledge that was assumed by a message or a text (Bransford, 1994). Through the SIOP model, we urge teachers to activate students' background knowledge explicitly and provide linkages from their experiences to the concepts or text. The interactive emphasis of the SIOP model (see Chapter 6 for specific features) enables teachers to elicit students' background knowledge and discuss ideas, issues, concepts, or vocabulary that are unfamiliar to them.

Concepts Linked to Students' Background

Tying new information to students' own background experiences, both personal (including cultural) and academic, makes the information take on new meaning. Teachers may provide explicit links to students' background by asking questions that preview an upcoming topic—such as, "Have you ever seen a rat?" or "How do people usually feel about rats? Why?" or "Have you ever been sick?"—and then directly relating it to the text by saying, "Well, today we're going to read about some rats. Let's see how similar the rats in the story are to the ones you've just described from your experience."

Teaching Scenarios

The teachers have their own plans for teaching the unit on *Mrs. Frisby and the Rats of NIMH* (see Figure 3.2). Their individual approaches to teaching the unit and SIOP scores are described below.

FIGURE 3.2   **Literature Unit: Mrs. Frisby and the Rats of NIMH (6th grade)**

The lessons described in this chapter take place in a large urban middle school with a large population of English language learners. The number of ELLs in this school enables classes to be grouped homogeneously by students' English proficiency level. Students in all three classes described here are advanced beginners, which means their English proficiency is beyond the beginning stages of acquisition but not quite at an intermediate level. Most of the students immigrated from rural areas in Latin America and have low literacy levels due to interrupted schooling experiences.

As part of a literature course, Mrs. Jarmin, Mr. Ramirez, and Miss Paige are required to teach a variety of American literature novels. The first book in the series is *Mrs. Frisby and the Rats of NIMH,* and the teachers will spend 5 to 10 days on the unit. The story is about Mrs. Frisby, a field mouse, who is worried about her younger son, Timothy. He has had pneumonia and is too weak and frail to be moved. But if the Frisby's don't move immediately, they'll all be killed. Mrs. Frisby hears about the wonderful Rats of NIMH who are strong, smart, and able to do almost anything. The story chronicles the adventures of the family and the Rats of NIMH.

The objectives for this unit include (1) students will read an extended text, and (2) students will use their prior knowledge as a tool for understanding the text. Even though these objectives may seem somewhat vague, the teachers felt strongly that these students needed to have the experience of reading an extended text because materials written at their literacy levels tend to be short, simple stories. The teachers are planning to introduce the novel by showing the video version of the story. Seeing the video prior to reading the text will provide students with an overall understanding of the story, and will provide exposure to new vocabulary associated with the text. Following the viewing of the video, the teachers will introduce the text that the class will read together. Each teacher may provide activities of their own choosing to reinforce the concepts and vocabulary covered in the story.

Example 1   Miss Paige began the first lesson of the unit by asking, "Have you ever seen a rat?" The students were quite interested in this topic and readily shared their experiences. Students brainstormed a variety of characteristics of the rats they had had experience with, either personal experiences or through other means such as television and movies. Miss Paige then drew a semantic map and, with the students' input, categorized the various characteristics of the rats they knew about and recorded the students' experiences. When the semantic map was complete and the students had a good understanding of rats, Miss Paige then directly related it to the text by showing the book and saying, "Well, in this book we're going to read about some rats. Let's see how similar the rats in the story are to the ones you've just described." Then, she explained to the students that prior to reading the book, they would see a video, *The Secret of NIMH.*

SIOP Evaluation: Miss Paige received a "4" on the SIOP for this indicator. She spent time eliciting students' background knowledge about rats, creating an interest level that would facilitate learning. A novel, such as *Mrs. Frisby and the Rats of NIMH,* may be difficult for ELLs to understand, yet by linking the topic to their own experiences the teacher helped to enhance student comprehension.

FIGURE 3.3   SIOP Evaluation for Miss Paige: Concepts Linked

④	3	2	1	0	NA
7. Concepts explicitly linked to students' background experiences		**Concepts loosely linked** to students' background experiences		**Concepts not explicitly linked** to students' background experiences	

Example 2   At the beginning of the first lesson of the unit, Mrs. Jarmin began by telling the class that they would be reading an interesting book in which the main characters were rats. Then Mrs. Jarmin asked, "Who has ever seen a rat?" Several students told of their experiences seeing rats or having them as pets. After that Mrs. Jarmin told the class that they would see a video based on the novel they would read later and began showing the video.

SIOP Evaluation: Mrs. Jarmin received a "2" on this SIOP indicator. She made an effort to activate the students' prior knowledge, but it was not done in an explicit or systematic way. While Miss Paige organized the information using a semantic map for students to see and make reference to later, Mrs. Jarmin merely conducted a verbal discussion about a few students' experiences. English language learners benefit from visual clues given during a discussion and Mrs. Jarmin did not provide any visual assistance for those learners with limited English proficiency. Further, she did not organize the information in a useful way that would make the information accessible and meaningful to all the students in class.

FIGURE 3.4   SIOP Evaluation for Mrs. Jarmin: Concepts Linked

4	3	②	1	0	NA
7. Concepts explicitly linked to students' background experiences		**Concepts loosely linked** to students' background experiences		**Concepts not explicitly linked** to students' background experiences	

Example 3   Mr. Ramirez began the first lesson of the unit by distributing the text to the students. He asked what the students thought the book would be about and they suggested that it would be something about rats. He told them that they would first watch a video based on the book before actually reading the text, then Mr. Ramirez showed the video.

SIOP Evaluation: Mr. Ramirez received a "0" on the SIOP for this indicator. Although the video did provide background information for the students, Mr. Ramirez did not provide students with an introduction to the video or to the book. Further, he did not provide any opportunity for the students to link their backgrounds or experiences to the unit.

FIGURE 3.5   SIOP Evaluation for Mr. Ramirez: Concepts Linked

4	3	2	1	(0)	NA
7. **Concepts explicitly linked** to students' background experiences		**Concepts loosely linked** to students' background experiences		**Concepts not explicitly linked** to students' background experiences	

Links Made between Past Learning and New Concepts

It is also important for teachers to make explicit connections between new learning and the material, vocabulary, and concepts previously covered in class. The teacher must build a bridge from previous lessons to new learning for students to cross over. We know that many students do not automatically make such connections, and all students benefit from having the teacher explicitly point out how past learning is related to the information at hand (Tierney & Pearson, 1994). Links between past and new learning can be made through a discussion—such as, "Who remembers what we learned about _____? How does that relate to our story?"— or by reviewing graphic organizers or other written reminders about the information. By preserving and referring to word banks, outlines, and graphic organizers, teachers have tools for reminding students of previous learning.

Teaching Scenarios

The practice of linking past learning with new concepts is approached differently by each of the three teachers previously introduced.

Example 1   As you recall, Mrs. Jarmin activated students' backgrounds with a semantic map listing students' knowledge of rats. Now, during the second day of the unit, Mrs. Jarmin and the class began reading the story. Mrs. Jarmin paused after the first chapter and brought out a Venn diagram from an earlier lesson that illustrated the way fiction and fantasy are similar, yet not all fiction involves fantasy. She asked the students how they would describe this story so far, as fiction or as fantasy. Looking at the descriptors listed on the Venn diagram, they decided the story was fantasy. Mrs. Jarmin then told the students that, especially because fan-

tasy can sometimes be confusing, they would construct a graphic organizer to keep track of the characters as they proceeded through the story, as well as to provide visual clues for plot events and vocabulary in the story. She asked students to think of words to describe the characters—Timothy, Martin, Cynthia, Teresa, and Mrs. Frisby—from the first chapter. As students mentioned the adjectives, Mrs. Jarmin began writing them on chart paper as a graphic organizer.

SIOP Evaluation: Mrs. Jarmin received a "4" on this SIOP item. Not only did she provide a direct link between past learning and new learning by showing the Venn diagram, she began constructing a graphic organizer that would be an important tool for activating students' knowledge as they proceeded through the book. Each day the students will be oriented to the characters in the story, and will be reminded of events covered in the book.

FIGURE 3.6 SIOP Evaluation for Mrs. Jarmin: Links Made

④	3	2	1	0	NA
8. **Links explicitly made** between past learning and new concepts		**Few links made** between past learning and new concepts		**No links made** between past learning and new concepts	

Example 2   As Miss Paige was reading the first chapter with her students, she paused after every few paragraphs to check for understanding, elaborate, define words, and paraphrase parts of the story. Occasionally she would remind students of something they had discussed in another lesson. For example, when Mrs. Frisby is described as a widow, Miss Paige said, "Who remembers what a widow is? We talked about that word when we read *The Witches* by Roald Dahl. Remember the grandma who was a widow? What does that mean?" Then Miss Paige wrote the word on a piece of chart paper that she continued to use as a word bank throughout the unit, adding words the students identified as unfamiliar.

SIOP Evaluation: Miss Paige received a "2" on this SIOP indicator. Although she made a few links between past learning and new vocabulary, it was done orally and she did not make explicit links to new concepts. Miss Paige did, however, develop a word bank that assisted students' learning by reminding them of the meaning of words used in the story.

FIGURE 3.7   SIOP Evaluation for Miss Paige: Links Made

4	3	②	1	0	NA
8. Links explicitly made between past learning and new concepts	Few links made between past learning and new concepts			No links made between past learning and new concepts	

Example 3   Mr. Ramirez read the first chapter with the students, asked a number of comprehension questions, cleared up one student's confusion about which character was ill, and reviewed the chapter completely after reading it with the students.

SIOP Evaluation: Mr. Ramirez received a "0" on the SIOP indicator. He did not make any attempt to link previous learning to what the students were currently reading about, nor did he establish any system for reviewing the material during subsequent lessons.

FIGURE 3.8   SIOP Evaluation for Mr. Ramirez: Links Made

4	3	2	1	⓪	NA
8. Links explicitly made between past learning and new concepts	Few links made between past learning and new concepts			No links made between past learning and new concepts	

Key Vocabulary Emphasized

Vocabulary development is critical for English language learners because we know that there is a strong relationship between vocabulary knowledge in English and academic achievement (Saville-Trioke, 1984). To be most effective, vocabulary development should be closely related to the subject matter students are studying. As you will see, the one teacher in this chapter, Miss Paige, who taught vocabulary well, embedded the new words within the context of the text, providing students with a rich contextual environment in which to learn new terms and expand their English vocabulary.

There are two aspects to vocabulary development to attend to when using the SIOP. One involves selecting several key terms on which to focus from the lesson's material, and the other is explicitly teaching "school language"—or the vocabulary associated with activities such as identify, define, compare, and summarize—the kinds of terms that are typically used in classroom tasks and discussions.

Developing Content Language

There is little benefit to selecting 25 to 30 isolated vocabulary terms and asking ELLs to copy them from the board and look up their definitions in the dictionary. Many of the words in the definitions are also unfamiliar to these students, rendering the activity meaningless. Although using the dictionary is an important school skill to learn, the task must fit the students' learning needs. The number of terms should be tailored to the students' English and literacy levels, and they should be presented in context, not in isolation. For students with minimal literacy skills, using the dictionary to find words can serve to reinforce the concept of alphabetizing and it familiarizes them with the parts of a dictionary; however, defining words should not be the only strategy used. Effective sheltered instruction teachers support the understanding of dictionary definitions so that the task is meaningful for students. In fact, many effective teachers introduce dictionary skills to students by using words that are already familiar to them.

There are a myriad of meaningful and useful ways that vocabulary can be taught to English language learners. The following section describes approaches to vocabulary development and word study that are especially helpful to ELLs. When used regularly, they provide students with multiple exposures to key language and vocabulary through meaningful practice and review.

Contextualizing Key Vocabulary Sheltered teachers peruse the material and select several key terms that are critical to understanding the lesson's most important concepts. The teacher introduces the terms at the outset of the lesson, systematically defining or demonstrating each and showing how that term is used within the context of the lesson. Experienced SI teachers know that having students understand the meaning of several key terms completely is more effective than having a cursory understanding of a dozen terms.

Another way of contextualizing words is to read with students in small groups and, as they come across a term they do not understand, pause and explain it to them, using as many examples, synonyms, or cognates as necessary to convey the meaning.

Vocabulary Self-Selection Following the reading of a content text, according to Ruddell (1997), students self-select key vocabulary that is essential to understanding content concepts. Words may be selected by individuals, partners, or small groups, and they are eventually shared and discussed by the entire class. A class list of vocabulary self-selection (VSS) words for a particular lesson or unit is mutually agreed on by the teacher and the students, and these are reviewed and studied throughout. They also may be entered into a word study notebook and students may be asked to demonstrate their knowledge of these words through written or oral activities. Ruddell (1997) has found that when students are shown how to identify key content vocabulary, they become adept at selecting and learning words they need to know. Vocabulary self-selection is an effective method for teaching and reviewing content vocabulary because students learn to trust their own judgments about which content words are the most important to learn. This approach is most appropriate for students who are high-intermediate and advanced English language learners.

Personal Dictionaries Similar to VSS, personal dictionaries are created as an individual vocabulary and spelling resource for students at all levels of English proficiency. Generally used with students who have more advanced English proficiency, ELLs read together in partners or small groups and write unknown words they encounter in their personal dictionaries. The teacher works with each group and discusses the words students have written in their dictionaries, providing correction or clarity as needed.

Word Wall During a lesson, key vocabulary is reviewed by directing students to a Word Wall where relevant content vocabulary words are listed alphabetically, usually on a large poster, sheet of butcher paper, or pocket chart (Cunningham, 1995). Originally designed as a method for teaching and reinforcing sight words for emergent readers, Word Walls are also effective for displaying content words related to a particular unit or theme. The words are revisited frequently throughout the lesson or unit and students are encouraged to use them in their writing and discussions.

Cunningham (1995) recommends that teachers judiciously select words for a Word Wall and that the number be limited to those of greatest importance. We would add that teachers should resist the temptation to have multiple Word Walls in one classroom because the walls quickly become cluttered with words that are difficult to sort through, especially for ELLs. One Word Wall, carefully maintained and changed as needed, is what we recommend. Some teachers, with students' input, regularly remove words from a Word Wall to keep the number of words at a reasonable number. Every Friday, or every other Friday, for example, the students jointly decide which words they no longer need on the wall.

Concept Definition Map   The Concept Definition Map is a great way to learn and remember content vocabulary and concepts (Buehl, 1995). Even though it is a simple graphic, it can be used to discuss complex concepts. For example, a class is studying the American Revolution in social studies. To clarify the meaning of "revolution," the class could complete a Concept Definition Map, as shown in Figure 3.9.

Cloze Sentences   Cloze sentences can be used to teach and review content vocabulary. Students read a sentence that has strong contextual support for the vocabulary word that has been omitted from the sentence. Once the meaning of the word is determined and possible replacement words are brainstormed, the teacher (or a student) provides the correct word. For example, "During a _____, which can be violent or peaceful, a group of people tries to overthrow an existing government or social system." (*revolution*)

FIGURE 3.9   Concept Definition Map

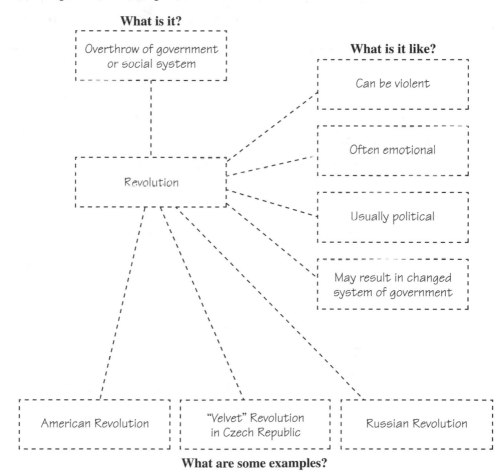

Word Sorts   During a Word Sort, students categorize words or phrases, which have been previously introduced, into groups predetermined by the teacher (Bear, Invernizzi, Templeton, & Johnston, 2000). Words or phrases are typed on a sheet of paper (46-point type on the computer works well). Students cut the paper into word strips and then sort the words according to meaning, similarities in structure (e.g., words ending in -tion, -sion, or -tation), derivations, or sounds.

For example, the following words related to the American Revolution are listed in mixed order on a sheet of paper: revolution, tension, frustration, taxation, representation, vision, plantation, mission, participation, solution, passion, transition, nation, and so on. After you discuss the meanings of the words, have students cut out each of the words and sort them according to spelling pattern (see Figure 3.10a). The objectives here would be twofold: to introduce words related to content concepts and to reinforce spellings and word structure.

FIGURE 3.10a   Word Sorts: American Revolution—Example 1

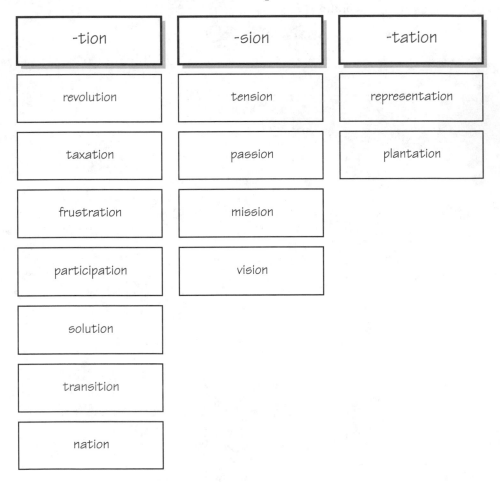

-tion	-sion	-tation
revolution	tension	representation
taxation	passion	plantation
frustration	mission	
participation	vision	
solution		
transition		
nation		

Another example of a Word Sort for the American Revolution might involve words and phrases related to content concepts such as right to bear arms, muskets, George Washington, rifles, Thomas Jefferson, democracy, Thomas Payne, knives, taxation, King George, bayonets, freedom of religion, Paul Revere, self-governance, cannons. After students cut apart the words and phrases, they sort them into groups and identify an appropriate label for each (e.g., People, Weapons, Issues) (see Figure 3.10b).

This categorizing activity also can be completed as a List–Group–Label activity (Vacca & Vacca, 1998) when students brainstorm words related to the topic and then determine possible categories or labels for the words. The brainstormed words are then reviewed when they are rewritten under the various labels.

Word Generation This activity helps ELL students and others learn and/or review new content vocabulary through analogy. For example, write "-port" on the board. Invite students to brainstorm all the words they can think of that contain "port." Examples might include report, import, export, important, portfolio, Port-a-Potty, Portland, deport, transport, transportation, support, airport, and so on. Analyze the meaning of each brainstormed word and ask students to figure out what words containing "-port" might mean "to carry." If they cannot figure it out, it's fine to tell them the meaning. Then, go back and revisit each word to see if

FIGURE 3.10b   Word Sorts: American Revolution—Example 2

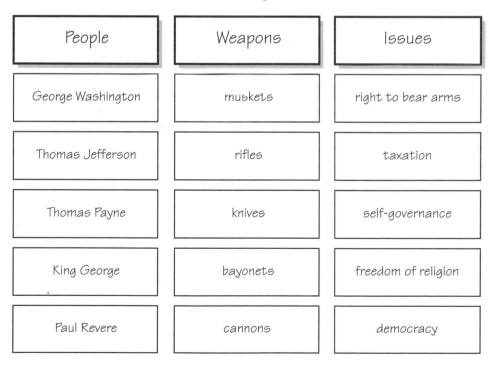

People	Weapons	Issues
George Washington	muskets	right to bear arms
Thomas Jefferson	rifles	taxation
Thomas Payne	knives	self-governance
King George	bayonets	freedom of religion
Paul Revere	cannons	democracy

the definition "to carry" has something to do with the word's meaning. Note that we did not define "port" first; rather, we recommend that students generalize meanings of content words from words that they already know that contain the same syllable or word-part.

Word Study Books   A Word Study Book is a student-made personal notebook containing frequently used words and concepts. Bear et al. (2000) recommend that the Word Study Book be organized by English language structure, such as listing together all the words studied so far that end in -tion, -sion, and -tation. We support this notion and believe that Word Study Books can also be used for content study where words are grouped by meaning (e.g., American Revolution-related words).

Developing School Language

The issue of making "school language" comprehensible to students is an important one. Teachers often give students instructions and assume the terms used in the instructions are meaningful to the students. In a science class, we observed that the teacher did an excellent job of preparing a hands-on lesson that incorporated many of the features of the SIOP. However, as the lesson was introduced, the teacher said, "The purpose of this lesson is for you to better understand why some things float while others sink. Before we're done, you'll be able to calculate and predict whether something will be buoyant enough to float." The teacher did well in stating the objective of the lesson in a way the students could understand, but the students were lost when the teacher used unfamiliar terms such as "calculate," "buoyant," and "predict."

Teaching Scenarios

Examples of lessons from the three previously introduced sixth-grade teachers are given here to illustrate whether, and how, they teach both content vocabulary and school language.

Example 1   As mentioned previously, Mrs. Jarmin began the unit with an oral discussion of students' experiences with rats. She told the class they would see a video, *The Secret of NIMH*, based on the novel they were going to read. Before showing the video, Mrs. Jarmin wanted to teach the students some terms they would encounter during the unit. Working with small, rotating groups, she used a reciprocal teaching strategy (Palinscar & Brown, 1984) and began with the words "predicting," "clarifying," and "questioning" posted on the wall. Mrs. Jarmin distributed three index cards which described each of the three terms to each student in the group.

First she asked students to look at the card that gave guidelines for "predicting." She read, "Let's look at the title." The teacher paused and asked the students what the title was. The students showed her the title of the book. She continued reading, "Look at all the visual clues on the page." Again she stopped to make sure the students understood and asked them the meaning of "visual clues." Because the students weren't sure, she told them it means "pictures, graphs, and the like." Then she read, "What do you think we'll be reading about?" Mrs. Jarmin told the students to follow the guidelines and tell her what they would "predict" the book is about.

FIGURE 3.11   Activity based on *Reciprocal Teaching* (Palinscar and Brown, 1984)

Predicting

Let's look at the title. Look at all the visual clues on the page. What do you think we'll be reading about?

Clarifying

One of the words I wasn't sure about was _____.

Questioning

What is the main idea?

She reiterated the information on the card, telling the students to (1) look at the title, (2) look at the pictures, and (3) think about what we'll read about. She left the group to think while she checked on another group. When she returned, she said, "What do you think we'll be reading about? I . . ."; and a student began his sentence with, "I think we'll be reading about some rats." Mrs. Jarmin asked him to explain how he came to that answer and then replied, "Good. Who has more information they want to share?" One student made a comment about the mice. The teacher wrote the words, mice and rats, on the board and asked, "What will the story be about?"

Some students seemed confused by those words, so the teacher asked them to look at the title. They had a brief discussion about how mice and rats differ. Once the distinction was made, they moved on to the card about "clarifying." The teacher read, "One of the words I wasn't sure about was _____." Mrs. Jarmin then distributed a photocopy of the summary of the story to the students and told them to use a highlighter to identify the words they didn't understand. The teacher circulated among other groups as the students read the summary and highlighted unfamiliar words.

When she returned, she asked the students to tell her their highlighted words as she wrote them on the board. She said, "Let's see if there are other words that can be used in place of the highlighted words. We'll see which words we already know and the ones we don't know we'll look up in the thesaurus. A thesaurus is a book like a dictionary that helps us clarify words." The words the students didn't know are listed in Figure 3.12:

FIGURE 3.12   Vocabulary Word List

NIMH–a place

Scarce–_____

Asparagus–a vegetable

Frail–_____

Abandoned–left behind

The group went through the list, with Mrs. Jarmin asking if anyone knew the meaning of the words. One student recognized that "NIMH" is the name of a place and that "asparagus" is a vegetable; so the teacher wrote those definitions beside the words. Since nobody knew the meaning of "frail" and "scarce," Mrs. Jarmin drew a line, indicating that the students will find those words in the thesaurus. Then the students looked up each word together. The first student to find the word called out the page number the word was on for the others. As a group, the students decided on a word or two to denote meaning. When they finished defining all the words, the teacher drew their attention to the final card about "questioning." She read, "What is the main idea?" and then said, "Now that we have predicted what the story will be about and we've clarified some terms, what do you think will be the main idea of the story?"

The students were familiar with the main idea of the story and knew how to clarify words they didn't understand. So, before starting the video based on the novel, Mrs. Jarmin showed a transparency on the overhead projector that listed 10 words she identified as key vocabulary. Each group of students was asked to look up two of the words in their thesaurus. The class discussed the definitions the students read and Mrs. Jarmin wrote a short definition next to each word on the overhead. She then told the students to copy the words on a paper and to put a check next to each word as they heard it while watching the video.

At the conclusion of the video, she asked students which vocabulary words they had heard and marked while viewing the video. Mrs. Jarmin wrote the words on a Word Wall and then reviewed the meaning of each word with the class, providing synonyms and drawing a picture if necessary to convey meaning as they had done in the clarifying exercise. The paper Word Wall remained posted throughout the reading of the novel and Mrs. Jarmin often drew students' attention to one of the posted words as they came across it in the text.

SIOP Evaluation: Mrs. Jarmin received a "4" on the SIOP for Key Vocabulary Emphasized. She took time to introduce students, not only to the story and associated vocabulary, but also to ways of "doing school." The introduction took only 15 minutes or so to do, but it taught students some valuable skills that are required in school, but are not always explicitly taught. Also, she made new vocabulary words meaningful by defining terms before watching the video and then asking students to identify the terms within the context of the video. The words were written, posted and referred to frequently throughout the unit. In this way, the key vocabulary terms became an integral part of the unit.

FIGURE 3.13   SIOP Evaluation for Mrs. Jarmin: Key Vocabulary

④	3	2	1	0	NA
9. **Key vocabulary emphasized** (e.g., introduced, written, repeated, and highlighted for students to see)		**Key vocabulary** introduced, but not emphasized		**Key vocabulary** not emphasized	

Example 2   After watching the video, Miss Paige showed a transparency listing 10 key terms from the story that she was certain the students did not understand. As she pointed to each word, she asked the class if they knew what the word meant. At least one student knew the meaning of 2 of the 10 vocabulary terms, indicating that Miss Paige had done an adequate job of selecting key vocabulary words for which the students needed direct instruction. She discussed each term and wrote a brief definition next to the word on the transparency.

SIOP Evaluation: Miss Paige received a "1" on this SIOP indicator. Although she did write down a number of key vocabulary terms and discussed them, there was no further reference to the list nor did she have students copy the list for their own reference. It became a vocabulary-building activity done in isolation of any context, rendering it less effective than if she had used the transparency throughout

FIGURE 3.14 SIOP Evaluation for Miss Paige: Key Vocabulary

4	3	2	①	0	NA
9. **Key vocabulary emphasized** (e.g., introduced, written, repeated, and highlighted for students to see)		**Key vocabulary** introduced, but not emphasized		**Key vocabulary** not emphasized	

the unit, reviewing and repeating the words, and having them available for students to see.

Example 3 After viewing the video during the first lesson of the unit, Mr. Ramirez began the second day's lesson by writing 20 vocabulary terms on the board. He told the students that they were to copy each term into their notebooks and look up the definition of each term in the dictionary. The students spent the second day completing this activity.

SIOP Evaluation: Mr. Ramirez received a "0" on the SIOP for Key Words Emphasized. First, rather than selecting a manageable number of key terms, he simply selected 20 words that he assumed the students didn't know. He didn't discuss the terms with the students or support them in their understanding of new vocabulary. Given these students' low literacy and English proficiency levels, an optimal number of new terms ranges from 5 to 12. The large number of terms coupled with the vocabulary contained within the definitions becomes overwhelming. Second, considering the students' academic and English proficiency levels, copying terms from the board and looking up their definitions in the dictionary is not very meaningful. Frequently this type of exercise results in students' papers filled with misspelled words and incomplete sentences since the majority of words, both the vocabulary terms and their definitions, are unfamiliar to these students. Finally, the more decontextualized the activity, the more problematic learning becomes. That is, the more directly related the activity is to the learning objective, the more likely it is that student learning will take place. In this lesson, the activity was not

FIGURE 3.15 SIOP Evaluation for Mr. Ramirez: Key Vocabulary

4	3	2	1	⓪	NA
9. **Key vocabulary emphasized** (e.g., introduced, written, repeated, and highlighted for students to see)		**Key vocabulary** introduced, but not emphasized		**Key vocabulary** not emphasized	

closely aligned to the context of the story. Both the vocabulary terms and their, often multiple, definitions were unfamiliar to the students, as was the formal lexicon of the dictionary that was supposed to clarify the terms. The activity had little or no meaning for these students.

Summary

The importance of building background has been well established and is one of the easier components of the SIOP to incorporate into teaching. Simply taking a few minutes to jump-start students' schema, find out what they know or have experienced about a topic, and linking it directly to the lesson's objective will result in greater understanding for English language learners.

Discussion Questions

1. Some educators argue the importance of connecting new information to English language learners' own cultural backgrounds in order to make content concepts meaningful. Others disagree, stating that students relate more to popular American influences ("adolescent culture") than they do to their parents' traditional cultural practices. What are some merits and problems with both positions? What about ELLs born in the United States who have never lived in their native cultural setting?

2. Reflect on how you learn new vocabulary. In what settings and around which people are you most comfortable using the new word(s)? What happens if you don't frequently use the word(s)? What are the implications of this process of learning new words to teaching key vocabulary to ELLs?

3. Was the concept of developing "school language" a new idea to you? Discuss the importance of explicitly teaching school language to English language learners, and give specific examples of the kinds of terminology teachers frequently assume students know. Draw from the language of classroom routines and the language of specific subjects.

4. Think about a joke or cartoon that you didn't understand, such as from a late-show monologue or a political cartoon. Why was it confusing or unamusing? What information would you have needed for it to make sense? What are the implications for teaching content to all students, including English language learners?

4 Indicators of Instruction: Comprehensible Input

FIGURE 4.1: Instruction Section of the SIOP: Comprehensible Input

4	3	2	1	0	NA
10. **Speech** appropriate for students' proficiency level (e.g., slower rate, enunciation, and simple sentence structure for beginners)		**Speech** sometimes inappropriate for students' proficiency level		**Speech** inappropriate for students' proficiency level	

4	3	2	1	0	NA
11. **Explanation** of academic tasks clear		**Explanation** of academic tasks somewhat clear		**Explanation** of academic tasks unclear	

4	3	2	1	0	NA
12. Uses a variety of **techniques** to make content concepts clear (e.g., modeling, visuals, hands-on activities, demonstrations, gestures, body language)		Uses some **techniques** to make content concepts clear		Uses few or no **techniques** to make content concepts clear	

This subsection of the SIOP Instruction section reflects one of the components that distinguish effective sheltered instruction from high-quality nonsheltered instruction. As you have seen in the SIOP items discussed so far, it is true that sheltered instruction shares many of the features of high-quality nonsheltered instruction. However, an effective sheltered teacher takes into account the unique characteristics of English language learners (ELLs). For these students, the teacher makes verbal communication more understandable by consciously attending to students' linguistic needs. Making adjustments to speech so that the message to the student is understandable is referred to as *comprehensible input* (Krashen, 1985). Comprehensible input is important and should be measured throughout the lesson to ensure that students are taking in and understanding what is being communicated to them.

Background

One way that communication is made more understandable is by using speech that is appropriate to students' proficiency level. The teacher enunciates and speaks more slowly, but in a natural way, for students who are beginning English speakers. More repetition may be needed for beginners and, as students gain more proficiency in English, the teacher adjusts her speech for the students' level.

These linguistic modifications are made in concert with a variety of techniques that make the message clear. The teacher also avoids jargon and idiomatic speech as much as possible. Effective sheltered teachers use gestures, body language, pictures, and real objects to accompany their words; for example when saying "We're going to learn about the three forms of water," the teacher holds up three fingers. Showing one finger she says, "One form is liquid," and shows a glass of water. Holding up two fingers she says, "the second form is ice," and shows an ice cube. Holding up three fingers she says, "and the third form is steam," and shows a picture of a steaming cup of coffee. These simple gestures and visual aids assist students in organizing and making sense of information that is presented verbally.

Another technique that facilitates English language learners' comprehension of the message is to provide a model of a process or of what is expected of students, as discussed in Chapter 2. For example, as the teacher discusses the process of water taking on the form of ice, she shows or draws a model of the process as it is being described. When students are later instructed to record conditions under which the change in ice from a solid to a liquid are accelerated or slowed, the teacher shows an observation sheet that is divided into three columns on the overhead projector. The teacher has a number of pictures (e.g., lamp, sun, and refrigerator), which depict various conditions such as heat and cold. She demonstrates the first condition, heat, with a picture of the sun. She models how students will describe the condition in the first column (e.g., _____ *heats*). Then she asks students what effect the sun, or heat, has on ice. They answer and in the second column she records how the ice changed (e.g., _____ *melted*), and in the third column she indicates if the process was accelerated or slowed by the condition (e.g., _____ *accelerated*). Providing a model as the students are taken through the task verbally eliminates ambiguity and gives the message in more than one way. Students are then able to complete the rest of the worksheet.

Hands-on activities provide students with an alternative form of expressing their understanding of information and concepts. Oftentimes ELLs have learned the lesson's information but have difficulty expressing their understanding in English, either orally or in writing. Further, hands-on activities can be used to

FIGURE 4.2   Unit: Buoyancy (9th grade)

The following lessons take place in an urban high school where English language learners comprise 35% of the student population. In the classrooms described, all the students are beginning to advanced beginning speakers of English, and they have varying levels of literacy in their native languages.

Ninth-grade teachers, Mr. Lew, Mrs. Castillo, and Mr. Dillon, are all teaching a unit on *buoyancy*—the ability to float. The science text addresses the question of why some objects float while others sink, and reviews the concepts of *mass*—a quantity of matter of non-specific shape—and *volume*—the capacity of a three-dimensional object. The goal is for students to understand that an object will float as long as the mass doesn't exceed the object's capacity, or volume. Students have calculated mass–volume ratios previous to this unit, although the application of these concepts to buoyancy is new. You will see in the scenarios that the teachers have their own way of helping students understand that an object's ability to float is based on its mass–volume ratio.

reinforce the concepts and information presented, with a reduced linguistic demand on these students.

As mentioned in Chapter 3, vocabulary development is critical for English language learners. There is a correlation between vocabulary development and academic achievement, so it behooves SI teachers to present content vocabulary to students in a way that can be comprehended and retained.

In the scenarios that follow, you will see examples of teachers who use comprehensible input strategies to varying degrees of effectiveness (for a unit on buoyancy see Figure 4.2).

Appropriate Speech for ELLs

For this item, speech refers to (1) rate and enunciation and (2) complexity of speech. The first aspect addresses *how* the teacher speaks and the second aspect refers to *what* is said, such as level of vocabulary used, complexity of sentence structure, use of idioms, and the like.

Students who are at the beginning levels of English proficiency benefit from teachers who slow down their rate of speech and enunciate clearly while speaking. As students become more comfortable with the language and acquire higher levels of proficiency, a slower rate isn't as necessary. In fact, for advanced and transitional students, teachers should use a rate of speech that is normal for a regular classroom. Effective sheltered teachers adjust their rate of speech and enunciation to their students' level of English proficiency.

Also, sheltered teachers carefully monitor the vocabulary and sentence structure they use with ELLs in order to match the students' proficiency level, especially with students at beginning levels of English proficiency. Use of idioms—

sayings that cannot be translated exactly such as, "He's gone head over heels for her"—creates difficulty for students who are trying to make sense of a new language. English language learners are better served when teachers use language that is straightforward and clear, and is accompanied by a visual representation. Paraphrasing and repetition are useful techniques. Cognates are often useful in promoting comprehension for students whose native language has a Latin base. For example, using "calculate the mass/volume ratio" (*calcular* in Spanish) may be easier for some students to understand than "figure out the mass/volume ratio." Furthermore, teachers should use simple sentence structures like subject–verb–object with beginning students and reduce or eliminate embedded clauses.

Teaching Scenarios

Each of the following teachers will make a science lesson on buoyancy (Colburn & Echevarria, 1999) meaningful and comprehensible for the students in their classes to varying degrees.

Example 1   As Mr. Lew began the lesson, he drew students' attention to the objective written on the board and told students that the purpose of the unit was to understand why some objects float and others sink. As he said the word "float," he pointed at an orange floating in the aquarium at the front of the room, and as he said the word "sink," he dropped a peeled orange into the water—it sank to the bottom. Then he repeated while pointing at the corresponding object, "Some things float and others sink." He went on to tell the students that at the end of the unit they would be able to calculate and predict whether something is buoyant enough to float.

The words "float," "sink," "calculate," "predict," and "buoyant" were written in a word list for students to see. This list included content vocabulary (buoyant, float, sink) as well as functional language (calculate, predict). Because many of his students were recent immigrants and had gaps in their educational backgrounds, Mr. Lew was careful to make sure students not only knew the meaning of content vocabulary, but also knew the meaning of words associated with the academic tasks—predict and calculate.

Throughout the lesson, Mr. Lew used language structures and vocabulary that he believed the students could understand at their level of proficiency. He slowed his normal rate of speech to make himself better understood by the students and he enunciated clearly. Also, he avoided the use of idioms, and when he sensed that students did not understand him, he paraphrased to convey the meaning more clearly. He repeated important words frequently and wrote them for students to see.

SIOP Evaluation: Mr. Lew received a score of "4" on this item. He slowed his rate of speech and enunciated clearly when he addressed beginning speakers; he adjusted his speech for the other, more proficient speakers of English. He used a natural speaking voice, but paid attention to his rate of speed and enunciation.

Further, Mr. Lew adjusted the level of vocabulary and complexity of the sentences he used so that students could understand. Since most students were beginning English speakers, he selected words that were appropriate to his students' proficiency level. Although the science book highlighted nearly 15 terms for the unit on buoyancy, Mr. Lew had learned from experience that it is better for his students to learn a smaller number of words thoroughly than to give superficial treatment to dozens of content-associated vocabulary. His students will be able to use and apply the selected words and their concepts because they will have a complete understanding of their meaning.

FIGURE 4.3   SIOP Evaluation for Mr. Lew: Appropriate Speech for ELLs

④	3	2	1	0	NA
10. **Speech** appropriate for students' proficiency level (e.g., slower rate and enunciation, and simple sentence structure for beginners)		**Speech** sometimes inappropriate for students' proficiency level		**Speech** inappropriate for students' proficiency level	

Example 2   As is her practice, Mrs. Castillo wrote the objective, "Find the mass/ volume ratio for objects that float," on the board. She began the lesson by discussing the fact that some things float and others sink, giving examples of objects that float, such as a large ship, and others that sink, such as a small coin. Then she asked the class if they knew what makes some objects float and others sink. A few students guessed, but nobody was able to give an accurate explanation. During the discussion, Mrs. Castillo paid attention to her rate of speech and she tried to use sentences that were less complex than those she would naturally use; however, some of the students still seemed confused while she was talking.

Mrs. Castillo told the students to read the first three pages of their text to themselves and they would discuss it when they'd finished. After the students indicated that they were done reading, Mrs. Castillo asked students if there were any words in the text they did not know. Several students called out unfamiliar words, and the teacher wrote them on the overhead sheet. Then she assigned students at each table a word to look up in the glossary. After several minutes, she asked the students what they had found. Only about half of the unfamiliar words were included in the glossary, because the other words were not science terms per se, but words such as "therefore" and "principle." Mrs. Castillo orally gave students the definitions of those words that were not in the glossary, and then summarized the information the students read in the text for 10 minutes. As she talked, she occasionally spoke too fast for many of the students to understand and she used long, detail-laden sentences in her summary. When she noticed that students were not paying attention, she slowed her rate of speech to make it understandable and to regain students' interest.

SIOP Evaluation: Mrs. Castillo received a score of "2" on this SIOP indicator. Her rate of speech and enunciation vacillated between that used with native speakers and a rate her students could understand. She didn't consistently adjust her speech (rate or complexity) to the variety of proficiency levels in the class. She was aware that her ELLs needed extra attention in understanding the language, but she only addressed their needs by asking for unfamiliar vocabulary. She could have paraphrased, using simpler sentence structure, and she could have used synonyms for words that appeared too difficult for students to understand.

FIGURE 4.4   SIOP Evaluation for Mrs. Castillo: Appropriate Speech for ELLs

4	3	②	1	0	NA
10. **Speech** appropriate for students' proficiency level (e.g., slower rate and enunciation, and simple sentence structure for beginners)		**Speech** sometimes inappropriate for students' proficiency level		**Speech** inappropriate for students' proficiency level	

Example 3   Mr. Dillon began the lesson by having students open their science text to the chapter on buoyancy. He told them that in this unit they would learn what makes objects buoyant. He gave a five-minute oral introduction to the concepts behind buoyancy, discussing the fact that if the object's mass exceeds its volume it will sink. Mr. Dillon used a rate and speaking style that was appropriate for native speakers, but not the beginning English speakers in his class. He then directed the students' attention to 13 vocabulary terms written on the board and told the class to copy each word, look up the definition in the glossary, and copy the definition onto their papers.

After students looked up vocabulary words in the glossary, Mr. Dillon asked them to put the paper in their homework folders. He told them that they needed to take the words home and their homework assignment was to use each word in a sentence. He emphasized that students needed to complete their homework because he had been frustrated by low homework response rates in this class.

Then Mr. Dillon turned to the science text, telling students to open their books to the beginning of the chapter. He proceeded to lecture from the text, asking students questions to stimulate a class discussion. Most students were reluctant to speak up. After talking about the material on the first five pages of the text, Mr. Dillon gave students a worksheet about buoyancy. He told them they could work in pairs or alone to calculate the mass/volume ratio of the objects shown on the worksheet. He said, "You remember how to calculate mass/volume ratios? First you determine the volume of the object, and then you take the mass and divide it by the volume. OK, just calculate the ratios for each object shown on the worksheet, and when you've finished, you can begin doing your homework."

SIOP Evaluation: Mr. Dillon received a "0" on the SIOP. He did not make any effort to adjust his oral presentation to the needs of the English language learners in his class. He lectured about new, complex concepts without regard to his rate of speech or complexity of speech, the variables that impact ELLs' ability to comprehend information in class. Also, copying definitions for new terms and requiring students to create original sentences is an inordinately difficult task for ELLs. Unwittingly, Mr. Dillon set the students up for failure and then was frustrated by the low number of completed homework assignments. While he believed students chose not to complete assignments, in reality they *could not* complete the type of assignment he gave.

Further, Mr. Dillon did not discuss the lesson content or class and homework assignments in any meaningful or understandable way for ELLs. He thought that discussing the material in the chapter would make the concepts clear for his students, and he asked them questions during his lecture. Unfortunately, his efforts were lost on the English language learners who needed richer, comprehensible development of the lesson's concepts to understand the text or lecture. Also, the few students who participated in the discussion gave the teacher the inaccurate impression that the class was able to follow along with what was discussed.

FIGURE 4.5   SIOP Evaluation for Mr. Dillon: Appropriate for ELLs

4	3	2	1	⓪	NA
10. **Speech** appropriate for students' proficiency level (e.g., slower rate and enunciation, and simple sentence structure for beginners)		**Speech** sometimes inappropriate for students' proficiency level		**Speech** inappropriate for students' proficiency level	

Explanation of Academic Tasks

English language learners at all levels (and native English speakers) do better in academic situations when the teacher gives clear instructions for assignments and activities. Moreover, the more practice students have with the types of tasks found in content classes, the better prepared they will be when they exit the language support program. It is critical for ELLs to have instructions presented in a step-by-step manner, preferably accompanied by a visual representation or demonstration of what is expected. According to case study data collected from ELLs in sheltered classes (Echevarria, 1998), teachers *do* make a difference in the way they present information to students. The following are some student comments:

- "She doesn't explain it too good. I don't understand the words she's saying because I don't even know what they mean."

- "She talks too fast. I don't understand the directions."
- "He talks too fast. Not patient."
- "It helps when he comes close to my desk and explains stuff in the order that I have to do it."

These students' comments illustrate the importance of providing a clear explanation of teachers' expectations for lessons, including delineating the steps of academic tasks. This point cannot be overstated. In our observations of classes, many "behavior problems" are often the result of students not being sure what they are supposed to do. A cursory oral explanation of an assignment can leave many students without a clue as to what to do to get started. The teacher, frustrated with all the chatter, scolds students, exhorting them to get to work. However, students do not know *how* to get to work and oftentimes do not know how to articulate that fact to the teacher.

Teaching Scenarios

The three teachers' lessons on buoyancy continued:

Example 1   As the lesson progressed in Mr. Lew's class, the students were told that, working in small groups, they were to complete an activity. Mr. Lew was very explicit in his instructions. As he gave students instructions orally, he wrote each step on the overhead projector transparency. He said,

> First, you will get in your assigned groups and be ready to perform the role that has been assigned to each of you. Second, you will make shapes out of aluminum foil and try to get them to float [*he puts a small aluminum foil boat on the water and it floats*]. Third, you will calculate the object's volume [*the students already know how to do this*] and write it on the worksheet; and fourth, you will determine the maximum mass the boat will hold before it sinks. Finally, you will calculate the mass/volume ratio. You will write all of these numbers on the worksheet.

Then Mr. Lew told the students to watch as he demonstrated. He took a piece of aluminum foil and shaped it into a long, narrow boat. He pointed to #2 on the transparency, took the boat and filled its interior space with water, and then dumped the water into a measuring cup to calculate the volume of the boat. He wrote this number on the worksheet.

Mr. Lew went on to determine the maximum mass and the mass/volume ratio, writing each step on the overhead transparency as he did it. He told the students that they must make at least five different boat shapes during the experiment. He wrote the number "5" next to step #2 on the overhead.

After Mr. Lew showed students the steps for calculating mass/volume ratios described here, he gave students 30 seconds to get in their assigned group, get their items organized for the experiments, and begin working. Mr. Lew circulated around the classroom supervising the students and answering their questions. After about five minutes, Mr. Lew determined that all the groups except one were clear about the assignment. To clarify for the other group, Mr. Lew drew that group's attention to a group that was doing well. He asked one student to stand and explain the steps of what they were doing. As the student talked, Mr. Lew pointed to the step-by-step instructions on the overhead projector transparency. When the student finished explaining, Mr. Lew asked the confused group to explain what they were going to do. That brief peer-modeling situation clarified the assignment for the confused group and reinforced the other groups' understanding as well.

SIOP Evaluation: Mr. Lew received a "4" on the SIOP for Explanation of Academic Tasks. He walked the students through each step of the experiment, demonstrating what they were expected to do. When a group hadn't gotten started, he had other students model the steps of the assignment for the class, drawing their attention again to the overhead's instructions.

FIGURE 4.6 SIOP Evaluation for Mr. Lew: Explanation of Academic Tasks

④	3	2	1	0	NA
11. **Explanation** of academic tasks clear		**Explanation** of academic tasks somewhat clear		**Explanation** of academic tasks unclear	

Example 2 As described previously, Mrs. Castillo's teaching approach involved having students read through several pages of the chapter independently, pausing after every couple of pages to ask students to identify unfamiliar vocabulary. Students were assigned words to look up in the glossary, and the class discussed the meaning of the words. Mrs. Castillo would then summarize the text material read so far and move on to the next portion of the chapter.

SIOP Evaluation: Mrs. Castillo received a score of "1" on this item of the SIOP. She did not explain what was expected during the lesson to the students, but the expectation was inferred by the format she used: read material, discuss unknown terms, teacher summarizes material read. Since Mrs. Castillo followed the same format whenever the class read from the text, the students knew what was expected.

FIGURE 4.7 SIOP Evaluation for Mrs. Castillo: Explanation of Academic Tasks

4	3	2	①	0	NA
11. **Explanation** of academic tasks clear		**Explanation** of academic tasks somewhat clear		**Explanation** of academic tasks unclear	

Example 3   After the class completed the worksheet for calculating mass/volume ratios, Mr. Dillon went over the answers as a whole group. He began by demonstrating how to calculate the first problem. He wrote the numbers on the overhead and went through the process. When he finished he said, "If you got the same answer as I did, raise your hand." About half of the students raised their hands. Mr. Dillon determined that he needed to demonstrate a few more problems so that more students would understand the process. He continued with the next three problems, asking students what they did differently. Finally, he told the class to work in pairs to review their work, checking the final problems against the process he demonstrated.

SIOP Evaluation: Mr. Dillon received a score of "1" on this item of the SIOP. First, he made unsubstantiated assumptions about the students' knowledge and ability to complete tasks. He said, "You remember how to calculate mass/volume ratios? . . . OK, just calculate the ratios for each object. . . ." and left them to work independently. He demonstrated how to calculate ratios, but he should have done that kind of demonstration *before* asking students to do it independently. Teaching is more effective when a good model is demonstrated initially for students to see rather than a post hoc review of students' work and correcting their mistakes. The process of explaining the assignment *after* students completed the worksheet was particularly confusing for the class's English language learners who struggled to make sense of the assignment, only to find out that they had calculated most of the problems incorrectly.

For in-class assignments and for homework, Mr. Dillon did not make his expectations clear by modeling and discussing what students were to do. He should have provided a step-by-step explanation of the academic tasks he asked students to complete.

FIGURE 4.8   SIOP Evaluation for Mr. Dillon: Explanation of Academic Tasks

4	3	2	①	0	NA
11. **Explanation** of academic tasks clear		**Explanation** of academic tasks somewhat clear		**Explanation** of academic tasks unclear	

Use of Techniques

Effective SI teachers make content concepts clear and understandable for English language learners through the use of a variety of techniques that make content comprehensible. We have observed some teachers who teach the same way for English language learners as they do for native English speakers, except that they use pictures for ELLs. We believe that the actual teaching techniques a teacher uses have a greater impact on student achievement than having a lot of pictures

illustrating content concepts. High-quality sheltered lessons offer students a variety of ways for making the content accessible to them. Although it might be impossible for teachers to present a variety of interesting hands-on lessons that include visuals to illustrate every concept and idea in the curriculum each period of every day, there does need to be sufficient planning to incorporate such techniques and activities throughout the week's lessons.

The techniques we suggest in the SIOP are critical for providing meaningful, understandable lessons to students learning English, including adapting the content to students' proficiency levels (Chapter 2); highlighting key vocabulary (Chapter 3); using scaffolding techniques and providing opportunities for students to use strategies (Chapter 5); and providing activities that allow students to apply newly acquired content and language knowledge (Chapter 7).

Teaching Scenarios

Example 1   After all groups had completed at least five boats' mass/volume ratios, Mr. Lew showed a table with columns for mass and volume figures on the overhead. He asked students to pool their data by selecting two boats per group and reporting their mass and volume. A representative from each group wrote the figures in the appropriate columns on the overhead transparency. Then Mr. Lew told the class that they would use these data to construct a graph, plotting the maximum mass held by the boat on the y-axis and the boat's volume on the x-axis.

Each student then plotted the mass to volume ratios on their individual graphs. At the end of the lesson, Mr. Lew asked the students to look at the objective written on the board and then asked each student to write on his or her paper why some objects float and others sink.

SIOP Evaluation: Mr. Lew received a score of "4" on this item of the SIOP. He did an excellent job of providing visuals through the use of the tanks and aluminum foil, as well as by using the overhead projector. Not only did he write the vocabulary and assignment for students to see, he consistently referred back to the visual information. In addition to providing a clear explanation of the assignment, this technique teaches student to use visual clues to help gain understanding.

Mr. Lew walked students through each step of the experiment, demonstrating what they were expected to do. In general, behavior problems are reduced and student success with the task is higher when clear explanations and expectations about assignments are provided.

Also, Mr. Lew used graphing and writing effectively to review the concepts of the lesson. Notice that these academic tasks came after students were already familiar with the lesson's concepts, which increases the likelihood that students will be able to successfully complete academic tasks.

Finally, students were able to apply their knowledge through the hands-on activity, making the concepts of mass, volume, and buoyancy tangible, and thus more understandable. Measuring a boat's actual volume and determining maximum mass by adding to the mass by hand makes the concepts come alive for students. Compare the benefit of this hands-on activity to the other scenarios in which the students simply went through paper-and-pencil tasks. Surely those students learned and remembered less about buoyancy and mass-to-volume ratios than did the students in Mr. Lew's class.

FIGURE 4.9 SIOP Evaluation for Mr. Lew: Use of Techniques

④	3	2	1	0	NA
12. Uses a variety of **techniques** to make content concepts clear (e.g., modeling, visuals, hands-on activities, demonstrations, gestures, body language)		Uses some **techniques** to make content concepts clear		Uses few or no **techniques** to make content concepts clear	

Example 2 As mentioned previously, Mr. Dillon assigned students words to look up and define in writing and then use each word in an original sentence for homework. He lectured from the text and provided students with a worksheet that they completed alone or in pairs.

SIOP Evaluation: Mr. Dillon received a "2" for this item. He attempted to use a number of techniques to make concepts clear such as using the text as a basis for discussion, providing a worksheet that showed different sized boats and other objects, and some demonstration for the calculations. Also, he let students work in pairs to calculate the mass-to-volume ratios. Mr. Dillon should have used more visuals, modeled what he expected from the students, and provided a hands-on activity for this lesson. Some lessons, like this one, lend themselves easily to hands-on activities, but Mr. Dillon did not take advantage of the opportunity.

FIGURE 4.10   SIOP Evaluation for Mr. Dillon: Use of Techniques

4	3	②	1	0	NA
12. Uses a variety of **techniques** to make content concepts clear (e.g., modeling, visuals, hands-on activities, demonstrations, gestures, body language)		Uses some **techniques** to make content concepts clear		Uses few or no **techniques** to make content concepts clear	

Example 3   Mrs. Castillo continued the lesson following the same format as described previously. She asked students to read a portion of the text, paused to clarify unknown vocabulary, and summarized the part of the text students had read. When they completed the chapter, Mrs. Castillo selected several end-of-chapter questions for students to answer. She let students work in pairs or groups to complete the questions, and then they discussed the answers together.

SIOP Evaluation: Mrs. Castillo received a score of "0" on this SIOP indicator. Mrs. Castillo was a compassionate teacher who showed concern about the academic success of the English language learners in her class. Her effort to help ELLs included clarifying unknown vocabulary (in a somewhat random fashion), paraphrasing or summarizing the chapter (done orally without visuals or other contextual clues), reducing the number of end-of-chapter questions (done independently by students), and having the students work together in answering questions (with no systematic checks for understanding). Although she had good intentions and wanted her students to understand the concept of buoyancy, Mrs. Castillo did not use the kind of techniques that facilitated conceptual understanding for these students.

The atmosphere in Mrs. Castillo's classroom was warm and nonthreatening for ELLs. She chatted with students throughout the class, and showed genuine interest in their well-being. Although she enjoys working with students from diverse cultural backgrounds, she needs to develop effective techniques and strategies to further students' learning.

The lesson was almost entirely oral, which was difficult for the beginning English speakers in her class to follow. Having students read a portion of the text followed by her summary was a good idea, except that there were no techniques used to ensure students understood the text, which was too difficult for them to read independently. She also did not teach them skills so that eventually they could read texts on their own. The summary was given orally, which means beginning English speakers got little understanding from it. Mrs. Castillo should have used a more structured approach to reading the text and discussing the concepts therein. Finally, she should have adjusted the number of questions students had to answer to their ability level because there was a good chance the entire exercise was meaningless for many students since their English proficiency and reading levels were well below the level of the text and its questions. The students worked diligently on the assignment because they liked Mrs. Castillo and wanted to please her, but they needed assistance in making the information meaningful—assistance beyond that which Mrs. Castillo provided.

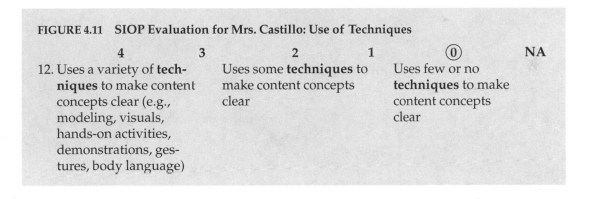

FIGURE 4.11   SIOP Evaluation for Mrs. Castillo: Use of Techniques

4	3	2	1	⓪	NA
12. Uses a variety of **techniques** to make content concepts clear (e.g., modeling, visuals, hands-on activities, demonstrations, gestures, body language)		Uses some **techniques** to make content concepts clear		Uses few or no **techniques** to make content concepts clear	

Summary

English language learners often report that teachers talk too fast and do not explain things well. We need to pay attention to these informants' comments, for they are our "customers." The effective SI teachers constantly modulate and adjust their speech when teaching English language learners to ensure that the context is comprehensible. Concepts are taught using a variety of techniques, including modeling, gestures, hands-on activities and demonstrations, so that students understand and learn the content material. Finally, effective sheltered teachers provide explanations of academic tasks in ways that make clear what students are expected to accomplish and that promote student success.

Discussion Questions

1. Have you recently been in a situation where you were not an "insider," and therefore you didn't understand what was being said? Compare that situation and your feelings about it to the use of jargon and idiomatic speech

within classrooms where there are English language learners. As a teacher, what can you do to make sure all students are able to follow a lecture or discussion?

2. It has been said that humans can "hold on" to no more than three oral directions at a time. Think of an academic task you might ask students to do and explain it clearly and simply in no more than three steps. What should you do if the task requires more than three steps?

3. Many times in classrooms, discipline problems can be attributed to students not knowing what they're supposed to be doing. What are some ways that a teacher can avoid having students confused about accomplishing academic tasks?

4. If someone were to explain something to you in a foreign language, what are some techniques they could use to make the message clearer?

5 Indicators of Instruction: Strategies

FIGURE 5.1 Instruction Section of the SIOP: Strategies

4	3	2	1	0	NA
13. Provides ample opportunities for students to use **strategies**		Provides students with inadequate opportunities to use **strategies**		No opportunity for students to use **strategies**	

4	3	2	1	0	NA
14. Consistent use of **scaffolding** techniques throughout lesson, assisting and supporting student understanding (e.g., think-alouds)		Occasional use of **scaffolding** techniques		No use of **scaffolding** techniques	

4	3	2	1	0	NA
15. Teacher uses a variety of **question types, including those that promote higher-order thinking skills** (e.g., literal, analytical, and interpretive questions)		Teacher infrequently poses **questions that promote higher-order thinking skills**		Teacher does not pose **questions that promote higher-order thinking skills**	

To this point, we have discussed elements of effective planning, background building, and content instruction for English language learners (ELLs). This chapter examines how we teach students to access information in memory, how we help them make connections between what they know and what they are learning, how we assist them in problem solving, and how we promote retention of newly

FIGURE 5.2   Unit: The Rain Forest (7th grade)

The three classrooms described in the teaching vignettes in this chapter are hetero-geneously mixed with English language learners who have intermediate and advanced fluency, and native English speakers. The middle school is in a suburban community with approximately 75% of the student population who are Hispanic English language learners.

Mrs. Montoya, Mrs. Fletcher, and Miss Lee, seventh-grade science teachers, are each teaching several lessons on the tropical rain forest. They are all using the same arti-cle taken from a science news magazine designed for middle school students. District content standards for seventh-grade science include the following guiding questions:

1. Where are the tropical rain forests on Earth?
2. Why are rain forests needed to support life on Earth?
3. Why are rain forests being destroyed?
4. What is the effect of the destruction of the rain forests?
5. What can we do to protect our rain forests?

The illustrated teaching vignettes take place during the first and second days of the unit on the rain forest.

---

learned information. This involves the explicit teaching of strategies that facilitate the learning process. Techniques and methods for learning and retaining informa-tion are systematically taught, reviewed, and assessed in effective sheltered class-rooms.

The lessons on the tropical rain forest that follow illustrate how three seventh-grade science teachers incorporate the teaching of strategies into their classrooms (see Figure 5.2).

Background

As introduced in Chapter 3, researchers have learned that information is retained and connected in the brain through "mental pathways" that are linked to an indi-vidual's existing schema (Anderson, 1984; Barnhardt, 1997). If the schemata for a particular topic are well developed and personally meaningful, new information is easier to retain and recall, and proficient learners initiate and activate their asso-ciations between the new and old learning.

In cognitive theory, this initiation and activation are described as the men-tal processes that enhance comprehension, learning, and retention of informa-tion. Competent language learners actively engage these cognitive skills, and researchers know these learners are effective, in part, because they have special ways of processing the new information they are learning. These mental processes are called *learning strategies* because they are "the special thoughts or behaviors that individuals use to help them comprehend, learn, or retain new information" (O'Malley & Chamot, 1990, p. 1).

Strategies

There is a growing body of research evidence to indicate that learning strategies include the following three types (O'Malley & Chamot, 1990):

1. **Metacognitive Strategies.** The process of purposefully monitoring our thinking is referred to as metacognition (Baker & Brown, 1984). Metacognition is characterized by (1) matching thinking and problem-solving strategies to particular learning situations, (2) clarifying purposes for learning, (3) monitoring one's own comprehension through self-questioning, and (4) taking corrective action if understanding fails (Dermody & Speaker, 1995). The use of metacognitive strategies implies awareness, reflection, and interaction; and strategies are used in an integrated, interrelated, and recursive manner (Dole, Duffy, Roehler, & Pearson, 1991; Vogt & Verga, 1998).

2. **Cognitive Strategies.** These are directly related to individual learning tasks and they are used by learners when they mentally and/or physically manipulate material to be learned, or when they apply a specific technique to a learning task (Pressley, Johnson, Symons, McGoldrick, & Kurita, 1989; O'Malley & Chamot, 1990). For example, taking notes or creating a personal semantic map while reading or listening to a lecture has been found to enhance learning for many people.

3. **Social/Affective Strategies.** These are identified in the research literature on cognitive psychology as the social and affective influences on learning (O'Malley & Chamot, 1990). For example, learning can be enhanced when people interact with each other to clarify a confusing point or when they participate in a group discussion or cooperative learning group to solve a problem.

In a somewhat different scheme, Muth and Alvermann (1999, p. 233) suggest there is a continuum of strategies that occur during the teaching–learning process (see Figure 5.3)—teacher-centered, teacher-assisted, peer-assisted, and student-centered.

The ultimate goal is for students to develop independence in self-monitoring and self-regulation through practice with peer-assisted and student-centered strategies. Many English language learners, however, have difficulty initiating an active role in using these strategies because they are focusing mental energy on their developing language skills. Therefore, SI teachers must scaffold ELLs by providing many opportunities for them to use a variety of strategies that have been found to be especially effective.

FIGURE 5.3   Continuum of Strategies

Teacher-Centered	Teacher-Assisted	Peer-Assisted	Student-Centered
Lecture	Drill and practice	Role playing	Rehearsal strategies
Direct instruction	Discovery learning	Peer tutoring	Repeated readings
Demonstration	Brainstorming	Reciprocal teaching	Selective underlining
Recitation	Discussion	Cooperative learning	Two-column notes
			Elaboration strategies
			Mental imagery
			Guided imagery
			Creating analogies
			Organizational strategies
			Clustering
			Graphic organizers
			Outlining

The national ESL Standards for Pre-K–12 Students (TESOL, 1997) recognize the importance of ELL's learning strategies. One standard for each of the three goals—to use English in social settings, to use English to achieve academically in all content areas, and to use English in socially and culturally appropriate ways—highlights strategic knowledge:

Goal 1, Standard 3: Students will use learning strategies to extend their communicative competence.

Goal 2, Standard 3: Students will use appropriate learning strategies to construct and apply their academic knowledge.

Goal 3, Standard 3: Students will use appropriate learning strategies to extend their sociolinguistic and sociocultural competence.

The ESL Standards' document (TESOL, 1997) provides guidance to teachers in terms of the types of behaviors students should exhibit in order to meet the standards. Our interest relates primarily to Goal 2, Standard 3, which refers to academic achievement. The following are some suggested behaviors for teachers to foster:

- Focusing attention selectively; that is, focusing on the "big picture" and most important information
- Situating new learning in context; that is, building on what students already know and what is familiar
- Applying self-monitoring and self-corrective strategies to build and expand a knowledge base; that is, knowing how to "fix-it" when comprehension is impeded

- Evaluating one's own success in a completed learning task; that is, self-assessing one's competence and knowledge
- Recognizing the need for and seeking assistance appropriately from others
- Imitating the behaviors of native English speakers to complete tasks successfully
- Knowing when to use native language resources (human and material) to promote understanding (TESOL, 1997, p. 91).

Whatever strategies are emphasized, learned, and used, it is generally agreed that they should be taught through explicit instruction, careful modeling, and scaffolding. However, Paris, Lipson, and Wixson (1983) suggest that teaching a variety of strategies is not enough. Rather, learners need not only *declarative* knowledge (What is a strategy?) but they also need *procedural* knowledge (How do I use it?), and *conditional* knowledge (When and why do I use it?). When teachers model strategy use and then provide appropriate scaffolding while children are practicing strategies, they are likely to become more effective strategy users (Pressley & Woloshyn, 1995).

When teaching strategies, effective sheltered teachers employ a variety of approaches, such as the following:

- **Mnemonics:** A memory system often involving visualization and/or acronyms
- **SQP2R:** An approach to content teaching and learning involving these steps (Vogt, 2000):
  1. **S**urveying (scanning the text to be read for 1–2 minutes)
  2. **Q**uestioning (having students generate questions likely to be answered by reading the text, with teacher guidance)
  3. **P**redicting (stating 1–3 things students think they will learn based on the questions that were generated)
  4. **R**eading (searching for answers to questions and confirming/disconfirming predictions)
  5. **R**esponding (answering questions and formulating new ones for the next section of text to be read)
- **PENS:** Students are taught to **P**review ideas, **E**xplore words, **N**ote words in a complete sentence, and **S**ee if the sentence is okay (Deshler, Ellis, & Lenz, 1996).
- **GIST**: This summarization procedure assists students in "getting the gist" from extended text (Muth & Alvermann, 1999). Together, students and teacher read a section of text printed on a transparency. After reading, assist students in underlining 10 or more words or concepts that are deemed "most important" to understanding the text. List these on the board and together write a summary statement or two using as many of the listed words as possible. Repeat the process through subsequent sections of the text. When finished, write an overall summary sentence for the entire text that was read.

- **Rehearsal Strategies**: Rehearsal is used when verbatim recall of information is needed (McCormick & Pressley, 1997; Muth & Alvermann, 1999). Visual aids, such as flashcards, engage students during rehearsal; and strategies, such as underlining and note-taking, help students commit information to memory.
- **Graphic organizers:** These are graphic representations of key concepts and vocabulary. Teachers present them as schematic diagrams of information being taught and students use them to organize the information they are learning. Examples include Venn diagrams, timelines, flow charts, semantic maps, and so forth.
- **Comprehension strategies:** Dole, Duffy, Roehler, and Pearson (1991) recommend that students' comprehension of text is enhanced when teachers incorporate strategy instruction that includes prediction, self-questioning, monitoring, determining importance, and summarizing. These strategies were identified in what has come to be known as the "proficient reader research" because: (1) proficient readers use them in all kinds of text; (2) they can be taught; and (3) the more they are taught and practiced, the more likely students are to use them independently in their own reading. In their study involving at-risk students, Keene and Zimmerman (1997) report that reading test scores can be elevated through scaffolded instruction of these strategies.

One of the most widely accepted methods for teaching strategies to English language learners is the Cognitive Academic Language Learning Approach (CALLA) created by Chamot and O'Malley (1987, 1994). It is an instructional model for content and language learning that incorporates student development of learning strategies. Developed initially for intermediate and advanced ESL students in content-based ESL classes, it has had wider application over the years in sheltered classes as well. The CALLA method incorporates the three previously identified categories of learning strategies: metacognitive, cognitive, and socio-affective. Through carefully designed lesson plans tied to the content curriculum, teachers explicitly teach the learning strategies and have students apply them in instructional tasks. These plans are based on the following propositions (O'Malley & Chamot, 1990, p. 196):

1. Mentally active learners are better learners
2. Strategies can be taught
3. Learning strategies transfer to new tasks
4. Academic language learning is more effective with learning strategies

Teaching Scenarios

The following vignettes illustrate the strategy instruction of three teachers.

Example 1   After distributing the magazine article on the tropical rain forest to his class, Mr. Montoya engaged his students in a preview-and-predict activity. He asked the students to take one minute to individually preview the text material by examining illustrations, photographs, bold print, italicized print, and so forth. This was a familiar process for his students, and when directed all engaged in the preview. At the end of one minute, Mr. Montoya stopped the process and directed the students to work with a partner to write three things they thought they would learn from the article. When finished, the partners shared their predictions with another pair and the lists were expanded. Eventually, all groups reported their predictions while Mr. Montoya listed them on the board.

The teacher then began reading the first section of the article aloud while the students followed along in their copies of the text. When he concluded reading, he modeled a summarizing strategy, *GIST*, by identifying the most important words and concepts in the section just read. He quickly listed these on another part of the board and together the class formulated a summary of what was read.

At this point, Mr. Montoya referred students back to the list of predictions on the board. Next to each prediction that was confirmed in the reading, a "+" was written, while predictions that were disconfirmed were marked with a "–." Predictions that were unlikely to be discussed in the remainder of the article were erased. A few additional predictions were then generated by the class prior to Mr. Montoya's directions to quietly read the next section of the text with a partner or in a triad.

When students finished the group reading activity, they discussed with their partners or group members the most important words and/or concepts and summarized what they had read. They then checked their predictions according to the process Mr. Montoya had previously modeled.

SIOP Evaluation: Mr. Montoya received a "4" on the SIOP for Strategies. He taught and modeled two important processing strategies, prediction and summarization. Mr. Montoya modeled both processes first and then encouraged the students to work with each other while putting them to use as they read the rain forest article.

FIGURE 5.4   **SIOP Evaluation for Mr. Montoya: Strategies**

④	3	2	1	0	NA
13. Provides ample opportunities for students to use **strategies**		Provides students with inadequate opportunities to use **strategies**		No opportunity for students to use **strategies**	

Example 2   Mrs. Fletcher began her lesson by distributing the rain forest article to the students. She told them the title, "Our Burning Forests." She asked the students to predict from the title and opening photograph what they though the article would be about. One boy said, "It looks like the jungle." Another said, "I think it's about parrots." Mrs. Fletcher then began reading the article, stopping once to

ask the class, "What do you think will happen to the animals in this rain forest?" At the conclusion of the article, she asked each of the students to write a paragraph on what they learned about rain forests.

SIOP Evaluation: Mrs. Fletcher received a "1" for the Strategies indicator. She did ask students to make predictions from the title of the article but did not build on or reinforce the two students' predictions, nor did she seek other predictions during the text reading. We often see teachers ask for predictions and then think that's all that's needed for strategy practice.

   Further, Mrs. Fletcher did not assist students in note-taking nor did she provide a graphic organizer or other means for students to organize information they were supposed to learn. She also could have strengthened the lesson by periodically stopping her oral reading to reinforce important concepts and discuss predictions that were confirmed or disconfirmed. Even though Mrs. Fletcher had the students write a paragraph about the article at the end of the reading, she missed the opportunity to model a summarizing strategy throughout.

FIGURE 5.5   SIOP Evaluation for Mrs. Fletcher: Strategies

4	3	2	①	0	NA
13. Provides ample opportunities for students to use **strategies**		Provides students with inadequate opportunities to use **strategies**		No opportunity for students to use **strategies**	

Example 3   Miss Lee introduced the magazine article by presenting a brief lecture on the rain forest and by showing a variety of photographs. She then divided the students into groups of four and asked one person in each group to read the article to the group members. When the students were finished, they independently wrote the answers to 10 fill-in-the-blank questions.

SIOP Evaluation: Miss Lee received a "0" for the Strategies item. At no point during her lesson were students required to engage in using strategies, and she did very little to assist them in learning the material. Students were required to complete the questions with little or no scaffolded support.

FIGURE 5.6   SIOP Evaluation for Miss Lee: Strategies

4	3	2	1	⓪	NA
13. Provides ample opportunities for students to use **strategies**		Provides students with inadequate opportunities to use **strategies**		No opportunity for students to use **strategies**	

Scaffolding Techniques

Scaffolding is a term associated with Vygotsky's (1978) notion of the Zone of Proximal Development (ZPD). In essence, the ZPD is the difference between what a child can accomplish alone and what he or she can accomplish with the assistance of a more experienced individual. In the classroom, teachers scaffold instruction when they provide substantial amounts of support and assistance in the earliest stages of teaching a new concept or strategy, and then decrease the amount of support as the learners acquire experience through multiple practice opportunities.

There are two types of scaffolding that can be used effectively with English language learners. One is *verbal scaffolding,* in which teachers, aware of ELLs' existing levels of language development, use prompting, questioning, and elaboration to facilitate students' movement to higher levels of language proficiency, comprehension, and thinking. Effective teacher–student interaction promotes confidence when it is geared to a student's language competence. The following are examples of verbal scaffolding:

- **Paraphrasing**—restating a student's response in order to model correct English usage
- **Using "think-alouds"**—carefully structured models of how effective strategy users think and monitor their understandings (Baumann, Jones, & Seifert-Kessell, 1993)
- **Reinforcing contextual definitions**—an example would be: "Aborigines, the people native to Australia, were being forced from their homes."

In addition to this important verbal scaffolding, effective teachers incorporate instructional approaches that provide procedural scaffolding. These include, but are not limited to, the following:

1. Using an instructional framework that includes explicit teaching, modeling, and practice opportunities with others, and expectations for independent application (see Figure 5.7)
2. One-on-one teaching, coaching, and modeling

FIGURE 5.7 Scaffolding Model: Teach, Model, Practice, Apply

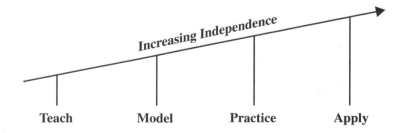

FIGURE 5.8   Scaffolding Model: Grouping

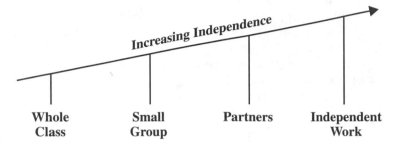

3. Small group instruction with children practicing a newly learned strategy with another more experienced student
4. Partnering students for reading activities, with a more experienced reader assisting one with less experience

Teaching Scenarios

Each of the three teachers in the preceding vignettes attempted to support their students' learning, though they succeeded to varying degrees. Note the differences in the scaffolding they provided.

Example 1   In the previously described scenario, Mr. Montoya provided considerable scaffolding for his students. He built background and generated predictions with the preview-and-predict activity. He also incorporated a variety of grouping configurations in the lesson: whole class, small groups, and partners. Students had the opportunity to confer with each other, receiving support and assistance if necessary. Mr. Montoya also carefully modeled the predicting and summarizing strategy activities for the students prior to requiring application. The reading demands of the article were reduced when students were allowed to read it together in pairs or triads.

FIGURE 5.9   SIOP Evaluation for Mr. Montoya: Scaffolding Techniques

④	3	2	1	0	NA
14. Consistent use of **scaffolding** techniques throughout lesson, assisting and supporting student understanding (e.g., think-alouds)		Occasional use of **scaffolding** techniques		No use of **scaffolding** techniques	

SIOP Evaluation: Mr. Montoya received a "4" for Scaffolding Techniques. He incorporated a wide variety of techniques, providing support with the expectation that his students would be able to eventually apply the strategies independently.

Example 2 You may recall that Mrs. Fletcher asked her students to make predictions from the title of the article on the rain forest, and she stopped reading only once during the lesson to ask for another prediction. She also read the article orally to the class.

SIOP Evaluation: Mrs. Fletcher received a "1" for Scaffolding Techniques. She provided her students with limited scaffolding by eliciting the few predictions. Her oral reading of the text significantly reduced the reading demands of the text. However, if she continues to read everything aloud to the students, she won't be gradually reducing her support and the students will be less likely to become independent readers. Therefore, her scaffolding might have been more effective if she had begun reading the article to the students and then had them complete the reading with a partner. Obviously, this presumes that the article's difficulty is such that the students could successfully read it with help from one another.

FIGURE 5.10   SIOP Evaluation for Mrs. Fletcher: Scaffolding Techniques

4	3	2	①	0	NA
14. Consistent use of **scaffolding** techniques throughout lesson, assisting and supporting student understanding (e.g., think-alouds)		Occasional use of **scaffolding** techniques		No use of **scaffolding** techniques	

Example 3 Again referring back to the previous scenarios, Miss Lee gave a brief lecture on the rain forest accompanied by photographs. She had the students read the article in groups, taking turns. After the article was completed, the students independently completed a fill-in-the-blank worksheet.

SIOP Evaluation: Miss Lee received a "2" on the SIOP for Scaffolding Techniques. The photographs she displayed during her lecture provided additional support for students who had little background knowledge about the topic of rain forests. By having the students complete the reading by taking turns in their groups, the reading demands were reduced. Had Miss Lee just lectured, with no accompanying photographs, required the students to independently read the article, and then required them to complete the worksheet by themselves, she would have received a "0" on the SIOP for this indicator.

FIGURE 5.11   SIOP Evaluation for Miss Lee: Scaffolding Techniques

4	3	②	1	0	NA
14. Consistent use of **scaffolding** techniques throughout lesson, assisting and supporting student understanding (e.g., think-alouds)		Occasional use of **scaffolding** techniques		No use of **scaffolding** techniques	

Questioning

Another way that teachers can promote strategy use is by asking questions that promote critical thinking. More than 40 years ago, Bloom and colleagues (1956) introduced a taxonomy of educational objectives that includes six levels: Knowledge, Comprehension, Application, Analysis, Synthesis, Evaluation. This taxonomy was formulated on the principle that learning proceeds from concrete knowledge to abstract values, or from the denotative to the connotative (Nagel, Vogt, & Kaye, 1998). Educators adopted this taxonomy as a hierarchy of questioning that, when used in the classroom, elicits varied levels of student thinking. A similar hierarchy of comprehension collapsed the six levels into three, referred to as Literal, Interpretive, and Applied (Ruddell, 1997).

Over the years, teachers have been encouraged to vary the levels of oral and written questions with special attention to those at the top four levels of Bloom et al.'s taxonomy. However, researchers have found that of the approximately 80,000 questions the average teacher asks annually, 80% of them are at the Literal or Knowledge level (Gall, 1984; Watson & Young, 1986). This is especially problematic with English language learners. As children are acquiring proficiency in English, it is tempting to rely on simple questions that result in yes/no or other one-word responses.

It is possible, however, to reduce the linguistic demands of responses while still promoting higher levels of thinking. For example, in a study of plant reproduction, the following question requires little thought: "Are seeds sometimes carried by the wind?" A nod or one-word response is almost automatic if the question is understood. A higher-level question such as the following requires analysis: "Which of these two seeds would be more likely to be carried by the wind: the round one or smooth one? Or this one that has fuzzy hairs?" Encouraging students to respond with higher levels of thinking requires teachers to consciously plan and incorporate questions at a variety of levels.

Teaching Scenarios

In the following scenarios, each of the three teachers employs questioning with varying degrees of effectiveness.

Example 1   Mr. Montoya began the second day's lesson on the rain forest by introducing three titles the students would read in discussion circles. He gave a "book talk" for each book, building interest and curiosity. The teacher had chosen which students would be in each of the discussion circles, with six per group. Group membership was determined primarily by the students' reading levels and English proficiency, as well as other factors such as leadership skill, participation, and motivation.

Only Mr. Montoya knew that the three titles varied considerably in reading difficulty. *Life in the Rain Forests* (Baker, 1997) was an easier selection, while *Learn About Rain Forests* (Green, 1998) was deemed to be of average difficulty. *Tropical Rain Forests: Our Endangered Planet* (Mutel & Rogers, 1993) was the most challenging of the selections. Not wanting to group students solely by ability, Mr. Montoya attempted to heterogeneously mix many of the students, but the English language learners were placed in groups with the books that had more considerate ("student-friendly") content.

Multiple copies of each book were made available to the groups. Mr. Montoya introduced the discussion circle activity by carefully explaining four questions he had written on the board:

1. Why are we dependent on the rain forests for our survival on Earth?
2. Compare and contrast the arguments of foresters and environmentalists. With which argument do you most agree? Why?
3. Imagine the Earth in a hundred years. How would you describe it if the present rate of deforestation continues?

4. Pretend you are the President of the United States. You are writing a letter to the president of the lumber company that is responsible for burning many acres of rain forest. What would you say in your letter to convince her to stop destroying the rain forest and practice sustainable lumber development?

The students began reading their books together, volunteering to read to others in the group. After the students read for approximately 20 minutes, Mr. Montoya asked them to complete the section of the book they were reading, and to focus their attention on the four questions. They were to come to consensus in their answers to the questions, based on what they had learned to this point.

SIOP Evaluation: Mr. Montoya received a "4" on the SIOP for Questioning. By providing the varied levels of books to the students, he attempted to meet their reading needs while still expecting each of them to think critically about the questions he assigned. Note the varied levels of the questions: The first is a knowledge-level question, the second requires analysis and evaluation, the third requires application and synthesis, and the fourth requires synthesis and evaluation. Mr. Montoya effectively reduced the texts' difficulty, not the levels of his questions.

FIGURE 5.12   SIOP Evaluation for Mr. Montoya: Questioning

④	3	2	1	0	NA
15. Teacher uses a variety of **question types, including those that promote higher-order thinking skills** (e.g., literal, analytical, and interpretive questions)		Teacher infrequently poses **questions that promote higher-order thinking skills**		Teacher does not pose **questions that promote higher-order thinking skills**	

Example 2   In the next class, Miss Lee reinforced what the students had read in the magazine article by showing a video on the rain forests in the Amazon. When the students completed viewing the video, Miss Lee distributed a study guide and the copy of the article that had been read the previous day. The study guide included the following questions:

1. How much of the Earth's surface is covered by rain forests?
2. What percent of the Earth's species are found in rain forests?
3. What are three products that are produced from the rain forests?
4. Why are the rain forests being burned or cut?
5. Which people are doing the burning and cutting?

6. One of the birds found in the rain forest is a _____.
7. Global warming is believed to be caused by _____.
8. I hope the rain forests are not all cut down because _____.

SIOP Evaluation: Miss Lee received a "1" for the Questioning indicator. Questions 1 through 7 are essentially knowledge-level questions, those with answers that could be found in the rain forest article or by viewing the video. Question 8, however, requires some application of the content concepts.

FIGURE 5.13   SIOP Evaluation for Mrs. Fletcher: Questioning

4	3	2	①	0	NA
15. Teacher uses a variety of **question types, including those that promote higher-order thinking skills** (e.g., literal, analytical, and interpretive questions)		Teacher infrequently poses **questions that promote higher-order thinking skills**		Teacher does not pose **questions that promote higher-order thinking skills**	

Example 3   Mrs. Fletcher opened her second day of study on the rain forest by distributing the paragraphs the students had written the previous day. After a brief discussion of the contents of the papers, Mrs. Fletcher showed the video on the rain forest. At the conclusion of the video, the teacher said, "Please put your papers away. Let's move on to the next lesson."

SIOP Evaluation: Mrs. Fletcher received a "0" for Questioning. In this particular lesson, she made no effort to promote critical thinking about the video or the topic.

FIGURE 5.14   SIOP Evaluation for Miss Lee: Questioning

4	3	2	1	⓪	NA
15. Teacher uses a variety of **question types, including those that promote higher-order thinking skills** (e.g., literal, analytical, and interpretive questions)		Teacher infrequently poses **questions that promote higher-order thinking skills**		Teacher does not pose **questions that promote higher-order thinking skills**	

Summary

In some of our classes we frequently tell preservice candidates preparing to be teachers, "Just because the students can't read doesn't mean they can't think!" A similar adage to this might be said of English language learners, "Just because they can't speak English proficiently doesn't mean they can't think!"

In this chapter, we have described how to promote critical and strategic thinking for all students, but most especially for ELLs. Learning is made more effective when teachers actively assist students in developing metacognitive, cognitive, and social/affective strategies, those that promote self-monitoring and problem solving. We believe that students with developing English proficiency should not be denied effective, creative, and generative teaching while they are learning the language. By conscientiously sheltering instruction through strategy teaching and modeling, by appropriately scaffolding support, and by thoughtfully asking questions that require students to interpret, apply, and synthesize, we increase the chances that English language learners will become critical thinkers.

Discussion Questions

1. Describe a learning situation you participated in in which the teacher modeled how to do something through demonstration. What worked and what didn't? How could the teacher have made things more clear?
2. Strategies are an important part of a teacher's repertoire. What are effective ways to teach students the use of strategies to enhance their learning? With a partner, demonstrate how to teach effectively a mnemonic strategy to English language learners.
3. The concept of scaffolding is often confusing. Consider the term to represent the construction process in which scaffolds are put in place to support a building. As the building becomes more complete, less scaffolding is necessary. When the building can stand on its own, the scaffolding is completely removed. The same may be said for teaching. How does the building analogy apply to teaching new information to English language learners?
4. Here's a factual question a teacher might ask based on a social studies text: "Who was the first President of the United States?" Given the topic of the presidency, what are several additional questions you could ask that promote higher-order thinking? Why is it important to use a variety of questioning strategies with English language learners?

6 Indicators of Instruction: Interaction

FIGURE 6.1   Instruction Section of the SIOP: Interaction

4	3	2	1	0	NA
16. Frequent opportunities for **interaction** and discussion between teacher/student and among students, which encourage elaborated responses about lesson concepts		**Interaction** mostly teacher-dominated with some opportunities for students to talk about or question lesson concepts		**Interaction** primarily teacher-dominated with no opportunities for students to discuss lesson concepts	

4	3	2	1	0	NA
17. **Grouping configurations** support language and content objectives of the lesson		**Grouping configurations** unevenly support the language and content objectives		**Grouping configurations** do not support the language and content objectives	

4	3	2	1	0	NA
18. Consistently provides sufficient **wait time for student responses**		Occasionally provides sufficient **wait time for student responses**		Never provides sufficient **wait time for student responses**	

4	3	2	1	0	NA
19. Ample opportunities for students to **clarify key concepts in L1** as needed with aide, peer, or L1 text		Some opportunity for students to **clarify key concepts in L1**		No opportunity for students to **clarify key concepts in L1**	

English language learners (ELLs) benefit from structured opportunities to use the target language (English) in multiple settings and across content areas. Because of the large number of English language learners in schools today, *all* teachers are teachers of English, even if their content specialization is science, math, or social studies. For students learning English, teachers must create ample opportunities to practice using *academic* language, not simply social uses of language. And the language must be meaningful to students; it is not just the quantity of exposure to English that affects learning, but it is the quality as well (Wong-Fillmore & Valadez, 1986).

Background

Studies have indicated that, in most classrooms, teachers dominate the linguistic aspect of the lesson, leaving students severely limited in terms of opportunities to use language in a variety of ways (Cazden, 1986; Goodlad, 1984; Sirotnik, 1983). In a study of programs for ELLs (Ramirez, Yuen, Ramey & Pasta, 1991), it was found that the classes were characterized by excessive teacher talk. When students were given an opportunity to respond, it usually involved only simple information-recall statements, restricting students' chance to produce language and develop complex language and thinking skills. Instead of teachers talking and students listening, sheltered content classes should be structured so that students are interacting in their collaborative investigation of a body of knowledge (Diaz, 1989).

We find that it is interesting and helpful to analyze actual transcripts from lessons to demonstrate the kind of teacher dominance that is so prevalent in classrooms. The following transcripts are from a pilot study (Echevarria, Greene & Goldenberg, 1996) in middle school social studies classes. The teachers were videotaped teaching the same content about consumerism to English language learners, the first using a typical approach found in mainstream classes and the other using a sheltered approach. Both classes had approximately 25 students and in this lesson they were learning how to read labels on clothing and on a bottle of antiseptic.

> *Mainstream Lesson*
> TEACHER: Look at the piece of clothing at the bottom. It says (*he reads*), "This shirt is flame-resistant," which means what?
> STUDENT: Could not burn.
> STUDENT: Won't catch fire.
> TEACHER: It will not burn, won't catch fire. Right (*continues reading*). "To retain the flame-resistant properties"—what does "to retain" mean?
> STUDENT: (*unintelligible*)
> TEACHER: To keep it. All right. "In order to keep this shirt flame-resistant (*he reads*), wash with detergent only." All right (*he reads*). "Do not use soap or bleach. Tumble dry. One hundred percent polyester." Now, why does it say, "Do not use soap or bleach"?
> STUDENT: 'Cause it'll take off the . . .

TEACHER: It'll take off the what?

STUDENTS: (*fragmented responses*)

TEACHER: It'll take off the flame-resistant quality. If you wash it with soap or bleach, then the shirt's just gonna be like any old shirt, any regular shirt, so when you put a match to it, will it catch fire?

STUDENT: No.

TEACHER: Yes. 'Cause you've ruined it then. It's no longer flame-resistant. So the government says you gotta tell the consumer what kind of shirt it is, and how to take care of it. If you look at any piece of clothing: shirt, pants, your shirts, um, your skirts, anything. There's always going to be a tag on these that says what it is made of and how you're going to take care of it. OK. And that's for your protection so that you won't buy something, and then treat it wrong. So labeling is important. All right. Let's review. I'll go back to the antiseptic. What did we say indications meant? Indications? Raise your hands, raise your hands. Robert?

STUDENT: What's it for.

TEACHER: What is it for, when do you use this? OK. What do directions, what is that for, Victor?

STUDENT: How to use . . .

TEACHER: How to use. OK, so indications is when you use it (*holds one finger up*), directions is how you use it (*holds another finger up*), and warnings is what?

STUDENTS: (*various mumbled responses*)

TEACHER: How you don't use it. This is what you don't do.

The teacher in this case tended to finish sentences for the students and accept any form of student comment without encouraging elaborated responses.

Sheltered Instruction

TEACHER: Most clothing must have labels that tell what kind of cloth was used in it right? Look at the material in the picture down there (*points to picture in text*).[1] What does it say, the tag right there?

STUDENT: The, the, the . . .

TEACHER: The tag right there.

STUDENT: (*Reading*) "Flame-resis . . ."

TEACHER: Resistant.

STUDENT: "Flame-resistant. To retain the flame-resistant properties, wash with detergent only. Do not use soap or bleach. Use warm water. Tumble dry."

---

[1]The teacher explained then that they would be doing an activity in which they would read labels for information.

TEACHER: "One hundred percent . . ."

STUDENT: "Polyester."

TEACHER: Now, most clothes carry labels, right? (*pointing to the neck of her sweater*). They explain how to take care of it, like dry clean, machine wash, right? It tells you how to clean it. Why does this product have to be washed with a detergent and no soap or bleach?

STUDENT: Because clothes . . .

TEACHER: Why can't you use something else?

STUDENTS: (*several students mumble answers*)

STUDENT: (*says in Spanish*) Because it will make it small.

TEACHER: It may shrink, or (*gestures to a student*) it may not be . . . what does it say?

STUDENT: It's not going to be able to be resistant to fire.

TEACHER: Exactly. It's flame-resistant, right? So, if you use something else, it won't be flame-resistant anymore. How about the, uh, look at the *antiseptic* (*holds hands up to form a container*)—the picture above the shirt, the antiseptic?

STUDENT: Read it?

TEACHER: Antiseptic (*Teacher reads*), and other health products you buy without a prescription often have usage and warning labels. So what can you learn from this label? Read this label quietly please, and tell me what you can learn from the label. Read the label on that antiseptic. (*Students read silently.*)

TEACHER: What can you learn from this label?

STUDENT: It kills, oh I know.

TEACHER: Steve?

STUDENT: It kills germs.

STUDENT: Yeah, it kills germs.

TEACHER: It kills germs. You use it for wounds, right? What else?

STUDENTS: (*various enthusiastic responses*)

TEACHER: One person at a time. OK, hold on. Veronica was saying something.

STUDENT: It tells you in the directions that, you could use it, that like that, 'cause if you use it in another thing, it could hurt you.

TEACHER: It could hurt you. OK, what else? Ricardo?

STUDENT: If you put it in your mouth, don't put it in your mouth or your ears or your eyes.

TEACHER: Very good. Don't put it in your mouth, ears, and eyes. OK, for how many days should you use it? No more that what?

STUDENT: No more than ten days.

STUDENT: Ten days.

TEACHER: So don't use it—you have to follow what it says so don't use it more than ten days. Now, the next activity you're going to do . . .

FIGURE 6.2   Unit: Third-Grade Math

The third-grade teachers in this chapter, Mrs. White, Mr. Yacoob, and Mrs. Thomas, work in a suburban school that has a 24% ELL population. Their classes have an even distribution of English language learners, approximately 10% ELLs each. Most of those students are at the intermediate to advanced intermediate levels of English proficiency, and still benefit from having teachers use sheltered techniques to increase their understanding of lessons.

The teachers in this school plan math units around the district's content standards. The lessons described in the scenarios that follow are part of a unit on subtraction with regrouping designed to meet the mathematics content standard: "Students will understand the numeration system by relating counting, grouping, and place-value concepts." The teachers each have their own methods for teaching subtraction with regrouping, as seen in the lessons that follow.

The sheltered teacher allowed for a balance of teacher-to-student talk and encouraged student participation. The sheltered teacher asked questions, waited for students' responses, and restated or elaborated on the responses. The three teachers in this chapter also vary in their classroom interaction (see Figure 6.2).

Opportunities for Interaction

This item emphasizes the importance of balancing linguistic turn-taking between the teacher and students, and among students. As mentioned previously, we have clear evidence that teachers tend to do most of the talking in class. While teachers certainly have knowledge to share and discuss with students, learning is more effective when students have an opportunity to participate fully in lessons by discussing ideas and information. Students benefit from using the target language and practicing expression of their ideas, opinions, and answers in English. Effective SI teachers structure their lessons in ways that promote student discussion and they strive to provide a more balanced linguistic exchange between themselves and their students. It can be particularly tempting for teachers to do most of the talking when students are not completely proficient in their use of English, but these students are precisely the ones who need opportunities to practice using English the most.

Effective sheltered teachers also encourage elaborated responses from students when discussing the lesson's concepts. The teacher elicits more extended student contributions by using a variety of techniques that will take students beyond simple yes or no answers and short phrases (Echevarria, 1995b; Goldenberg, 1992–1993). Some of these techniques include asking students to expand on their answers by saying, "Tell me more about that"; and by asking direct questions to prompt more language use such as, "What do you mean by . . ." or "What else. . . ." Another technique is to provide further information through questions

such as: "How do you know?" "Why is that important?" "What does that remind you of?" Other techniques include offering restatements such as, "In other words . . . is that accurate?" and by frequently pausing to let students process the language and formulate their responses. Some teachers often call on other students to extend a classmate's response.

Making these techniques a part of a teacher's repertoire requires practice. The teachers with whom we've worked report that they had to consciously practice overcoming the temptation to speak for students or to complete a student's short phrase. The preceding transcript showed how the first teacher spoke for the students instead of encouraging students to complete their thoughts. The following segment from the transcript provides an example:

TEACHER: What do "directions," what is that for, Victor?

STUDENT: How to use . . .

TEACHER: How to use. OK, so "indications" is when you use it, "directions" is how you use it, and "warnings" is what?

STUDENTS: (various mumbled responses)

TEACHER: How you don't use it. This is what you don't do.

In this segment, the mainstream teacher could have encouraged a more balanced exchange between himself and the students. First, he did not encourage students to completely express their thoughts; he accepted partial and mumbled answers. Secondly, he answered for the students, dominating the linguistic aspect of the lesson. It is easy to imagine how students could become disinterested, passive learners in a class in which the teacher accepts minimal participation and does the majority of the talking.

The sheltered teacher approached students–teacher interaction differently:

TEACHER: What can you learn from this label?

STUDENT: It kills, oh I know.

TEACHER: Steve?

STUDENT: It kills germs.

STUDENT: Yeah, it kills germs.

TEACHER: It kills germs. You use it for wounds, right? What else?

STUDENTS: (*various enthusiastic responses*)

TEACHER: One person at a time. OK, hold on. Veronica was saying something.

STUDENT: It tells you in the directions that, you could use it, that like that, 'cause if you use it in another thing, it could hurt you.

TEACHER: It could hurt you. OK, what else? Ricardo?

STUDENT: If you put it in your mouth, don't put it in your mouth or your ears or your eyes.

TEACHER: Very good. Don't put it in your mouth, ears, and eyes. OK, for how many days should you use it? No more than what?

STUDENT: No more than ten days.

STUDENT: Ten days.

TEACHER: So don't use it—you have to follow what it says, so don't use it more than ten days. Now, the next activity you're going to do . . .

The sheltered teacher let the students have time to express their thoughts (e.g., student says, "It kills . . . It kills germs."). The teacher could have completed the sentence for the student, but she waited for him to complete his answer. Also, the sheltered teacher encouraged and challenged the students more than the mainstream teacher did by asking twice, "What else?" Finally, the teacher nominated students who volunteered to talk and repeated what they said so that the class could hear a full response (e.g., Veronica).

Effective sheltered teachers make sure that they provide frequent opportunities for meaningful exchanges among students and balance the amount of talk evenly between the teacher and students. Further, effective SI teachers consciously strive to draw out elaborated responses from the English language learners in their classes.

Moreover, effective teachers plan instruction so that students have opportunities to speak with one another to accomplish academic tasks. Through meaningful interaction, students can practice speaking and making themselves understood. That implies asking and answering questions, negotiating meaning, clarifying ideas, giving and justifying opinions, and more. Students may interact in pairs, triads, and small groups. Literature circles, think-pair-share, jigsaw readings, debates, and science experiments are only a sample of the types of activities teachers can include in lessons to foster student–student interaction.

Teaching Scenarios

In planning their lessons, each of the third-grade teachers considered opportunities for student interaction to varying degrees, as seen in the vignettes that follow.

Example 1   Mrs. White began teaching the unit on regrouping by reviewing key vocabulary, such as place-value, digit, and difference. She then showed a subtraction problem that required regrouping (20 – 13 = ?) on the overhead transparency. She told the class that they would have 30 seconds to work with a partner to figure out how they might solve the subtraction problem.

After 30 seconds, Mrs. White directed students' attention to the problem on the overhead and told them to see if their ideas matched her explanation. She then placed another transparency on the overhead that had three columns, one representing the 1s place, one for the 10s place and one for the 100s place. She asked the students which place the 20 from 13 went in and she placed three cubes in the 1s column.

She continued this process until the problem was accurately represented by place-value blocks (cubes and sticks) in the columns on the overhead. Then Mrs. White took the class through the steps of regrouping, modeling the process on the overhead as she discussed it with the class. The discussion was balanced between teacher talk and student talk and included a lot of verbal prompting on the teacher's part. For example, she said, "Why can't I take three away from zero? Then, what would I do next? Why? Okay, so are you saying that I borrow one ten and give it to the ones place? Is that correct? Jade, can you tell me in your own words what Gabriela just told us?"

After she checked that all the students had an understanding of the steps for subtracting with regrouping, she grouped the students by fours and gave each group of four students a worksheet that resembled the columns on the overhead (see Figure 6.3a and b) with the number 200 written in the columns at the top. They were also given a game board with columns, number cubes (similar to dice), and enough place-value blocks (cubes and sticks) to represent the number 200 on the game board.

Mrs. White then gave a detailed explanation of how to play a game in which students rolled the number cubes, put them side by side to make a two-digit number, and then they were to decide which digit was in the 1s place and 10s place. Students then subtracted the number from 200, using regrouping and followed the model the teacher had demonstrated. The group that removed all blocks from the game board first won. This regrouping activity gave students the opportunity to practice speaking English through play and problem solving for nearly 30 minutes.

FIGURE 6.3a   Math Manipulatives and Activity Lesson on Subtraction with Regrouping

Name _____   Date _____

Hundreds	Tens	Ones
2	0	0

FIGURE 6.3b Math Manipulative Worksheet

Name _____

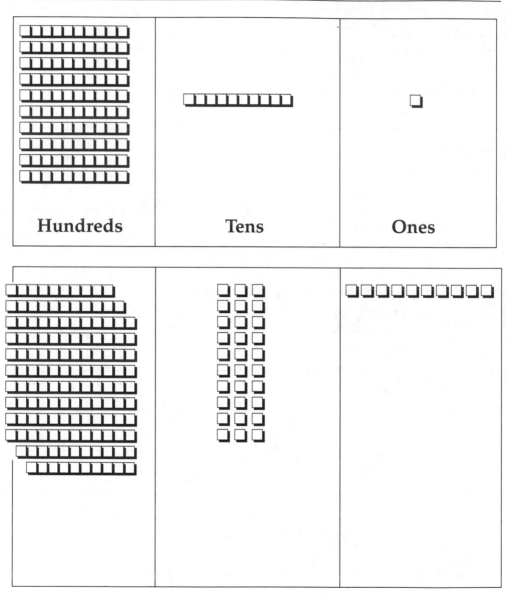

SIOP Evaluation: Mrs. White received a score of "4" on this item of the SIOP. Not only did she involve students in the whole group discussion by using techniques to draw out elaborated language, she also made sure that students had plenty of opportunities (nearly 30 minutes) to talk about the lesson's concept among themselves. She created opportunities for students to engage in meaningful interaction about the lesson's concepts, while at the same time practice using English.

FIGURE 6.4   SIOP Evaluation for Mrs. White: Interaction

④	3	2	1	0	NA
16. Frequent opportunities for **interaction** and discussion between teacher/student and among students, which encourage elaborated responses about lesson concepts		**Interaction** mostly teacher-dominated with some opportunities for students to talk about or question lesson concepts		**Interaction** primarily teacher-dominated with no opportunities for students to discuss lesson concepts	

Example 2   Mr. Yacoob introduced the unit on subtraction with regrouping by drawing a sketch of a house on the overhead projector transparency. Then he asked the students if they or their parents had ever borrowed something from a neighbor. He gave the example of his mother cooking and when she realized she was out of an ingredient, she went next door and got it from a neighbor. Several students gave examples of getting items from or giving items to neighbors. Mr. Yacoob then told the students that today they would learn a way of subtracting that involved regrouping, or using other resources. He wrote a problem on the overhead: $52 - 7 = \_\_$. Then he asked the class, holding up two fingers, "Can I subtract seven from two?" He went on to discuss the issue of only having 2 of something and needing to subtract 7.

Mr. Yacoob explained that he could go next door (pointing to the 5) and use a 10 to regroup the 1s. He gave the class a brief review of the 1s, 10s, and 100s place. Then he explained that they would be using a 10 from the 10s place. Mr. Yacoob solved the problem for the class, explaining each step as he did it. He spent the next 15 minutes solving several problems, reinforcing each step of the regrouping process and calling on individual students to explain the step-by-step process. At times, he encouraged students to elaborate on their responses and at other times he tended to accept one or two word responses or completed students' sentences for them. After he was sure the class understood how to subtract with regrouping, he told the students to get into their groups and spend 10 minutes completing 15 subtraction problems from their textbook, helping one another as needed.

SIOP Evaluation: Mr. Yacoob received a "3" on the SIOP for this item. He planned a lesson that included opportunities for students to interact with him and each other. During the whole group portion of the lesson, Mr. Yacoob involved students in the discussion by calling on individuals and asking them to explain the process of regrouping. At times he encouraged students to elaborate on their responses and at other times he tended to accept one or two word responses or he completed students' sentences for them.

Students were also given the opportunity to use academic language in their groups. Students assisted one another in solving the assigned subtraction problems. However, overall the lesson tended to be teacher-dominated. Student groups were an effective way to provide opportunities for interaction but Mr. Yacoob only allowed 10 minutes for students to work together and the rest of the class time was teacher directed whole-group instruction.

FIGURE 6.5   SIOP Evaluation for Mr. Yacoob: Interaction

4	③	2	1	0	NA
16. Frequent opportunities for **interaction** and discussion between teacher/student and among students, which encourage elaborated responses about lesson concepts		**Interaction** mostly teacher-dominated with some opportunities for students to talk about or question lesson concepts		**Interaction** primarily teacher-dominated with no opportunities for students to discuss lesson concepts	

Example 3   Mrs. Thomas introduced the unit on regrouping by having students open their books to the first page on subtraction with regrouping. She then, on the chalkboard, showed the students how to regroup. She explained each step as she performed it. Then she said, "Do you understand how this is done? Let me do a couple more problems so you're sure." Mrs. Thomas proceeded to complete three more problems on the board. Then she told the students to complete the first five problems in their books and they would correct them together.

Students completed the problems independently and then Mrs. Thomas wrote each problem on the board. She asked for volunteers to come to the board and solve a problem. Several students came forward and completed the subtraction problems on the board. Then Mrs. Thomas had the class focus their attention on the board as she went through each problem to check its accuracy. Students corrected their own papers as each problem was reviewed. After Mrs. Thomas believed her students understood the process of subtraction with regrouping, she assigned the remaining 20 problems on the page, telling students that the ones they didn't finish in class would be homework.

SIOP Evaluation: Mrs. Thomas received a "0" on the SIOP item related to interaction and discussion. The lesson represented what we have learned about many classrooms from the research: It was primarily teacher-dominated with few or no opportunities for students to discuss the lesson's concepts. The ELLs in Mrs. Thomas's class did not practice using English, and especially not academic English. They were in what is called a "passive language-learning environment" (Ramirez et al., 1991). Students passively listened to instruction and the large group format probably inhibited them from speaking out or asking questions.

FIGURE 6.6   SIOP Evaluation for Mrs. Thomas: Interaction

4	3	2	1	⓪	NA
16. Frequent opportunities for **interaction** and discussion between teacher/student and among students, which encourage elaborated responses about lesson concepts		**Interaction** mostly teacher-dominated with some opportunities for students to talk about or question lesson concepts		**Interaction** primarily teacher-dominated with no opportunities for students to discuss lesson concepts	

Grouping Configurations

Over the years, we have learned that homogeneous grouping for instruction (low group, average group, high group) has serious academic and social effects for students who are not in the top group (Hiebert, 1983). Frequently referred to as "tracking," the practice of providing instruction to students in instructional groups segregated by ability or performance level has been found to be inequitable because it often differentiates across socioeconomic and ethnic lines, and it promotes differentiated expectations for students' success. When working with low-achieving groups, teachers have been found to talk more, use more structure, ask lower-level questions, cover less material, spend more time on skills and drills, provide fewer opportunities for leadership and independent research, encourage more oral than silent reading, teach less vocabulary, and allow less wait time during questioning, plus they spent twice as much time on behavior and management issues.

In many schools, it has become common practice to group English language learners with low-achieving students regardless of academic ability and performance. However, all students, including ELLs, benefit from instruction that frequently includes a variety of grouping configurations. Whole-class groups are beneficial when they develop classroom community and provide a shared experience for everyone. Flexible small groups promote the development of multiple perspectives and encourage collaboration. Partnering encourages success because it provides practice opportunities, scaffolding, and assistance for classmates (Flood, Lapp, Flood, & Nagel, 1992; Tompkins, 1997).

Effective sheltered classes are characterized by a variety of grouping structures, including individual work, partners, triads, small groups of four or five, cooperative learning groups, and whole-group. Groups also vary in that they may be homogeneous or heterogeneous by gender, language proficiency, language background, and/or ability. There are times that it may be most effective to have students grouped by language-proficiency level. For example, if a teacher's goal is for students at beginning levels of English proficiency to practice using a particular language structure within the context of a social studies lesson, such as present progressive (-*ing* form), then it may be useful to have those students grouped together for that lesson. Likewise, when developing the skills of students with low levels of literacy, it makes sense to have those with similar ability grouped together for a particular lesson. Grouping all ELLs together regularly is *not* good practice, especially when a bilingual aide teaches them almost exclusively. In SI classes, ELLs are given the same access to the curriculum and the teacher's expertise as native English speaking students.

Using a variety of grouping configurations also facilitates learning in a couple of ways. One, the variety of groups helps to maintain students' interest. It is difficult for some students to stay focused when the classroom is always set up the same way with the teacher talking to the whole class or having students work individually on their own. Moving from a whole group to cooperative groups or partners adds variety to the learning situation and increases student involvement in the learning process.

Second, varying grouping structures increases the chance that a student's preferred mode of instruction will be matched. For instance, some students work best with a partner, getting somewhat distracted in a large group. Other students are stimulated by the many perspectives shared in a large group and do well in that setting.

It is recommended that at least two different grouping structures be used during a lesson, depending on the activity and objectives of the lesson.

Teaching Scenarios

The third-grade teachers in this chapter implemented grouping structures to support the objectives of the lesson to varying degrees, as you will see in the scenarios that follow.

Example 1   In her lesson on subtraction with regrouping, Mrs. White made sure that students were given the opportunity to participate in a variety of grouping structures. She began the lesson with the whole group, ensuring that all students were given the same initial instruction. Within the whole-group format, she gave students the opportunity to brainstorm with a partner. After Mrs. White provided whole-group instruction, she had students work in their preassigned groups of four, practicing regrouping by playing the subtraction game.

SIOP Evaluation: Mrs. White received a "4" on the SIOP for this item. She used the right amount of grouping structures—not too many but enough to support the language and content objectives she had established for the lesson. The large group instruction accompanied by visuals, modeling, and student–teacher interaction was effective for delivering new information to the class. The discussion between partners was appropriate because it provided students with a more comfortable situation for discussing new information. Most students would prefer not to hazard a guess in front of an entire class, but may feel more confident sharing their ideas with a partner. Finally, Mrs. White had students work in groups of four during the game. This type of structure is effective for teaching students to cooperate and work together toward a common goal, plus it provides time for students to talk together about an academic topic. The groups were small enough for the teacher to spot a student who did not understand regrouping (content objective).

Finally, the variety of grouping configurations facilitated oral discussion of the lesson's concepts (language objective). Overall, the groups Mrs. White used fully supported the language and content objectives of the lesson.

FIGURE 6.7   SIOP Evaluation for Mrs. White: Grouping

④	3	2	1	0	NA
17. **Grouping configurations** support language and content objectives of the lesson		**Grouping configurations** unevenly support the language and content objectives		**Grouping configurations** do not support the language and content objectives	

Example 2   The lesson Mr. Yacoob taught included two types of groupings, whole class and small group. He prefers to conduct direct teaching for the first one-half to three-fourths of the lesson and then have students work together for the remainder of the time.

SIOP Evaluation: Mr. Yacoob received a "2" on the SIOP item related to grouping. The small group structure provided students with a nonthreatening means of discussion and questioning. But the lesson in its entirety did not fully support the language and content objectives. Students easily "slip through the cracks" of instruction when there is heavy reliance on whole-class instruction (more than half the lesson). More variety in grouping configurations would have yielded a higher rating for Mr. Yacoob.

Another concern was that Mr. Yacoob relied on the same lesson format every day (whole-class, direct instruction followed by small groups). While this does ensure that two grouping configurations are met, the groupings are not varied from day to day. This practice leads to boredom on the students' part and may limit the interaction of those students who work best with partners or even inhibit those who do better individually. Grouping configurations should vary across a week of instruction.

FIGURE 6.8   SIOP Evaluation for Mr. Yacoob: Grouping

4	3	②	1	0	NA
17. **Grouping configurations** support language and content objectives of the lesson		**Grouping configurations** unevenly support the language and content objectives		**Grouping configurations** do not support the language and content objectives	

Example 3   As described previously, Mrs. Thomas conducted a whole-group lesson by demonstrating on the board how to work out subtraction problems with regrouping. Then she had students solve problems independently, correcting the problems on the board as a group. Finally, students completed their work individually.

SIOP Evaluation: Mrs. Thomas received a "0" on this SIOP indicator. She employed what would be considered a recitation approach to teaching (Tharp & Gallimore, 1988). She did not afford her students any opportunity to experience different grouping configurations. They worked independently or listened to the teacher's instruction.

The type of instructional format Mrs. Thomas used tends not to promote active learning. Students passively listened to instruction and the large-group format may have inhibited them from speaking out or asking questions. Recitation teaching restricts opportunities for students to use language to express their ideas in meaningful ways. It is possible, even probable, that some students in Mrs. Thomas's class had questions about the process of subtraction with regrouping, or needed clarification about exactly what they were expected to do. But the very structure of the teaching environment limited the learning of those students who have difficulty focusing on the instruction when it is done exclusively in front of the class in a large-group setting. Some students cannot see the board well, others are distracted by all the competing noise and movement in the classroom, and still others require more active involvement to maintain their attention. Also, whole-group instruction limits the time all students have to talk and thus practice English.

Effective SI teachers plan lessons that allow students to work in groups, sharing ideas, discussing the academic tasks, and using English to interact with peers.

FIGURE 6.9   SIOP Evaluation for Mrs. Thomas: Grouping

4	3	2	1	⓪	NA
17. **Grouping configurations** support language and content objectives of the lesson		**Grouping configurations** unevenly support the language and content objectives		**Grouping configurations** do not support the language and content objectives	

Wait Time

Wait time is the length of time between utterances during an interaction. In classroom settings, it refers to the length of time that teachers wait for students to respond before interrupting, answering a question themselves, or calling on someone else to participate. Wait time varies by culture; it is appropriate in some cultures to let seconds, even minutes, lag between utterances, while in other cultures utterances can even overlap one another. In U.S. classrooms, the average length of wait time is clearly *not* sufficient. Imagine the impact of wait time on ELLs who are processing ideas in a new language and need additional time to formulate the phrasings of their thoughts.

Effective sheltered teachers consciously allow students to express their thoughts fully, without interruption. Many teachers in U.S. schools are uncomfortable with the silence that follows their questions or comments, and they immediately fill the void by talking themselves. This situation may be especially pertinent in sheltered classes where ELLs need extra time to process questions in English, and then to formulate their response. Although teachers may be tempted to fill the silence, ELLs benefit from a patient approach to classroom participation, in which teachers wait for students to complete their verbal contributions.

While effective sheltered teachers provide sufficient wait time for ELLs, they also work to find a balance between wait time and moving a lesson along. Some students may become impatient if the pace of the class lags. One strategy for accommodating impatient students is to have the more advanced students write down their responses while waiting, and then they check their answers against the final answer.

Teaching Scenarios

The length of wait time varied from teacher to teacher in the scenarios that follow.

Example 1   Mrs. White was careful to make sure she allowed students time to formulate their thoughts and express their ideas. During the whole-group instruction, she paused after asking questions and called on students who volunteered with a response, and gently prompted those who did not volunteer. After asking a question of both types of students, Mrs. White patiently waited for their responses, providing verbal scaffolding as needed. For example, when Mrs. White asked why three could not be subtracted from zero, one girl shyly said, "Can't take nothing." Mrs. White responded with, "OK, so if there is nothing, or zero, what?" (She waited while the student formulated her sentence.) The student then replied, "You can't take away." Mrs. White said, "Good. If there is nothing in the one's place, or zero, then there's nothing to take away, right? Then what do you do?" She waited for another student to volunteer and give his answer.

SIOP Evaluation: Mrs. White received a "4" for the SIOP for Wait Time. She understood the importance of allowing students sufficient wait time, and she consciously practiced patience in waiting for students' responses. It may be quite tempting to interrupt or answer for students, especially as they struggle to express their ideas in English. However, the importance of enough wait time cannot be overstated. One teacher with whom we worked reported that she put her hand over her mouth after asking a probing question to remind herself to keep quiet and let the students answer in their own time.

FIGURE 6.10   SIOP Evaluation for Mrs. White: Wait Time

④	3	2	1	0	NA
18. Consistently provides sufficient **wait time for student responses**		Occasionally provides sufficient **wait time for student responses**		Never provides sufficient **wait time for student responses**	

Example 2   Mr. Yacoob occasionally provided sufficient wait time when the students and teacher interacted. At the beginning of the lesson, when asking about the students' experiences with borrowing from neighbors, Mr. Yacoob patiently waited for students to express their stories. However, as the lesson progressed and Mr. Yacoob became concerned about completing the lesson, he tended to cut students off verbally and finish their sentences for them.

SIOP Evaluation: Mr. Yacoob received a score of "2" on this indicator. Sometimes he provided sufficient wait time and other times he did not. Wait time was a feature of sheltered instruction that Mr. Yacoob was working on because his speaking style was one in which he tended to interrupt the speaker, making overlapping comments as the speaker talked. He and his family were accustomed to this type of speaking pattern, but Mr. Yacoob became aware that his natural speaking pattern did not foster students' participation, especially in his ELLs. He observed how students shut down after he interrupted them, and he had difficulty coaxing them to participate afterward. Mr. Yacoob has made progress in the area of wait time, and needs to continue doing so.

FIGURE 6.11   SIOP Evaluation for Mr. Yacoob: Wait Time

4	3	②	1	0	NA
18. Consistently provides sufficient **wait time for student responses**		Occasionally provides sufficient **wait time for student responses**		Never provides sufficient **wait time for student responses**	

Example 3   Given the type of recitation instruction Mrs. Thomas used in the lesson, there was little oral student participation. She had students come to the board to explain their answers, but when a student hesitated or couldn't think of a word, Mrs. Thomas completed the sentence for him or her.

SIOP Evaluation: Mrs. Thomas received a "0" on the SIOP for Wait Time. As a caring teacher, Mrs. Thomas thought she was helping students, especially the English language learners, by providing them with the vocabulary they were lacking. Her intent was to take the pressure off the speaker by completing sentences for them when she noticed they hesitated to formulate their own sentences. What Mrs. Thomas didn't understand is that ELLs require wait time to process language and to think about how to express their response. Students are deprived of opportunities to use language in meaningful ways when they are cut off and the answer is completed for them.

FIGURE 6.12   SIOP Evaluation for Mrs. Thomas: Wait Time

4	3	2	1	⓪	NA
18. Consistently provides sufficient **wait time for student responses**		Occasionally provides sufficient **wait time for student responses**		Never provides sufficient **wait time for student responses**	

Clarify Key Concepts in L1

Best practice indicates that English language learners benefit from opportunities to clarify concepts in their native language (L1). Although sheltered instruction involves teaching subject-matter material in English, students are given the opportunity to have a concept or assignment explained in their L1 as needed. Significant controversy surrounds the use of L1 for instructional purposes, but we believe that clarification of key concepts in students' L1 by a bilingual instructional aide, peer, or through the use of materials written in the students' L1 provides an important support for the academic learning of those students who are not yet fully proficient in English.

This item on the SIOP often has NA circled as a score because not all sheltered classes have the resources for or a need to use (especially for advanced ELLs) students' L1 to clarify concepts for them.

Teaching Scenarios

You will see, as described in the following class scenarios, that students had the opportunity to use their L1 to varying degrees. Notice the circumstances under which L1 was used effectively.

Example 1   In Mr. Yacoob's class there was a balanced, structured use of L1 within student groups. Groups were organized so that they included native English speakers with ELLs from the same language group. When ELLs needed clarification, the group worked together to come to understanding, using L1 as needed.

Also, Mr. Yacoob had Spanish math book texts available for students who needed additional clarification of regrouping.

SIOP Evaluation: Mr. Yacoob received a score of "4" on this SIOP item. The native language was not overused or restricted in his classroom. There was ample opportunity for students to use L1 for clarification.

FIGURE 6.13   SIOP Evaluation for Mr. Yacoob: Clarify Key Concepts in L1

④	3	2	1	0	NA
19. Ample opportunities for students to **clarify key concepts in L1** as needed with aide, peer, or L1 text	Some opportunity for students to **clarify key concepts in L1**		No opportunity for students to **clarify key concepts in L1**		

Example 2   Mrs. Thomas asked the students to solve five subtraction problems individually, then they corrected the problems on the board together as a class. After reviewing the problems on the board, students were asked to complete the remainder of the problems on their own. During the time students worked on their own, Mrs. Thomas was working at her desk. She didn't circulate among the students to monitor their work, which resulted in a lot of student-to-student talking, mostly in Spanish. Many times, from her desk, Mrs. Thomas reminded the class to be quiet, but she also told the students that if they had trouble solving a problem, they could ask each other for help. Mrs. Thomas didn't mind if students used their native language when helping one another.

SIOP Evaluation: Mrs. Thomas received a "1" on the SIOP for this item. She understood the notion that the most efficient learning takes place when students understand the instruction, and for English language learners the native language (L1) is often used for clarifying an instruction that was delivered in English. However, there was little monitoring of student learning during the time they were working on their own, so it was unclear if the talking was for academic or social purposes.

Mrs. Thomas received "1" point of credit on the SIOP because she intended to have students use Spanish to help each other. She could have increased her score by making sure that the use of students' L1, or any language, was structured around an academic purpose. During a sheltered lesson, the teacher uses English as the medium of instruction but students may use their L1 with a bilingual aide, and with peers for clarifying key concepts. Also, for those students literate in their native language, L1 texts are valuable resources. Simply allowing students to talk in any language is not a good instructional practice.

FIGURE 6.14   SIOP Evaluation for Mrs. Thomas: Clarify Key Concepts in L1

4	3	2	①	0	NA
19. Ample opportunities for students to **clarify key concepts in L1** as needed with aide, peer, or L1 text		Some opportunity for students to **clarify key concepts in L1**		No opportunity for students to **clarify key concepts in L1**	

Example 3   Mrs. White was a skillful teacher but was uncomfortable with students speaking other languages in her classroom. Although she had seen that allowing students to help one another in their native language seemed to be effective, she felt that she couldn't monitor on-task conversations if the students weren't speaking English at all times. She told the bilingual aide to offer assistance in English only so that students could maximize the amount of English input they received.

SIOP Evaluation: Mrs. White's score on this SIOP indicator was "0." It is not only the amount of input a student receives but the quality of the input. Mrs. White provided ample opportunities for students to practice hearing and using English in this lesson. If a student was confused about regrouping, the lesson's content objective, then he or she should have had the opportunity to have the concept clarified in an understandable way—through the language he or she understands best.

Mrs. White was clearly committed to having her students learn English by the excellent way that she scaffolded instruction, provided wait time, and designed the lesson in a way that maximized interaction. However, clarifying concepts in the L1 will only enhance understanding of the content, and doesn't detract from the students' opportunity to learn English.

FIGURE 6.15   SIOP Evaluation for Mrs. White: Clarify Key Concepts in L1

4	3	2	1	⓪	NA
19. Ample opportunities for students to **clarify key concepts in L1** as needed with aide, peer, or L1 text		Some opportunity for students to **clarify key concepts in L1**		No opportunity for students to **clarify key concepts in L1**	

Summary

For English language learners, teachers need to create ample opportunities for students to practice using academic English, among themselves and with teachers.

Incorporating a number of grouping configurations into lessons often facilitates using English in ways that support the lessons' objectives.

The evidence is clear that for most teachers, balancing the interchange between themselves and their students continues to be challenging. Effective sheltered teachers plan for and incorporate structured opportunities for students to use English in a variety of ways.

Discussion Questions

1. Think of a content concept that you might be teaching. Describe three different grouping configurations that could be used for teaching and learning this concept. How would you organize the members of each group? How would you monitor student learning? What would you want students to do while working in their groups? How would the grouping configurations facilitate learning for ELLs?

2. Either videotape your own classroom while you're teaching a lesson or observe another teacher's classroom for a 15-minute segment. Estimate the proportion of teacher talk and student talk. Given the ratio of teacher–student talk, what are some possible ramifications for English language learners in the class?

3. English language learners are often reticent to contribute to class discussions. An important role for a sheltered teacher is to encourage ELLs to participate in nonthreatening ways. What are some specific techniques you can use to encourage students to elaborate on their responses and express their thoughts fully? What can you do to ensure sufficient wait time for students to formulate and express their thoughts?

4. The use of primary language (L1) instruction is controversial today. What are the pros and cons of primary language support in sheltered classrooms? Why do you think this is such a contentious issue?

Indicators of Instruction: Practice/Application

FIGURE 7.1   Instruction Section of the SIOP: Practice/Application

4	3	2	1	0	NA
20. Provides **hands-on** materials and/or manipulatives for students to practice using new content knowledge		Provides few **hands-on** materials and/or manipulatives for students to practice using new content knowledge		Provides no **hands-on** materials and/or manipulatives for students to practice using new content knowledge	

4	3	2	1	0	NA
21. Provides activities for students to **apply content and language knowledge** in the classroom		Provides activities for students to **apply** either **content or language knowledge** in the classroom		Provides no activities for students to **apply content or language knowledge** in the classroom	

4	3	2	1	0	NA
22. Uses activities that integrate all **language skills** (i.e., reading, writing, listening, and speaking)		Uses activities that integrate some **language skills**		Uses activities that apply to only one **language skill**	

One common memory that most adults share is of learning to ride an adult bike. Even after riding smaller bicycles with training wheels, most of us were unprepared for the balancing act required for us not to fall down when riding a "big" bike. If you had an older brother or sister who talked you through the process, showed you how to balance, and perhaps even held onto the bike while you were steadying yourself, your independent practice time with the big bike was probably enhanced. Talking about the experience, listening to someone else describe it,

FIGURE 7.2   Unit: Ecosystems (11th grade)

The three eleventh-grade general biology classrooms described in the teaching vignettes in this chapter are in a large urban high school. Approximately 65% of the students in the classes are English language learners and they are nearly all in the beginning and advanced-beginning stages of English language fluency. The other students in the classes are heterogeneously mixed.

The general biology standards for the eleventh grade require that teachers include the study of ecosystems, water and nutrient cycling, symbiosis, life cycles, and decomposition. Scientific processing skills include making observations, recording data, forming hypotheses, making models, project design, and experimentation. For the scenarios described in this chapter, the teachers have designed an extended unit on *ecosystems* (ecological communities that, together with their environment, form a unit) and *symbiosis* (a close relationship between two or more species that may or may not benefit each other). The lessons extend over several days.

observing other riders, and then practicing for yourself all worked together to turn you into a bicycle rider. That feeling of accomplishment, of mastering something new through practice and application, is a special feeling that most of us have experienced as learners.

Background

In this chapter, we discuss how sheltered teachers provide English language learners (ELLs) with the types of hands-on experiences, guidance, and practice that can lead to mastery of content knowledge. The teaching vignettes demonstrate how three high school general biology teachers, all of whom have large numbers of ELLs in their classes, designed biology lessons on ecosystems (see Figure 7.2).

Hands-On Materials and/or Manipulatives for Practice

As previously mentioned, riding a bike is usually preceded by practicing with training wheels and working with a more experienced bike rider. Obviously, the more practice one has on the bike the more likely one is to become a good bike rider. Now, think about learning to play a musical instrument.

Some years ago, an entrepreneur decided to market a piano-teaching course that included a cardboard sheet printed with piano keys. Students were supposed to practice the piano on the paper keyboard by following the directions printed in the course manual. The black-and-white keys on the keyboard were printed and dotted lines represented where students were supposed to place their fingers during practice sessions. It was little surprise that the paper keyboards didn't catch on even though the course manual clearly described in incremental steps how to play the piano, because even with hours of practicing on the paper keyboard, students were still unable to play the piano well. In this case, it wasn't just the *practice* that was important. Without hearing the sounds during practice, learning to play the piano was an artificial and nearly impossible task.

When learning to ride a bicycle, play the piano, or articulate how convex lenses differ from concave, students have a greater chance of mastering content concepts and skills when they are given multiple opportunities to practice in relevant, meaningful ways. When this practice includes "hands-on" experiences including manipulatives, practice sessions are enhanced. Madeline Hunter (1982), a renowned expert in teaching methods, coined the term "guided practice" to describe the process of the teacher leading the student through practice sessions prior to expecting independent application. She suggested that we keep the following four questions (and their answers) in mind as we plan lessons involving hands-on practice for students (pp. 65–68):

1. How much material should be practiced at one time? *Answer:* A short meaningful amount. Always use meaning to divide your content into parts.
2. How long in time should a practice period be? *Answer:* A short time so the student exerts intense effort and has intent to learn.
3. How often should students practice? *Answer:* New learning, massed practice. Older learning, distributed practice. [Hunter explains that massed practice means several practice periods scheduled close together. Distributed practice means spacing practice periods farther and farther apart, such as when we review previously learned material.]
4. How will students know how well they have done? *Answer:* Give specific knowledge of results [i.e., specific feedback].

Although all students benefit from guided practice, English language learners make more rapid progress in mastering content objectives when they are provided with multiple opportunities to practice with hands-on materials and/or manipulatives. These may be organized, created, counted, classified, stacked, experimented with, observed, rearranged, dismantled, and so forth. Practicing by manipulating learning materials is what is important for ELLs because it enables them to connect abstract concepts with concrete experiences.

Obviously, the type of manipulative employed for practice depends on the subject being taught. For example, in a tenth-grade geometry class in which students are learning how to solve proofs, content objectives might justify paper-and-pencil practice. However, if it is possible to incorporate hands-on practice with manipulatives, students' learning will probably be enhanced. Being told how to ride a bike or play the piano, reading about how to do so, or watching a video of someone else engaged in bike riding or piano playing is much different from riding down the sidewalk or listening to musical sounds you have produced yourself. Whenever possible and appropriate, use hands-on manipulatives for practice.

Teaching Scenarios

In this section, we will compare how the three teachers provided their students with practice opportunities.

Example 1   Ms. Dowden decided that the best way for her students to understand and apply newly learned content about ecosystems was to have them read about, discuss, and write detailed observations about, and create their own models of, ecosystems. She began the first lesson by introducing content vocabulary and then students read the section of the biology textbook on ecosystems together in small groups. Ms. Dowden reviewed the key concepts by writing them on the board.

Because Ms. Dowden realized that many of the content concepts and key vocabulary in this unit were new and complex, she believed she could best meet everyone's needs, including ELLs and English proficient students by dividing the class into two groups. As older adolescents, her students were able to work independently and most had experience with computers and the Internet, even though the amount of experience they had varied. Ms. Dowden directed students with higher levels of academic and English proficiency to some library references and Internet websites related to science and biology. These students were instructed to read and research the topic of ecosystems and symbiosis and design a method for creating an ecosystem using a variety of inexpensive and accessible materials they could find around their homes. Ms. Dowden pledged her assistance in helping them with the research and the project, but she urged them to work together as partners and in groups to create sustainable ecosystems. She explained how students were to write and submit their plans including materials, timeline, and so forth. Once they created their ecosystems, they were to monitor the changes that occurred within them, and eventually, they would include their findings on the districtwide general biology website.

While a third of the students were independently researching the library and the Internet, Ms. Dowden worked with the English language learners and a few other students. She introduced them to a website on the classroom computer that included information about ecosystems. She had printed a few pages from the website and together students read these, comparing the information to what they learned in their textbooks. Ms. Dowden then introduced a project in which students were to create their own "ecocolumns"—stacked ecosystems made from plastic bottles (*Bottle Biology*, 1993). Simplified directions in the form of an illustrated sequence map provided steps for creating the ecocolumns along with a list of materials that were needed. The ELLs volunteered to bring materials from home, including soil, water, plants, compost, spiders, fruit flies, snails, and two large plastic soda bottles for each ecocolumn.

The following day, while Ms. Dowden modeled the process, the ELLs began creating their own ecocolumns from the soda bottles that were each cut into three sections. Chambers were created using the sections of the plastic bottles and an aquarium with water and rocks was prepared for the bottom section of the ecocolumn. Above it was a soil or decomposition unit, and above that was a plant or animal habitat. The top of the system included air holes and a precipitation funnel. Ms. Dowden modeled the creation of the ecocolumns, demonstrating each step of the process.

The students then created their own ecosystems; as they were doing so, Ms. Dowden encouraged them to discuss what was working and what wasn't, and why. Over the next two weeks, all students were expected to observe their ecosystems, including root and soil changes and the effects of light and water. Ms. Dowden provided models of data-recording sheets that showed what students might be observing and what they should record on the overhead. All students, including those who independently created their ecosystems, used the models as guides. The ELLs used specially designed data sheets on which they recorded their data in a simplified format.

The students who designed their own ecosystems completed a "bioessay" to explain the effects of different substances on seed germination and plant development (*Bottle Biology*, 1993, p. 79). The ELLs were encouraged to list the changes that occurred as a result of competition among the species in their ecosystems; that is, "Did one species do better than another, and if so, how do you know? Which appeared to be symbiotic? How do you know?" The ELLs were also encouraged to contribute their findings to the general biology website.

Throughout this unit, Ms. Dowden emphasized to all students that there was no right or wrong way to build the ecosystem and/or the ecocolumn. Change was considered to be a natural part of the experience and students were encouraged to work together to determine what happened with their own systems and why.

SIOP Evaluation: Ms. Dowden received a "4" for Hands-On Manipulatives and Practice indicator. All students in Ms. Dowden's class, regardless of English proficiency, were expected to master the content concepts related to ecosystems and symbiosis. Also, all students were expected to create their own ecosystems; however, the ELLs were provided with materials and clear directions, including modeling, to assist them in building their ecocolumns. The hands-on experimentation by all students reinforced the content concepts and key vocabulary, and the meaningful practice made concrete what could have been abstract for the English language learners.

FIGURE 7.3   SIOP Evaluation for Ms. Dowden: Hands-On Manipulatives and Practice

④	3	2	1	0	NA
20. Provides **hands-on** materials and/or manipulatives for students to practice using new content knowledge		Provides few **hands-on** materials and/or manipulatives for students to practice using new content knowledge		Provides no **hands-on** materials and/or manipulatives for students to practice using new content knowledge	

Example 2   Mr. Nguyen approached the subject of ecosystems from a different perspective. After students read the chapter in the textbook, Mr. Nguyen provided photographs, illustrations, and procedural steps for creating an ecosystem that was essentially a covered terrarium—a container for plants and small animals. The materials he used to build the ecosystem included a glass tank, a variety of small plants, some sand, small rocks, soil, a turtle, a horned toad, and meal worms. He poured a small amount of water into the system and put the terrarium under a soft sunlamp. He presented a brief lecture on how the various species within the ecosystem might support each other within it.

Mr. Nguyen then showed a video on a variety of ecosystems that exist on Earth. Students were given a study guide to use during the video that included two columns for structured note-taking. Over the next two weeks, each student was required to complete a standard lab observation report about the changes that occurred within the ecosystem. Throughout, students were encouraged to work in groups on writing up their observations and findings, and the most vocal students were enthusiastic participants during the shared discussions.

SIOP Evaluation: Mr. Nguyen received a "2" for Hands-On Manipulatives and Practice. Although he modeled the creation of an ecosystem (the covered terrarium), he incorporated a "one-size-fits-all" approach by having everyone do the same thing. Because native English speakers represented one-third of his class, and the rest of the students were in the beginning to advanced beginning stages of English proficiency, the most vocal and competent English speakers assumed primary responsibility for monitoring the changes in the ecosystem (terrarium). Therefore, ELLs may have concluded the unit with few opportunities to participate in a hands-on manner, thus they most likely had limited mastery of the content and key vocabulary concepts.

FIGURE 7.4   SIOP Evaluation for Mr. Nguyen: Hands-On Manipulatives and Practice

4	3	②	1	0	NA
20. Provides **hands-on** materials and/or manipulatives for students to practice using new content knowledge		Provides few **hands-on** materials and/or manipulatives for students to practice using new content knowledge		Provides no **hands-on** materials and/or manipulatives for students to practice using new content knowledge	

Example 3   Miss Delgado taught the lessons on ecosystems by having students work as partners to read the textbook chapter. She pointed out key vocabulary and orally reinforced the key concepts. To illustrate an ecosystem, she drew a layered ecosystem on the blackboard that included decaying plant matter, insects, and small animals. Students were directed to copy her illustration off the board and to label the various species within the ecosystem. Miss Delgado then showed a video on ecosystems and symbiosis. Each student was required to write a paragraph explaining how various species on the Earth support and contribute to each other's sustenance and viability.

SIOP Evaluation: Miss Delgado received a "1" on the SIOP for Hands-On Manipulatives and Practice. Although she attempted to illustrate an ecosystem on the board, students were mostly passive while they copied her illustration and when they watched the video. Few of the students had the opportunity to practice using their newly learned content information or key vocabulary. It is therefore doubtful that ELLs had a clear understanding of ecosystems or that students could apply what they had learned in any meaningful way.

FIGURE 7.5   SIOP Evaluation for Miss Delgado: Hands-On Manipulatives and Practice

4	3	2	①	0	NA
20. Provides **hands-on** materials and/or manipulatives for students to practice using new content knowledge		Provides few **hands-on** materials and/or manipulatives for students to practice using new content knowledge		Provides no **hands-on** materials and/or manipulatives for students to practice using new content knowledge	

Application of Content and Language Knowledge

Think again about the relationship between actually riding a bicycle and just watching someone else ride it, or about actually playing a piano and just reading step-by-step piano-playing instructions. As Hunter (1982) said:

> The difference between knowing how something should be done and being able to do it is the quantum leap in learning . . . new learning is like wet cement, it can be easily damaged. A mistake at the beginning of learning can have long-lasting consequences that are hard to eradicate (p. 71).

We all recall our own learning experiences in elementary, middle, and high school, and the university. For many of us, the classes and courses we remember best are the ones in which we applied our new knowledge in meaningful ways. These may have included activities such as writing a diary entry from the perspective of a character in a novel, creating a semantic map illustrating the relationships among complex concepts, or completing comprehensive case studies on children we assessed and taught. These concrete experiences forced us to apply new information and concepts in a personally relevant way. We remember the times when we "got it," and we remember the times when we gave it our all but somehow still missed the point.

For students acquiring a new language, the need to apply new information is critically important because discussing and "doing" make abstract concepts concrete. Application can occur in a number of ways, such as clustering, using graphic organizers, solving problems in cooperative learning groups, writing a journal, engaging in discussion circles, or a variety of other meaningful activities (Peregoy & Boyle, 1997). Mainly we must remember that we learn best by involving ourselves in relevant, meaningful application of what we are learning.

For English language learners, application must also include opportunities for them to practice language knowledge in the classroom. As previously mentioned, opportunities for social interaction promote language development, and these include discussion, working with partners and small groups, and "reporting out" information orally and in writing. For example, it is appropriate, depending on students' language proficiency, to ask students to explain a process to a peer using newly learned vocabulary. Activities such as describing the results of an experiment, specifying why a character reacted in a particular way, and listing the steps in a process all help ELLs produce and practice new language and vocabulary, as long as students are supported in a caring environment.

Whether to correct ELLs' language errors during practice time is a topic of controversy (Peregoy & Boyle, 1997). In general, consider students' stages of English language development when deciding to correct or not. For beginning English speakers, errors may be developmental and reflect students' native language use (e.g., not remembering to add past tense inflected endings to English verbs). Other errors may deal with placement of adjectives, sentence structure, plurals, and so forth. If errors impede communication, you can gently correct them by restating the sentence in correct form.

For example, Meeli, who recently emigrated from Estonia told her teacher, "My parents sends congratulations to you." She meant that her parents sent their greetings. In reply, Meeli's teacher responded, "Thank you. I think you mean 'greetings.' Please tell your parents I send them my greetings, too." Note that the confusion over the nouns, "congratulation" and "greetings" was corrected, but the teacher just modeled the appropriate usage of the verb "send" without making note of the correction. What is most important is that you be sensitive to errors that confuse communication; these usually can be corrected in a natural way.

Teaching Scenarios

In the preceding vignettes, the three general biology teachers incorporated varied approaches to application of content and language knowledge.

Example 1 Recall that Ms. Dowden provided her students with two different ways to apply their newly learned content, depending on their academic and language proficiency. One was to research and create an ecosystem; the other was to use illustrated, comprehensible directions to build an ecosystem patterned after the teacher's model. Throughout the unit, ELLs were encouraged to discuss, share, and work together to solve problems and create their data sheets. In the end, all students were required to apply their knowledge in a variety of ways (e.g., through writing data reports and orally sharing their findings), and to demonstrate it in a hands-on manner through their individual ecosystems.

SIOP Evaluation: Ms. Dowden received a "4" for the Application of Content and Language Knowledge indicator. Throughout the lessons, students were required to apply what they were learning, not only during the creation of their ecosystems, but also during discussion and through their submitted data sheets. ELLs had multiple opportunities to apply what they were learning and to practice English (e.g., sharing observations of changes with partners and groups). While Ms. Dowden provided independent research opportunities for English-fluent students, she carefully

FIGURE 7.6 SIOP Evaluation for Ms. Dowden: Application of Content and Language Knowledge

④	3	2	1	0	NA
21. Provides activities for students to **apply content and language knowledge** in the classroom		Provides activities for students to **apply** either **content or language knowledge** in the classroom		Provides no activities for students to **apply content or language knowledge** in the classroom	

scaffolded the learning for ELLs, but note she did not lessen her expectations that all her general biology students would master the content and language objectives.

Example 2   In his lesson on ecosystems, Mr. Nguyen provided his students with photographs, illustrations, and procedural steps for creating a terrarium. Even though he was the one who actually created the terrarium, his students noted changes within the ecosystem and reported on examples of symbiosis. Further, they completed data reports on their observations and Mr. Nguyen discussed what they were observing with students. They were encouraged to ask questions and to share their observations and hypotheses with other students.

SIOP Evaluation: Mr. Nguyen received a "3" on the SIOP for Application of Content and Language Knowledge. Students were involved as observers in the creation of the ecosystem, and they applied what they learned through their data sheets and in their discussions. Language knowledge was applied through oral interactions and in the writing of the data reports; however, there were few opportunities for students to engage in student–student interactions, which provide language practice and develop language proficiency. The video reinforced the textbook content concepts and the demonstration provided another level of scaffolding.

FIGURE 7.7   SIOP Evaluation for Mr. Nguyen: Application of Content and Language Knowledge

4	③	2	1	0	NA
21. Provides activities for students to **apply content and language knowledge** in the classroom		Provides activities for students to **apply** either **content or language knowledge** in the classroom		Provides no activities for students to **apply content or language knowledge** in the classroom	

Example 3   After students read the textbook chapter, Miss Delgado drew an illustration of a layered ecosystem on the board. Students copied the drawing and labeled species. They watched the video on ecosystems and symbiosis and each wrote a paragraph about what they had learned.

SIOP Evaluation: Miss Delgado received a "1" for Application of Content and Language Knowledge. Although there was no opportunity for students to apply their content knowledge in a hands-on way, they could demonstrate what they knew through their written paragraph. There were very few opportunities for students to practice or apply their language knowledge orally.

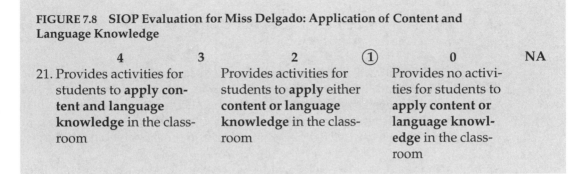

FIGURE 7.8   SIOP Evaluation for Miss Delgado: Application of Content and Language Knowledge

4	3	2	①	0	NA
21. Provides activities for students to **apply content and language knowledge** in the classroom		Provides activities for students to **apply** either **content or language knowledge** in the classroom		Provides no activities for students to **apply content or language knowledge** in the classroom	

Integration of Language Skills

Reading, writing, listening, and speaking are complex, cognitive language processes that are interrelated and integrated. As we go about our daily lives, we move through the processes in a natural way, reading what we write, talking about what we've read, and listening to others talk about what they've read and written. Most young children become grammatically competent in their home language by age five, and their continuing language development relates primarily to vocabulary, more sophisticated grammar usage (e.g., embedding subordinate clauses), and functional as well as sociocultural applications of language (e.g., using different language registers according to their audience, developing rhetorical styles) (Peregoy & Boyle, 1997; TESOL, 1997). Proficiency in reading and writing is achieved much later and differences exist among individuals in levels of competence. Students in particular need to learn academic language for use in school settings (see Chapter 1 for a detailed discussion).

For English language learners, students may achieve competence in written language earlier than oral language and ELLs do not need to be proficient speakers before they start to read and write. In fact, the language processes—reading, writing, listening, and speaking—are mutually supportive. The ESL Standards (TESOL, 1997) specifically recommend developing these language skills in a holistic manner, recognizing their interdependent nature. Although the relationships among the processes are complex, practice in any one promotes development in the others.

Effective sheltered teachers understand the need to create many opportunities for English language learners to practice and use all four language processes in an integrated manner. Throughout the day, ELLs benefit from varied experiences that incorporate reading, promote interactions with others, provide the chance to listen to peers' ideas, and encourage writing about what is being learned. Because students have different preferred learning styles, when teachers teach through different modalities and encourage students to practice and apply new knowledge through multiple language processes, they have a better chance of meeting students' needs and furthering both their language and content development.

Teaching Scenarios

Ms. Dowden, Mr. Nguyen, and Miss Delgado incorporated the language processes in their unit on the ecosystems in the following ways.

Example 1   For all of her students, Ms. Dowden facilitated the reading of the textbook chapter and the information on the website about ecosystems. The ELLs followed her demonstration on how to build their ecocolumns, discussing their work throughout. Each student kept a data sheet on observed changes in the eco-columns and they were expected to talk about their findings with each other.

SIOP Evaluation: Ms. Dowden received a "4" on the SIOP for Integration of Language Skills. Throughout the lessons in this unit, English language learners were reading, discussing, and writing about the process of building their ecosystems. The language processes were well integrated into the delivery of the biology content because students were not only reading and writing about what they were learning, but they also had spoken interactions with the teacher and with each other.

FIGURE 7.9   **SIOP Evaluation for Ms. Dowden: Integration of Language Skills**

④	3	2	1	0	NA
22. Uses activities that integrate all **language skills** (i.e., reading, writing, listening, and speaking)		Uses activities that integrate some **language skills**		Uses activities that apply to only one **language skill**	

Example 2   As you may recall, Mr. Nguyen directed his students to read the chapter in the textbook and he provided photographs, illustrations, and procedural steps for creating an ecosystem. He also presented a brief lecture on how the various species in the ecosystem might support each other within it. Mr. Nguyen then showed a video on a variety of ecosystems that exist on Earth and students were to complete a study guide and data sheet on their observations. Throughout, students were encouraged to work in groups when writing up their observations and findings.

SIOP Evaluation: Mr. Nguyen received a "3" on the SIOP for Integration of Language Skills. Throughout their lesson on ecosystems, English language learners were given the opportunity to read, write, listen, and discuss the content concepts. However, because he did not differentiate his instruction for ELLs, his less vocal students may have felt reluctant to fully participate in class discussions. In addition, Mr. Nguyen's lessons were teacher-dominated so students' opportunities for language practice were somewhat limited.

FIGURE 7.10   SIOP Evaluation for Mr. Nguyen: Integration of Language Skills

4	③	2	1	0	NA
22. Uses activities that integrate all **language skills** (i.e., reading, writing, listening, and speaking)		Uses activities that integrate some **language skills**		Uses activities that apply to only one **language skill**	

Example 3   Miss Delgado's lessons on ecosystems involved partner reading for the textbook chapter and a lecture with a blackboard illustration on the process of decomposition of plant material. Independently, students copied her illustration off the board and labeled the various species within the ecosystem. After Miss Delgado showed the video on ecosystems and symbiosis, students wrote paragraphs explaining how various species on the Earth support and contribute to each other's sustenance and viability.

SIOP Evaluation: Miss Delgado received a "2" for the Integration of Language Skills indicator. Her students read the textbook, listened to the mini-lecture, watched the video, and wrote paragraphs about their understandings. However, students had few chances to connect reading and writing activities with discussion, either with the teacher or each other. There were few opportunities for students to practice language and content concepts with each other.

FIGURE 7.11   SIOP Evaluation for Miss Delgado: Integration of Language Skills

4	3	②	1	0	NA
22. Uses activities that integrate all **language skills** (i.e., reading, writing, listening, and speaking)		Uses activities that integrate some **language skills**		Uses activities that apply to only one **language skill**	

Summary

With any type of new learning, practice and application of newly acquired skills are needed to ensure mastery of content concepts. Hands-on activities and materials, including manipulatives, enable students to forge connections between abstract and concrete concepts. Students make these connections most effectively when they use all language processes, including reading, writing, listening, and speaking, during practice and application.

Discussion Questions

1. Compare and contrast the following two teachers' approaches to teaching a lesson on nutrition.
   a. One teacher's approach involves a lecture, a diagram of the food pyramid, and a list of appropriate foods for each group. Students are then tested about their knowledge of the food pyramid.
   b. The other teacher's approach begins with students' maintaining a food diary for a week. Copies of the food pyramid are distributed and explained, and all students must analyze their food consumption according to the recommendations on the pyramid. With a partner, students must design a nutritionally sound weekly menu for each day of the following week, and they must be prepared to defend their food choices to peer group members.
   Which of the approaches to teaching this content concept is most appropriate for English language learners? How do you know? Be as specific as you can.
2. In the preceding example, the second teacher might have included some hands-on manipulatives to enhance the lesson further. Why would this have helped English language learners? What types of hands-on manipulatives might she have used? How could they have been incorporated into the lesson?
3. English language learners benefit from the integration of reading, writing, listening, and speaking. For those with limited English language proficiency, tell what may be difficult. Is it performance of all four skills? What adjustments and techniques can a teacher use to provide ELLs with successful experiences while they read, write, listen, and speak about new information they are learning? Include specific activities and examples in your answer.
4. With a large number of content standards in each subject area for which teachers and students are accountable, how is it possible to provide direct application and hands-on practice for lessons? What can teachers do to alleviate the conflict between "covering the content" and making it "accessible" for English language learners?

CHAPTER

8 Indicators of Instruction: Lesson Delivery

FIGURE 8.1 Instruction Section of the SIOP: Lesson Delivery

4	3	2	1	0	NA
23. **Content objectives** clearly supported by lesson delivery		**Content objectives** somewhat supported by lesson delivery		**Content objectives** not supported by lesson delivery	
4	3	2	1	0	NA
24. **Language objectives** clearly supported by lesson delivery		**Language objectives** supported somewhat by lesson delivery		**Language objectives** not supported by lesson delivery	
4	3	2	1	0	NA
25. **Students engaged** approximately 90% to 100% of the period		**Students engaged** approximately 70% of the period		**Students engaged** less than 50% of the period	
4	3	2	1	0	NA
26. **Pacing** of the lesson appropriate to the students' ability level		**Pacing** generally appropriate, but at times too fast or too slow		**Pacing** inappropriate to the students' ability level	

Background

This chapter addresses the way a lesson is delivered, how well the content and language objectives are supported during the lesson, to what extent students are engaged in the lesson, and how appropriate the pace of the lesson is to students' ability levels. You will see that this chapter parallels Chapter 2, Indicators of Lesson Preparation, because the two are closely related. The effectiveness of a lesson's delivery—the level of student participation, how clearly information is

FIGURE 8.2   **The Gold Rush (4th grade)**

> The classrooms described in the teaching vignettes in this chapter are all in a suburban elementary school with heterogeneously mixed students. English language learners represent approximately 30% of the student population and the children speak a variety of languages. In the fourth-grade classrooms of teachers Ms. Chen, Mrs. Hensen, and Mr. Hargroves, the majority of the ELLs are at the intermediate stage of English fluency.
>
> As part of the fourth-grade social studies curriculum, Ms. Chen, Mrs. Hensen, and Mr. Hargroves have planned a unit on the California Gold Rush. The school district requires the use of the adopted social studies series although teachers are encouraged to supplement the text with primary source materials, literature, and realia. The content topics for the Gold Rush unit include: westward expansion, routes and trails to the West, the people who sought their fortunes, hardships, settlements, the discovery of gold, the life of miners, methods for extracting gold, the impact of the Gold Rush, and so forth.
>
> Each of the teachers has created several lessons for this unit. The first teaching vignettes illustrated here are from a two-day lesson plan (approximately 45 minutes per day) on routes and trails to the West. Specifically, the content of this lesson covers the Oregon Trail, the Overland Trail, and the route around Cape Horn.
>
> The second set of vignettes is from another two-day lesson on how gold was extracted from California's mines and streams, and includes the topics of gold panning, the rocker, and mining.

communicated, students' level of understanding reflected in the quality of student work—often can be traced back to the preparation that took place before students entered the classroom. We will meet the teachers from Chapter 2 again and discuss how their level of preparation played out in lesson delivery (see Figure 8.2).

Content Objectives

As we discussed in Chapter 2, content objectives should be stated orally and in writing for students and teachers alike to see. In this way, written objectives serve to remind us of the focus of the lesson, providing a structure to classroom procedures. Written objectives also allow students to know the direction of the lesson. Throughout the lesson and at its conclusion, the teacher and students can evaluate the extent to which the lesson delivery supported the content objectives.

In this section we will examine how well the profiled teachers actually reflected the content objectives in their teaching. It is one thing to write objectives for students to see, but it is more important for the teacher to meet the objectives through the lesson delivery.

Teaching Scenarios

These fourth-grade teachers differed in the ways they focused their teaching on content objectives.

Example 1   Ms. Chen wrote the following objectives in her plan book for the first lessons in the unit on the Gold Rush: "The learner will be able to (1) identify the three main routes to the West on a map, and (2) articulate at least one distinct fact about each of the three trails." Ms. Chen began the lesson on the second day of the unit by telling the students:

> Yesterday, we learned that some explorers and adventurers decided that it would be easiest and fastest to travel to the West by boat. They went around Cape Horn. Others decided to go a different way. They chose to go across country by land.
>
> Today, we're going to learn about two more of the land routes to the West called the Overland Trail and the Oregon Trail [she writes the objective on the board]. You will show that you know where the routes were by coloring them on your map of the United States. You will also be able to tell a friend one important fact about each trail.

Ms. Chen asked the students to get into their preassigned groups of four. She then distributed a United States map to each group. She reviewed the Cape Horn route and asked for a student to come to the front of the room and indicate the route on the large map for the rest of the class. Then she had students color the route on their maps. Once all the groups had colored the first route on their maps, Ms. Chen directed their attention to their textbooks. Before beginning to read, Ms. Chen turned on the overhead projector and revealed a transparency with a skeleton outline of the chapter that students would complete. For example, the Overland Trail outline had the subheadings, "Location," "Characteristics," "Challenges," and "Advantages." Students were instructed to copy the outline on a piece of paper.

Ms. Chen then began reading the textbook section about the Overland Trail. As she read aloud and students followed along, Ms. Chen paused every few paragraphs and asked comprehension questions of the class. She elicited from students the information needed to complete the outline, and she modeled filling in the outline as students provided information. The students copied what she wrote on the overhead transparency onto their papers.

After completing the outline, Ms. Chen instructed the groups to draw the Overland Trail on their maps. After all groups had completed the task, Ms. Chen put another outline transparency on the overhead screen. This outline was for the Oregon Trail, and it had the same subheadings as the one for the Overland Trail. She told the class that she would read the textbook passage about the Oregon Trail, but they had to complete the outline in their groups. Ms. Chen read the passage, pausing to ask comprehension questions. When she was finished, she told the groups they would have 15 minutes to complete the outline.

Each group found the information in the passage and completed the outline. Then they colored the Oregon Trail on their maps. Finally, Ms. Chen asked that each student tell one distinct fact about each of the trails to their group. She circulated around the class to make sure students were using complete sentences and reporting distinct facts. Ms. Chen wrapped up the lesson by having each group share one fact that was reported in their group for the whole class, and no group could repeat a fact shared already by another group.

SIOP Evaluation: Ms. Chen received a "4" for this SIOP lesson. The lesson was focused on achieving the content objectives of identifying each of the three trails, and articulating at least one distinct fact about each trail. The objective was apparent throughout the delivery of the lesson and manifested through the reading, writing, and group discussion activities.

FIGURE 8.3 SIOP Evaluation for Ms. Chen: Content Objectives

④	3	2	1	0	NA
23. **Content objectives** clearly supported by lesson delivery		**Content objectives** somewhat supported by lesson delivery		**Content objectives** not supported by lesson delivery	

Example 2 Mr. Hargroves set the following objective for his first lessons on the Gold Rush: "The learner will be able to compare and contrast the three major routes to California."

He began the lesson by stating, "Today you will learn about the Overland Trail. Eventually you will need to compare and contrast the Overland Trail, the route around Cape Horn, and the Oregon Trail." Mr. Hargroves instructed the class to open their textbooks to the chapter on the Gold Rush. He then told students to read silently the first four pages of the chapter and he would discuss it with them when they finished. Most students completed the reading in 10 minutes and began talking among themselves while several students continued reading. After 15 minutes, Mr. Hargroves asked the students some comprehension questions, focusing on the Overland Trail. He used the wall map to show the location of all three trails, but spent time discussing the Overland Trail in more detail.

SIOP Evaluation: Mr. Hargroves received a "1" on this item of the SIOP. Review of his lesson plan book revealed that he planned a content objective for the unit, and he stated the objective for his students. However, the objective was multifaceted and affected several days' lessons. Mr. Hargroves seemed to deliver a lesson that prepared students to meet the objective by providing information about the Overland Trail which could be contrasted with other routes in subsequent lessons; however, since the lesson was so teacher-dominated, it was difficult to judge the level of student understanding.

FIGURE 8.4 SIOP Evaluation for Mr. Hargroves: Content Objectives

4	3	2	①	0	NA
23. **Content objectives** clearly supported by lesson delivery		**Content objectives** somewhat supported by lesson delivery		**Content objectives** not supported by lesson delivery	

Example 3   Mrs. Hensen did not set explicit content objectives for the Gold Rush lessons on routes and trails. She began the lesson with a brief lecture on the Overland Trail. She then distributed a map of the United States to each student. She told the students to color the Overland Trail on their maps, tracing the trail on the wall map for students to see. There was also an illustration of all three routes in the textbook. Mrs. Hensen then directed the students to independently read the paragraphs describing the route around Cape Horn and the Oregon Trail. When they were finished, students were told to color both trails onto their maps.

SIOP Evaluation: Mrs. Hensen received a "0" on the SIOP for Content Objectives. She did not provide a focus for the students. Certainly some students inferred that the lesson was about the three routes explorers took, but others, particularly the English language learners, may have been unsure about the purpose of the lesson or what was important to remember.

FIGURE 8.5   SIOP Evaluation for Mrs. Hensen: Content Objectives

4	3	2	1	(0)	NA
23. **Content objectives** clearly supported by lesson delivery		**Content objectives** somewhat supported by lesson delivery		**Content objectives** not supported by lesson delivery	

Language Objectives

As we discussed in Chapter 2, language objectives are an important part of effective sheltered lessons. Teachers and students benefit from having a clear, simple language objective written for them to see and stated for them to hear during the lesson. The objective may be related to an ESL Standard such as, "Students will write to communicate with different people for different reasons"; or it may be related to teachers' scope and sequence of language skills that their own students need to develop such as, "Students will use punctuation and capitalization to make their writing readable." Whatever language objective the teacher chooses, it needs to be recognizable in the lesson's delivery.

Teaching Scenarios

The three teachers incorporated language objectives into their lesson delivery to varying degrees.

Example 1   The lesson's language objective was to have students use complete sentences orally. Ms. Chen provided opportunities for students to meet the objective by encouraging class discussion, having students work in groups talking among themselves, and having each student use a sentence about important facts related to the lesson.

SIOP Evaluation: Ms. Chen received a "4" on this item of the SIOP. Students had several opportunities to meet the objective: during the whole-group discussion, while working in small groups, when each student gave their group important facts about the three routes, and when they reported out to the class a fact from their group. In addition to the objective, Ms. Chen's teaching developed language skills when she provided key terms in writing by using the outlining strategy, she asked students comprehension questions based on the text, and she gave students a structured assignment to complete in small groups that required reading, writing, speaking, and listening.

FIGURE 8.6   **SIOP Evaluation for Ms. Chen: Language Objectives**

④	3	2	1	0	NA
24. **Language objectives** clearly supported by lesson delivery		**Language objectives** supported somewhat by lesson delivery		**Language objectives** not supported by lesson delivery	

Example 2   Mr. Hargroves did not have a specific language objective for the lesson. Throughout the lesson, he had students working independently or listening to his oral discussion of information. He did repeat the names of routes and trails and other related terminology, but he didn't write any words on the board or an overhead transparency for students to see. He also used the wall map to reinforce his oral discussion by pointing to the trails, but he did not label any areas on the map. Because students were working independently throughout the lesson, there was no opportunity for language or vocabulary development.

SIOP Evaluation: Mr. Hargroves received a "0" on this SIOP item. The entire lesson was conducted orally and students did not have an opportunity to use language skills. Mr. Hargroves did make an effort to reinforce terminology by repeating words, but it would have been more effective had he written the words for students to see.

FIGURE 8.7   **SIOP Evaluation for Mr. Hargroves: Language Objectives**

4	3	2	1	⓪	NA
24. **Language objectives** clearly supported by lesson delivery		**Language objectives** supported somewhat by lesson delivery		**Language objectives** not supported by lesson delivery	

Example 3   Mrs. Hensen did not have an explicit language objective written in her plan book, nor did she mention any objectives during the lesson. Her teaching did not explicitly address the students' English language development needs.

SIOP Evaluation: Mrs. Hensen scored "0" on the SIOP indicator. Although she has taught ELLs for three years, she still has not incorporated the practice of selecting and teaching a language objective for each lesson into her teaching style. Students' language development needs were largely ignored during this lesson.

FIGURE 8.8 **SIOP Evaluation for Mrs. Hensen: Language Objectives**

4	3	2	1	(0)	NA
24. **Language objectives** clearly supported by lesson delivery	**Language objectives** supported somewhat by lesson delivery			**Language objectives** not supported by lesson delivery	

Students Engaged

In observing sheltered classrooms, we have come to appreciate the importance of academic engaged time. English language learners are the students who can least afford to have valuable time squandered through boredom, inattention, socializing, and other off-task behaviors. Time also is wasted when teachers are ill prepared; have poor classroom management skills; spend excessive amounts of time making announcements, passing out, and handing in papers; and the like. The most effective teachers minimize these behaviors and maximize time spent actively engaged in instruction (Mastropieri & Scruggs, 1994). English language learners who are working to achieve grade-level competence benefit from efficient use of class time. Further, many of these learners have had uneven schooling experiences, missing time in school due to circumstances beyond their control, and are then further disadvantaged by inefficient use of class time.

There are actually three aspects to student engagement that should be considered: (1) allocated time, (2) engaged time, and (3) academic learning time (Berliner, 1984). Allocated time reflects the decisions teachers make regarding the amount of time to spend studying a topic (e.g., math versus reading) and a given academic task (e.g., how much time to spend on reading comprehension versus decoding skills). As we have discussed throughout this book, effective sheltered instruction teachers plan for and deliver lessons that are balanced between teacher presentation of information and opportunities for students to apply the information in meaningful ways. Effective sheltered teachers use instructional time wisely.[1]

Engaged time refers to the time students are actively participating in instruction during the time allocated. The engaged time-on-task research has consistently

[1]We believe that it is reasonable to deliver lessons that engage students 90% to 100% of the period. Lessons where students are engaged less than 50% of the time are unacceptable and warrant a "0" on the SIOP indicator for student engagement.

concluded that the more actively students participate in the instructional process, the more they achieve. As Bickel and Bickel (1986) put it: "Students learn more when they are attending to the learning tasks that are the focus of instruction" (p. 493). Instruction that is understandable to ELLs, that creates opportunities for students to talk about the lesson's concepts, and that provides hands-on activities to reinforce learning captures students' attention and keeps them more actively engaged.

Academic learning time focuses on students' time-on-task, when the task is related to the materials they will be tested on. Creative, fun activities are not effective if they are unrelated to the content and language objectives of the lesson. According to Leinhardt et al. (1982):

> When teachers spend their time and energy teaching students the content the students need to learn, students learn the material. When students spend their time actively engaged in activities that relate strongly to the materials they will be tested on, they learn more of the material (p. 409).

Of course, sheltered teachers need to be explicit in their expectations and make certain that their English language learners understand which materials relate to upcoming assessments.

In summary, effective SI teachers need to plan to use the entire class period efficiently, teach in ways that engage students, and make sure students are engaged in activities that specifically relate to the material on which they will be assessed.

Teaching Scenarios

The following teachers' lessons were varied in their ability to engage students actively in the learning process.

Example 1 Ms. Chen was an enthusiastic teacher who planned lessons that used each minute of class time to its fullest. As illustrated in the lesson described previously, Ms. Chen spent time presenting material and allowed students to work together. Students were actively engaged throughout the lesson. They eagerly participated in whole-group and small group discussions and Ms. Chen made sure they were on task as she walked around the room. In addition, the content of the lesson was directly related to the district's content standards for the social studies information the students will be assessed on at the end of the unit.

SIOP Evaluation: Ms. Chen received a "4" for this item of the SIOP. The lesson she delivered met all the criteria for active student engagement: She used the allocated time in an effective way, basing the lesson on the text, teaching outlining and mapping skills, providing opportunities for interaction and application of concepts, and so forth. Students were actively engaged throughout and the material was relevant to the assessment.

FIGURE 8.9 SIOP Evaluation for Ms. Chen: Students Engaged

④	3	2	1	0	NA
25. **Students engaged** approximately 90% to 100% of the period		**Students engaged** approximately 70% of the period		**Students engaged** less than 50% of the period	

Example 2   The lesson that Mrs. Hensen taught consisted almost entirely of independent work by the students. Students were engaged during her brief lecture and when they were told to color the first route. When they were told to read the passages independently, some students were off-task, presumably because the reading level was beyond their independent reading levels. But when they began tracing the routes on the map most students were actively participating.

SIOP Evaluation: Mrs. Hensen received a "2" on the SIOP for this item. Students in her class were engaged approximately 70% of the period.

FIGURE 8.10   **SIOP Evaluation for Mrs. Hensen: Students Engaged**

4	3	②	1	0	NA
25. **Students engaged** approximately 90% to 100% of the period		**Students engaged** approximately 70% of the period		**Students engaged** less than 50% of the period	

Example 3   As described before, Mr. Hargroves instructed his class to read the first four pages of the chapter silently and he told students he would discuss it with them when they finished. Most students completed the reading in 10 minutes and began talking among themselves while several students continued reading. After 15 minutes, Mr. Hargroves asked the students some comprehension questions, focusing on the Overland Trail. He used the wall map to show the location of all three trails, but spent time discussing the Overland Trail in more detail.

SIOP Evaluation: Mr. Hargroves received a "0" on this item of the SIOP. His students were engaged less than 50% of the period. First, the time allocated for independent reading was inappropriately long because most students were finished and off-task for five minutes. Then, a strictly oral presentation of information creates difficulty for many students, but especially for ELLs. Finally, Mr. Hargroves did not use any activities or group interaction to engage students in meaningful ways during the instruction.

FIGURE 8.11   **SIOP Evaluation for Mr. Hargroves: Students Engaged**

4	3	2	1	⓪	NA
25. **Students engaged** approximately 90% to 100% of the period		**Students engaged** approximately 70% of the period		**Students engaged** less than 50% of the period	

Pacing

Pacing refers to the rate at which information is presented during a lesson. The pace of the lesson depends on the nature of the lesson's content, as well as the level of students' background knowledge. When working with ELLs, it can be challenging to find a pace that doesn't present information too quickly yet is brisk enough to maintain students' interest, especially when a variety of English proficiency levels are represented in the same classroom. Finding an appropriate pace requires practice, but becomes easier as teachers develop familiarity with their students' skills.

Teaching Scenarios

Finding the appropriate pace for a lesson requires practice. The following vignettes illustrate the extent to which these teachers have mastered pacing.

Example 1   Ms. Chen understood that the English language learners in her class may have needed a slower pace than the native English speakers. She moved the pace along by reading aloud and providing the outline on the overhead projector. In this way, she scaffolded instruction for the ELLs and all students were able to work at roughly the same pace. The groups of 4 to 5 students included both native English speakers and ELLs, with students assisting one another as needed.

SIOP Evaluation: Ms. Chen received a "4" on this item of the SIOP. She was cognizant of the issue of pacing and delivered a lesson at a pace that was appropriate for students' ability levels.

FIGURE 8.12   **SIOP Evaluation for Ms. Chen: Pacing**

④	3	2	1	0	NA
26. **Pacing** of the lesson appropriate to the students' ability level		**Pacing** generally appropriate, but at times too fast or too slow		**Pacing** inappropriate to the students' ability level	

Example 2   As described previously, after her brief lecture on the Overland Trail, Mrs. Hensen asked students to color the trail on their individual maps. Then she asked them to read independently and complete the other trails on their maps. While students were reading, Mrs. Hensen prompted them to complete the reading and begin their map work.

SIOP Evaluation: Mrs. Hensen received a "2" on the SIOP item for Pacing. The pace of the lecture may have been a bit fast for the ELLs, and the pace of the independent

FIGURE 8.13 SIOP Evaluation for Mrs. Hensen: Pacing

4	3	②	1	0	NA
26. **Pacing** of the lesson appropriate to the students' ability level		**Pacing** generally appropriate, but at times too fast or too slow		**Pacing** inappropriate to the students' ability level	

reading portion of the lesson may have been too slow. Although the pace of the lesson she delivered was not always appropriate, it was generally appropriate, warranting a score of "2."

Example 3   The pace of the lesson Mr. Hargroves delivered was slow and monotonous at times, especially when he lectured, yet he covered material too quickly at other times. Many students were off-task because of the problematic pace of the lesson.

SIOP Evaluation: Mr. Hargroves received a "0" for Pacing on the SIOP. Overall the pacing was inappropriate to the students' ability level—too slow to maintain interest and too quick for ELLs to understand the information presented orally.

FIGURE 8.14 SIOP Evaluation for Mr. Hargroves: Pacing

4	3	2	1	⓪	NA
26. **Pacing** of the lesson appropriate to the students' ability level		**Pacing** generally appropriate, but at times too fast or too slow		**Pacing** inappropriate to the students' ability level	

Summary

The importance of setting and meeting objectives cannot be overemphasized. Many teachers may feel comfortable having a general objective in mind and moving along with a lesson's flow, but that approach is not helpful for English language learners. Delivering a lesson geared to objectives that have been made clear to students benefits all. The teacher stays on-task and the students know what is important to focus on and remember. By incorporating a variety of techniques that engage students throughout the lesson, teachers not only give students opportunities to learn, practice, and apply information and language skills, but they also help to ensure meeting the lesson's objectives.

Pacing is another important aspect of lesson delivery and appropriate pace is critical for English language learners. Information that is presented at a pace suitable for native English speakers may render that information meaningless, especially for beginning English speakers. Finding the right pace for a lesson depends in part on the content of the lesson and students' prior knowledge about the topic. As illustrated in the lessons here, effective sheltered teachers accommodate the language and learning needs of their students.

Discussion Questions

1. Effective sheltered teachers not only plan content objectives for their lessons but they also *teach to them*. What does this mean? Why is it important? If you were observing a classroom in which the teacher was clearly teaching to content objectives, how might it look? What problems might arise in a classroom in which a teacher had no specific content objectives for a lesson? Be specific.

2. Suppose three new middle school students, all with limited English proficiency, joined a social studies or history class during mid-year. The other students in the class include a few former ELLs and native English speakers. What are some language objectives the teacher could write for each of the following content concepts?
    a. Economic trends during the Great Depression
    b. The relationship between the run on banks and the crash of the Stock Market
    c. Migration of people from the Dust Bowl of Oklahoma

3. How does a teacher or supervisor determine whether a majority of students, including English language learners, are engaged during a lesson? What techniques could be used to sustain engagement throughout the period? What should the teacher do if he or she senses that students are off-task? Why is sustained engagement so critical to ELLs' academic progress?

4. A sheltered teacher in a class with a mix of ELLs and native English speakers finds that she is having difficulty pacing lessons so that her English language learners complete tasks successfully. If she slows her pace too much, her native English speakers lose interest and are off-task. If she quickens her pace in order to keep those students engaged, her ELLs have difficulty keeping up. What suggestions could you give her about how to determine a pace that would be appropriate for all students? How should she organize her classroom to accomplish this?

9 Indicators of Review/Assessment

FIGURE 9.1 Review/Assessment Section of the SIOP

4	3	2	1	0	NA
27. Comprehensive **review** of key vocabulary		Uneven **review** of key vocabulary		No **review** of key vocabulary	

4	3	2	1	0	NA
28. Comprehensive **review** of key content concepts		Uneven **review** of key content concepts		No **review** of key content concepts	

4	3	2	1	0	NA
29. Regularly provides **feedback** to students on their output (e.g., language, content, work)		Inconsistently provides **feedback** to students on their output		Provides no **feedback** to students on their output	

4	3	2	1	0	NA
30. Conducts **assessment** of student comprehension and learning of all lesson objectives (e.g., spot checking, group response) throughout the lesson		Conducts **assessment** of student comprehension and learning of some lesson objectives		Conducts no **assessment** of student comprehension and learning of lesson objectives	

In elementary and secondary classrooms, scheduling time for review and assessment is often difficult. However, effective teachers realize that throughout a lesson and particularly at the end, it is important to determine how well students have understood and retained key vocabulary and content concepts. Teachers must know who is ready to move on and who will benefit from additional instruction and support. This determination is at the heart of effective assessment and instruction, and it is essential for English language learners' success.

This chapter describes how effective sheltered teachers incorporate review and assessment into their daily lessons. It also describes how Section III of the SIOP can be used to evaluate the effectiveness of these important elements of instruction.

Background

While review and assessment are frequently structured as separate elements in a lesson, they also happen concurrently, spontaneously, and throughout the lesson, not just in the last few minutes of the instructional period. Effective sheltered instruction involves reviewing important concepts, providing constructive feedback through clarification, and making instructional decisions based on student response. In the end, you must have enough information to evaluate the extent to which students have mastered your lesson's objectives. This teach, review, and assess process is cyclical and recursive (see Figure 9.2).

FIGURE 9.2   Effective Teaching Cycle for ELLs

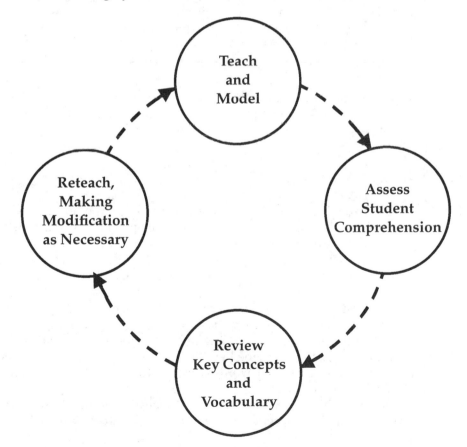

FIGURE 9.3   Unit: Egyptian Mummies (8th grade)

The classrooms described in the teaching vignettes in this chapter are all in a large urban middle school with a heterogeneously mixed student population. English language learners represent approximately 45% of the students who are in the teachers' eighth-grade classes and the majority are native Spanish speakers, most of whom are at an intermediate level of English proficiency.

The three eighth-grade language arts/social studies core teachers, Mr. Tran, Mr. Hughell, and Miss Johnston, are teaching an extended unit on Egypt. The lessons illustrated here are on the topic of Egyptian mummies using the book *Tales Mummies Tell* by Patricia Lauber. An ALA Notable Book, this nonfiction text tells about the process of mummification in fascinating detail through stories about Egyptian mummies.

Each of the teachers has planned a three-day lesson using the chapter titled "Mummy No. 1770: A Teenager" (Cooper et al., 1999). This chapter tells of a munmy that was in the possession of the Manchester Museum in England. Because very little was known about this mummy, the museum made it available to a group of scientists who wanted to use modern techniques for determining its age, its mummification process, and how the person had lived. The chapter describes what the scientists learned, including when the thirteen-year-old lived (A.D. 260), what she had eaten, what her life was like, how she died, and how her body was preserved.

The described teaching vignettes represent the second day of the lessons taught by Mr. Tran, Mr. Hughell, and Miss Johnston.

We will examine how three eighth-grade social studies teachers review and assess students' understanding of key vocabulary and content concepts in the following lessons about Egyptian mummies (see Figure 9.3).

Review of Key Vocabulary

In Chapter 2, we stated that effective teachers incorporate in their lesson plans techniques that support ELLs' language development. In Chapter 3, we discussed the importance of building background through teaching key content vocabulary as well as elements of language structure and functional language use. We suggested that language objectives should be identified in lesson plans, introduced to students at the beginning of a lesson, and reviewed throughout the lesson.

We can help develop key vocabulary by teaching and then reviewing terminology and concepts through *analogy*—the process of relating newly learned words to other words with the same structure or pattern. In Chapter 2, we gave the example of "photo" (meaning light) in a lesson on photosynthesis, and suggested referring students to other words with the same morpheme (e.g., photography). Reviewing key vocabulary also involves drawing students' attention to tense, parts of speech, and sentence structure. Repeating and reinforcing language patterns helps students become familiar with English structure.

Multiple exposures to new terminology also builds familiarity, confidence, and English proficiency. Words and concepts may be reviewed through paraphrasing, such as "Remember to *share your ideas;* that is, if you have something you want to say, tell it to the others in your group." Another example of a paraphrase is, "The townspeople were *pacifists,* those who would not fight in a war." Paraphrasing as review provides an effective scaffold for ELLs, especially after words and phrases have been previously defined and discussed in context.

Key vocabulary also can be reviewed more systematically. It is important to remember that it is ineffective to teach vocabulary through the "dreaded word list" on which students must write (or copy) dictionary definitions (Ruddell, 1997). Research findings are very clear—as stated previously, isolated word lists and dictionary definitions alone do not promote vocabulary and language development. We also know that students do not learn vocabulary words when the teacher just orally introduces and defines them and then expects students to remember the definitions. The more exposures students have to new words, especially if the vocabulary is reinforced through multiple modalities, the more likely they are to remember and use them.

An effective way to incorporate ongoing vocabulary study and review is through the use of individual Word Study Books (Bear et al., 2000). A Word Study Book is a student-made personal notebook that includes frequently used words and concepts. Bear et al. (1996) recommend that vocabulary in Word Study Books be organized by English language structure, such as listing together all the words studied so far that end in -tion, -sion, and -tation. This may be a useful framework. We also believe Word Study Books can also be used for content study where words are grouped by topic (e.g., American Revolution-related words). Some students may benefit by creating semantic maps of the words, for example, linking events to related verbs, adjectives, adverbs, and so forth.

Remember that we also need to help students become comfortable with "school talk" by introducing and modeling academic tasks throughout lessons and units. For example, if you are planning to have ELLs engage in literature discussion circles, it is important to review what "discussion" means, what "turn-taking" is, what it means to "share ideas," how questions are asked and answered, and so forth. Reviewing this terminology provides the necessary scaffolding so that students understand the expectations for their participation in routine activities.

Teaching Scenarios

The following vignettes illustrate how Mr. Tran, Mr. Hughell, and Miss Johnston incorporated review of key vocabulary into their second day's lesson on the chapter, "Mummy No. 1770: A Teenager."

Example 1   In Mr. Tran's lesson plan, he listed the following key vocabulary and content concept objectives for English language learners: "The learner will be able to (1) describe how scientists learned about Mummy No. 1770, (2) discuss five discoveries scientists made during the autopsy of the mummy, and (3) define and correctly use the following vocabulary: mummy, autopsy, evidence, embalming, amputation, tissue." Mr. Tran's lesson plan for the first day included the following activities:

1. Brainstorming words about mummies that students already knew
2. Creating a Word Wall with the brainstormed words
3. Group reading of the first five pages of the chapter
4. Adding new words to the Word Wall, selected by students from the reading (Vocabulary Self-Selection)
5. Completing the first section of a graphic organizer listing initial steps used by the scientists
6. Including on the graphic organizer words from the Word Wall (mummy, evidence, and autopsy)

On the second day of the lesson, the one observed for the SIOP evaluation, Mr. Tran began by referring back to the Word Wall. First, students as a whole class read the words aloud in sequence and again in random order. Mr. Tran asked for volunteers to give informal definitions for a few of the words, focusing on the key vocabulary he had selected to emphasize (mummy, evidence, autopsy). When needed, he clarified definitions, assisted students with pronunciations, and corrected errors.

Mr. Tran then asked students, grouped as partners, to review the graphic organizers they had begun the previous day in order to make corrections or additions about the steps scientists took in analyzing Mummy No. 1770. Students were reminded to include words from the Word Wall, especially the key vocabulary (mummy, evidence, autopsy). After the partner sharing, the entire class discussed the information on their graphic organizers.

Next, students reviewed the major discoveries scientists had made to this point and two were listed on the board. The teacher referred to illustrations on pages 5 through 7 of the chapter and asked students to predict what they think happened to the teenage girl and how scientists might have reached conclusions about her death. He wrote on the board, "What *evidence* did the scientists discover during the *autopsy* of the *mummy*?" and again reviewed the meaning of the key vocabulary words. With partners, students read the next four pages of the chapter, and recorded in two columns on a piece of paper, "Evidence scientists discovered about No. 1770's life" and "Evidence scientists discovered about No. 1770's death."

Following the reading, students reviewed their papers and the text to find additional words for the Word Wall. Among the words added were "embalming," "amputation," and "tissue." Mr. Tran wrote "embalm," "embalmer," and "embalming" on the board and discussed the differences in meaning. He also asked a volunteer to differentiate between the meaning of "tissue" in the text and the more common meaning—something one uses to blow one's nose.

Students then completed the second section of their graphic organizers, indicating the subsequent steps the scientists had taken to gather evidence from the mummy. Mr. Tran encouraged students to include the new key vocabulary

(embalming, amputation, and tissue) on the graphic organizer. He concluded the lesson by reviewing the steps taken by the scientists and determining the other major discoveries detailed in the text. These were discussed and added to those on the board from the previous day. Finally, Mr. Tran highlighted the six key vocabulary words in yellow on the Word Wall and these were reviewed one last time before the bell rang.

SIOP Evaluation: Mr. Tran received a "4" for the Review of Key Vocabulary indicator. He had clearly defined language and vocabulary objectives and throughout the lesson, his instruction and activities were congruent with these objectives. He built on what students already knew about mummies, incorporated student selection of important terms (VSS), while ensuring the key vocabulary words were included on the Word Wall (see Figure 9.4). He pointed out similarities in word structure and differences in word meaning (e.g., embalm/embalming and tissue/tissue).

Mr. Tran's English language learners were challenged to articulate the key vocabulary orally and in writing. However, even though many terms and phrases related to mummies were introduced; discussed in the text; and included on the Word Wall, graphic organizer, and worksheet, Mr. Tran limited the number of words students were expected to master to six. Note also that he repeatedly reinforced these words, at the beginning, in the middle, and again at the end of the lesson. By using the vocabulary in context, repeating the words orally, and writing the sentence on the board ("What *evidence* did the scientists discover during the

FIGURE 9.4   Use of a Word Wall

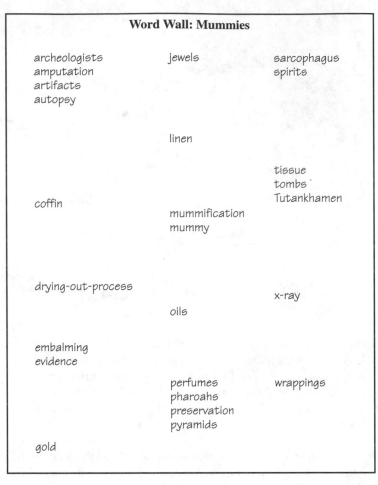

Word Wall: Mummies

archeologists   jewels   sarcophagus
amputation   spirits
artifacts
autopsy

                linen

                                  tissue
                                  tombs
coffin   Tutankhamen
                mummification
                mummy

drying-out-process
                                  x-ray
                oils

embalming
evidence

                perfumes   wrappings
                pharoahs
                preservation
                pyramids
gold

autopsy of the *mummy*?"), Mr. Tran reviewed not only the pronunciation but also the meanings of the words.

Finally, Mr. Tran expected students to use the new key vocabulary orally and in their writing during partner, small group, and whole-class discussion. Therefore, he could readily determine who had met the language and vocabulary objectives, and who had not.

FIGURE 9.5   SIOP Evaluation for Mr. Tran: Review of Key Vocabulary

④	3	2	1	0	NA
27. Comprehensive **review** of key vocabulary		Uneven **review** of key vocabulary		No **review** of key vocabulary	

Example 2   Mr. Hughell's lesson plan for this chapter on mummies noted the following objectives: "(1) Write a paragraph on what mummies teach scientists about how Egyptians lived, (2) explain how mummies were preserved, and (3) match 20 vocabulary words with their definitions." The plan for the first day of the lesson included:

1. Distributing a list of 20 words and definitions related to mummies along with page numbers on which the words could be found in the chapter
2. Reading aloud one-half of the chapter while students follow along
3. Having students find the first group of 10 vocabulary words in the chapter
4. Writing, with a partner, an original sentence for each word related to the topic of mummies

Mr. Hughell began the second day of the lesson by asking volunteers to read several of their vocabulary sentences written the previous day. As they read, he corrected definitions and errors in pronunciation. Mr. Hughell then gave students five minutes to review what had been read the previous day and asked volunteers to summarize what they had learned about Mummy No. 1770. Several students briefly responded and Mr. Hughell clarified points and made additions to the students' summaries.

He then asked for volunteers to read the next set of 10 words and definitions on the vocabulary list. He reminded students they would be tested on these words the following day with a matching quiz. The class next read the remainder of the text silently, encouraged by Mr. Hughell to ask for help if they found words they didn't understand. Following the reading, students worked with partners to write 10 more sentences for the words, which were identified in the text with page numbers, on the vocabulary list.

At the end of the period, Mr. Hughell quickly asked for a few volunteers to read their sentences, and asked if anyone had questions. Because not everyone had finished writing, he assigned the remaining sentences for homework and reminded students of the vocabulary quiz the next day. He also suggested that students review the entire chapter at home because in addition to the vocabulary quiz, they were going to be writing a paragraph in class on what scientists have learned from mummies.

SIOP Evaluation: Mr. Hughell received a "1" on the SIOP for the Review of Key Vocabulary indicator. He did review the vocabulary sentences from the first day, provided definitions and page numbers, and allowed students to write their sentences with partners. However, it is unrealistic to expect English language learners, as well as struggling readers, to master such a large number of vocabulary words through the approaches Mr. Hughell used. He did not assist students in learning the words through analogy or exploration of language structure, and provided very few exposures to the words. Mr. Hughell also expected students to be able to explain how mummies were preserved. Even with the five-minute silent review, many ELLs would be unable to do this orally without considerably more support and instruction.

Last, Mr. Hughell ran out of time at the end of the period and expected students to conduct their own review of the chapter at home. Obviously, this did not provide the type of scaffolding that English language learners need and did not represent effective review of language, vocabulary, and content.

FIGURE 9.6   SIOP Evaluation for Mr. Hughell: Review of Key Vocabulary

4	3	2	①	0	NA
27. Comprehensive **review** of key vocabulary		Uneven **review** of key vocabulary		No **review** of key vocabulary	

Example 3   Miss Johnston's lesson plans revealed one objective for the three-day lesson on mummies: "The learner will understand how mummies were made." The plan included the following for all three days: "(1) Read chapter on Mummy No. 1770, and (2) complete worksheet questions."

Miss Johnston began the second day of the lesson by calling on a student to summarize what had been read aloud the previous day. One student responded, "We read about how some guys in a museum unwrapped an old mummy." Another student added, "And scientists learned the mummy was a girl with no legs." Miss Johnston then distributed a new worksheet to students that had multiple-choice and fill-in-the-blank questions, along with two brief essay questions. Students were allowed to use their books while completing the worksheets, and if they finished early, they were given a word search with 10 words related to mummies. Miss Johnston circulated throughout the room answering questions and keeping students on-task. Toward the end of the period, she asked them to exchange papers and together they corrected the multiple-choice and fill-in-the-blank questions. The lesson concluded with students turning in their essays and being told to bring in shoe boxes and craft materials for dioramas that each would make on the following day.

SIOP Evaluation: Miss Johnston received a "0" on the SIOP for the Review of Key Vocabulary indicator. She had no language objectives for the lesson plan and did not introduce, teach, or review any key vocabulary to assist students in completing the worksheet. Some students (those who finished the worksheets early) practiced finding vocabulary on the word search. Most likely, struggling readers and ELLs

---

FIGURE 9.7   SIOP Evaluation for Miss Johnston: Review of Key Vocabulary

4	3	2	1	⓪	NA
27. Comprehensive **review** of key vocabulary		Uneven **review** of key vocabulary		No **review** of key vocabulary	

would not complete the word search since it was intended only for those who completed the worksheet quickly. It is important to note that word searches, while engaging, do not constitute effective review because students are expected to simply match spellings without knowing pronunciations or meanings, and without any teacher support.

Review of Key Content Concepts

Just as it is important to review key vocabulary periodically throughout a lesson, and especially at its conclusion, it is also essential that English language learners have key content concepts reviewed during and at the end of a lesson. Understandings are scaffolded when you stop and briefly summarize, along with students' help, the key content covered to that point. For example, you might say something like the following: "Up to this point, we learned that little was known about Mummy No. 1770 until it was donated to the museum. After the scientists completed the autopsy, they discovered three important things. Who remembers what they were?" This type of review is usually informal and it can lead into the next section of the text or a discussion: "Let's read this next section to see what else the scientists learned."

A more structured review might involve students summarizing with partners, written activities, or listing key points on the board. It is important to link the review to the content objectives so that you and the students stay focused on the essential content concepts. Toward the end of the lesson, a final review helps ELLs assess their own understandings and clarify misconceptions. Students' responses to review should guide your decisions about what to do next, such as a summative evaluation, or if needed additional re-teaching and assessing.

Teaching Scenarios

Mr. Tran, Mr. Hughell, and Miss Johnston, the three eighth-grade social studies teachers, had varied approaches to instruction and review as discussed next.

Example 1 You may recall that Mr. Tran's content objectives for the lessons on mummies included having students describe how scientists learned about Mummy No. 1770, and discuss five discoveries scientists made during the autopsy of the mummy. Mr. Tran began the second day of the lesson by reviewing key vocabulary on the Word Wall, followed by a partner review of the graphic organizers begun the previous day, which focused on how scientists learned from mummies. After this activity, Mr. Tran asked students to review the major discoveries that the scientists had made to this point.

Prior to assigning the second section of the text, Mr. Tran wrote on the board, "What *evidence* did the scientists discover during the *autopsy* of the *mummy*?" Students were directed to look for additional scientific discoveries as they read and to complete the next section of the graphic organizer. Toward the end of the lesson,

Mr. Tran asked students to review with their partners the steps taken by the scientists (from the graphic organizer) and to determine two more major discoveries detailed in the text. These were discussed and added to the two on the board from the previous day.

SIOP Evaluation: Mr. Tran received a "4" for the Review of Key Content Concepts indicator. Throughout the lesson, he consciously and consistently reviewed content directly related to his objectives. Students reviewed as a whole class and with partners, and opportunities were given for correcting errors on the graphic organizers and for clarifying misunderstandings. At the conclusion of the lesson, Mr. Tran reviewed the major discoveries.

FIGURE 9.8   SIOP Evaluation for Mr. Tran: Review of Key Content Concepts

④	3	2	1	0	NA
28. Comprehensive **review** of key content concepts		Uneven **review** of key content concepts		No **review** of key content concepts	

Example 2   Recall that Mr. Hughell wrote the following content objectives for his lessons on mummies: "(1) Write a paragraph on what mummies teach scientists about how Egyptians lived, and (2) explain how mummies were preserved." At the beginning of the second day's lesson following a brief review of vocabulary, Mr. Hughell gave students five minutes to review what had been read in the text the previous day. He asked for volunteers to summarize what they had learned about Mummy No. 1770 and how mummies were prepared. Several students responded with brief summaries and Mr. Hughell clarified some points and added to the students' summaries. At the end of the lesson, Mr. Hughell suggested that students review the entire chapter at home in order to prepare for a quiz and written assignment the next day.

SIOP Evaluation: Mr. Hughell received a "1" for the Review of Key Content Concepts indicator. He attempted to provide a review of the previous day's reading and had volunteers summarize what had been read. Most important, he clarified points and added information to their summaries. Because of running out of time at the end of the period, Mr. Hughell failed to review content concepts adequately as the lesson concluded. It was inappropriate for him to require English language learners to review at home an entire text chapter that had specialized terminology. The *teacher* is the one to provide this review prior to assessment and evaluation.

FIGURE 9.9   SIOP Evaluation for Mr. Hughell: Review of Key Content Concepts

4	3	2	①	0	NA
28. Comprehensive **review** of key content concepts		Uneven **review** of key content concepts		No **review** of key content concepts	

Example 3   Miss Johnston included one objective in her lesson plan: "The learner will understand how mummies were made." She intended to have the students read the chapter on mummies and complete a worksheet.

Recall that Miss Johnston began the second day's lesson by calling on students to summarize what had been read the previous day. Two students responded with very brief sentences. The worksheet was distributed and its questions were completed and corrected in class. The third day's plan was to have the class create a diorama.

SIOP Evaluation: Miss Johnston received a "0" for the Review of Key Content Concepts indicator. Although two students attempted to summarize the chapter, each gave only one sentence and they were not really summaries, just what the students recalled. Miss Johnston made no other attempts to review content concepts for her students. Her only objective was so vague ("students will understand . . .") that she herself may not have had clearly defined content concepts in mind.

FIGURE 9.10   **SIOP Evaluation for Miss Johnston: Review of Key Content Concepts**

4	3	2	1	(0)	NA
28. Comprehensive **review** of key content concepts		Uneven **review** of key content concepts		No **review** of key content concepts	

Providing Feedback

Periodic review of language, vocabulary, and content enables teachers to provide feedback to students that clarifies and corrects misconceptions and misunderstandings. Feedback also helps develop students' proficiency in English when it is supportive and validating. For example, teachers can model correct English usage when restating a student's response: "Yes, you're correct, the scientists *were confused* by what they thought was a baby's skull lying next to the mummy." Paraphrasing also supports students' understandings and validates answers if we add after the paraphrase, "Is this what you're thinking (or saying)?" If students are only able to respond to questions in one or two words, you can validate their answers in complete sentences: "You're right! *Embalming* is the process of preserving bodies."

Feedback is generally given orally or in writing, but teachers can also provide it through facial expressions and body language. A nod, smile of support, pat on the shoulder or encouraging look can take away fear of speaking aloud, especially for students who are beginning to develop English proficiency. Additionally, students can provide feedback to each other and the teacher can facilitate feedback by providing appropriate modeling.

Teaching Scenarios

In the previously described lesson on mummies, the three teachers provided feedback in varied ways.

Example 1   Mr. Tran began by reviewing words on the Word Wall. He asked volunteers to give informal definitions for a few words, focusing on the key vocabulary. When needed, Mr. Tran clarified definitions, assisted students with pronunciations, and gently corrected errors.

Additional feedback was provided by peers when students shared their graphic organizers with each other and were encouraged to make corrections and additions based on conversations with their partners. Mr. Tran concluded the lesson by asking students to review with their partners the steps taken by the scientists and to determine other major discoveries detailed in the text. These were discussed and added to the discoveries listed the previous day.

As a matter of practice, Mr. Tran walked around the room while students were working alone, with partners, or with groups. He frequently smiled, voiced encouragement, answered questions, and generally provided support for his students' efforts.

SIOP Evaluation: Mr. Tran received a "4" for the Feedback indicator. He scaffolded students' learning by clarifying, discussing, and correcting responses. He encouraged peer support and feedback when the graphic organizers were shared, and Mr. Tran used explanation and discussion to help students understand how to evaluate the importance of the scientists' discoveries. He moved around the classroom during the lesson, offering support and encouragement. Mr. Tran clearly used review, assessment, and feedback to develop his students' language proficiency and content knowledge.

FIGURE 9.11   SIOP Evaluation for Mr. Tran: Feedback

④	3	2	1	0	NA
29. Regularly provides **feedback** to students on their output (e.g., language, content, work)		Inconsistently provides **feedback** to students on their output		Provides no **feedback** to students on their output	

Example 2   At the beginning of Mr. Hughell's lesson on mummies, he asked for volunteers to read several of the vocabulary sentences they had written the previous day. As students read, Mr. Hughell corrected language errors when needed. He clarified content misconceptions and reminded students of correct definitions for vocabulary.

Mr. Hughell also asked volunteers to summarize what they had learned previously about Mummy No. 1770. Several students responded with brief summaries and Mr. Hughell gave explanations and added to the students' summaries. Students were then directed to read the remainder of the text silently and to ask for help if they found words they didn't understand.

SIOP Evaluation: Mr. Hughell received a "2" for the Feedback indicator. He frequently clarified misconceptions and gave clear corrections for students' errors. However, his feedback would have been more effective had it better scaffolded to students' developing language proficiency and content knowledge. That is, Mr. Hughell's feedback was primarily corrective rather than supportive. He essentially told students their answers were incorrect and then told them the correct ones, rather than assisting them in formulating the correct responses themselves. Mr. Hughell also directed students to read the text independently and to ask for help if needed. Many students, English language learners especially, may be reluctant to ask for help for fear of appearing incapable or because they don't know how to formulate the questions they need answered.

Because Mr. Hughell's classroom was also quite teacher-centered, and he delivered instruction mostly by standing at the front of the room, students had little opportunity to work together to provide each other with helpful feedback. His teaching would be more effective for ELLs if he created a more supportive classroom environment, and he could begin to give more sensitive feedback to his students' responses.

FIGURE 9.12   SIOP Evaluation for Mr. Hughell: Feedback

4	3	②	1	0	NA
29. Regularly provides **feedback** to students on their output (e.g., language, content, work)	Inconsistently provides **feedback** to students on their output			Provides no **feedback** to students on their output	

Example 3   Recall that Miss Johnston assigned her students the chapter on Mummy No. 1770 to read. At the beginning of the second day's lesson, she asked for two students to summarize what they had read the previous day. Two volunteered with very brief and incomplete sentences. Miss Johnston offered no further explanations at that time.

After she distributed the worksheets on mummies, Miss Johnston circulated throughout the room answering questions and keeping students on-task. Toward the end of the period, she asked students to exchange papers and together they corrected the multiple-choice and fill-in-the-blank questions. Miss Johnston read the correct answers as students marked their peers' papers.

SIOP Evaluation: Miss Johnston received a "1" for the Feedback indicator. She attempted to help students by answering questions while they were completing their worksheets. She also corrected the papers in class, providing correct answers for the questions. However, the amount of feedback she provided students was very limited and not particularly supportive. When she gave the correct responses to the worksheet questions, she provided little or no explanation. In all, English language learners received very little supportive feedback during the observed lesson.

FIGURE 9.13   SIOP Evaluation for Miss Johnston: Feedback

4	3	2	①	0	NA
29. Regularly provides **feedback** to students on their output (e.g., language, content, work)		Inconsistently provides **feedback** to students on their output		Provides no **feedback** to students on their output	

Assessment of Lesson Objectives

Within the context of lesson delivery for English language learners, we see review and assessment as an ongoing process, especially related to a lesson's language and content objectives. Historically, educators have blurred the line between assessment and evaluation, generally using the term "evaluation" for both formative and summative judgments. The teacher's role in evaluation was primarily as a judge, one who conveyed a value on the completion of a given task. This value was frequently determined from the results of periodic quizzes, reports, or tests that served as the basis for report card grades in elementary and secondary schools.

Today, however, many educators distinguish between assessment and evaluation (Ferrara & McTigue, 1992). *Assessment* is defined as "the gathering and synthesizing of information concerning students' learning," while *evaluation* is defined as "making judgments about students' learning. The processes of assessment and evaluation can be viewed as progressive: first, assessment; then, evaluation" (McLaughlin & Vogt, 1996, pp. 104, 106).

Assessment occurs throughout a lesson, as evidenced in lesson plans and in periodic review to determine if students are understanding and applying content concepts. Toward the end of the lesson, students' progress is assessed to see whether it is appropriate to move on or whether it is necessary to review and reteach. This type of assessment is *informal, authentic, multidimensional,* and includes *multiple indicators* that reflect student learning, achievement, and attitudes (McLaughlin & Vogt, 1996; O'Malley & Pierce, 1996).

Informal assessment involves on-the-spot, ongoing opportunities for determining the extent to which students are learning content. These opportunities may include teacher observations, anecdotal reports, teacher-to-student and student-to-student conversations, quick-writes and brainstorming, or any number of tasks that occur within regular instruction and that are not intended to be graded or evaluated according to set criteria.

Authentic assessment is characterized by its application to real life, where students are engaged in meaningful tasks that take place in real-life contexts (McLaughlin & Kennedy, 1993). Authentic assessment is usually *multidimensional* because teachers use different ways of determining student performance. These may include written pieces, audiotapes, student and parent interviews, videotapes, observations, creative work and art, discussion, performance, oral group responses, and so forth.

These multidimensional student performances usually involve *multiple indicators,* specific evidences related to the content objectives, goals, outcomes, or standards. For example, a student may indicate proficiency with a goal or objective through a piece of writing, through active participation in a group activity, and through insightful questions he asks during discussion. The teacher thus has more than one piece of evidence indicating he is progressing toward mastery of the particular content or language objective.

Periodic assessments before and during lessons can eventually lead to evaluation of a student's demonstrated performance for a goal, objective, or standard. This evaluation, while summative, also may be informal and take a variety of forms. Often, rubrics are used to ascertain a developmental level of performance for the particular goal, objective, or standard. For example, on a developmental rubric student performance may be characterized as "emergent," "beginning," "developing," "competent," or "proficient." Other rubrics may communicate evaluative information, such as "inadequate," "adequate," "thorough," or "exceptional" (McLaughlin & Vogt, 1996). Whichever rubric is used, results of assessment and evaluation are often shared with other interested stakeholders, such as parents and administrators, and with the students themselves.

Assessments can be individual or group administered. Individual oral or written responses tell you how one student is performing, while group responses may quickly tell you how the entire group is progressing. Group response is especially sensitive to the needs of ELLs, and there is a variety of methods for eliciting group responses, including some of our favorites:

- **Thumbs up/thumbs down:** Generally, this is used for questions that elicit "agree/disagree" responses. It can also be used for yes/no questions or true/false statements. Older students may be more comfortable responding with "pencils up/pencils down" (point of pencil up or down). Students can also indicate "I don't know" by making a fist, holding it in front of the chest, and wiggling it back and forth. The pencil used by older students can also be wiggled to indicate that the answer is unknown.
- **Number wheels:** A number wheel is made from tag board strips (5" × 1") held together with a round-head brass paper fastener. Each strip has a number printed on it, either 0 to 5 or 0 to 10, depending on your needs and students' ages. Students use their individual number wheels to indicate their answers to questions or statements that offer multiple-choice responses.

Possible answers are displayed on the board, overhead, or pocket chart and the teacher asks the questions or gives the statements orally.

For example, if you were teaching a lesson on possessives, you could write the following on the board:

1. boys
2. boy's
3. boys'

Each child has a number wheel and you say, "Show me the correct use of the word 'boys' in the following sentences. Remember that you can show me a "0" if you don't know the answer. Ready? 'The little boy's dog was hungry and was barking.' Show me!"

Students then find the number 2 strip and holding their number wheels in front of their chests, they display their answers. They repeat the process as you give the next sentence. Be sure to give plenty of "wait time" before giving the direction, "Show me!"

You may think that number wheels are only appropriate for younger students but middle school and high schools students enjoy working with them too, and they provide you with much needed information about students' understandings of language and content concepts.

- **Response boards:** Either small chalkboards or dry erase boards can be used for group responses. Each student has a board and writing instrument. You ask a question, students respond on their boards, and then turn them to face you when you say, "Show me!" Older students seem to prefer working with the dry erase boards and will willingly use them in a classroom in which approximations are supported and errors are viewed as steps to effective learning. Dry erase boards (12" × 12") can be inexpensively cut from "bathroom tile board," which is available at home and building supply stores.

Group response activities are very effective for assessing, reviewing, and providing feedback. If students are having difficulty with language and content concepts, and this is obvious from individual answers given during a group response activity, review and re-teaching are necessary.

Teaching Scenarios

Let's compare how the three teachers assessed their students' understandings and application of lesson objectives.

Example 1   Mr. Tran included multiple opportunities to assess his students' progress in meeting his key vocabulary and content concept objectives. These included:

1. The oral group reading of the Word Wall, in order and in random order
2. The informal definitions of the vocabulary
3. The review of the first section of the graphic organizer, first with partners and then with the whole class

4. The listing of the major scientific discoveries about Mummy No. 1770
5. The worksheet with the two columns, one for evidence about the girl's life and the other for evidence about the girl's death

Mr. Tran still had another day to complete his lesson as well as the final assessment of his students' performance on his language and content objectives.

SIOP Evaluation: Mr. Tran received a "4" for the Assessment indicator. He included group response and partner and whole-class reporting that he could readily assess, as well as individual written work. His assessments occurred throughout the lesson, and they were authentic, multidimensional, and included multiple indicators. Most important, his assessment was directly linked to his language and content objectives.

FIGURE 9.14   SIOP Evaluation for Mr. Tran: Assessment of Lesson Objectives

④	3	2	1	0	NA
30. Conducts **assessment** of student comprehension and learning of all lesson objectives (e.g., spot checking, group response) throughout the lesson		Conducts **assessment** of student comprehension and learning of some lesson objectives		Conducts no **assessment** of student comprehension and learning of lesson objectives	

Example 2   Mr. Hughell checked some of his students' work for the first half of the vocabulary sentences by having volunteers read their them aloud. He also asked for volunteers to summarize the previous day's reading, after giving them five minutes to review the text. At the end of his lesson, Mr. Hughell had some students read a few of their sentences written for the second half of the vocabulary list. He planned on evaluating students' understandings with a written paragraph and the matching quiz for vocabulary the following day.

SIOP Evaluation: Mr. Hughell received a "2" on the SIOP the Assessment indicator. It is not clear whether students could pronounce any of the vocabulary words because he never assessed whether students knew them. Even though he asked for volunteers to read their sentences, he had no way to know whether the rest of the students, particularly the English language learners, understood the meanings of the vocabulary. The matching test was not given until the last day of the lesson at the end of the period, too late for the assessment to guide review, feedback, and reteaching. The writing assignment also came too late to inform Mr. Hughell about his students' understandings during instruction. He attempted to match assessment and evaluation to his content objectives ("Write a paragraph on what mummies

teach scientists about how Egyptians lived; explain how mummies were preserved; match 20 vocabulary words with their definitions"). However, by the time
he discovered who had met them and who had not, the three-day lesson was
completed.

FIGURE 9.15 SIOP Evaluation for Mr. Hughell: Assessment of Lesson Objectives

4	3	②	1	0	NA
30. Conducts **assessment** of student comprehension and learning of all lesson objectives (e.g., spot checking, group response) throughout the lesson		Conducts **assessment** of student comprehension and learning of some lesson objectives		Conducts no **assessment** of student comprehension and learning of lesson objectives	

Example 3   Miss Johnston assessed student learning during her lesson by asking
two students to summarize the previous day's reading; they responded with one
sentence each that simply related a recalled fact. She had students exchange
papers to correct the worksheet with multiple-choice and fill-in-the-blank questions. She planned a diorama for the culminating activity for the lesson on mummies.

SIOP Evaluation: Miss Johnston received a "1" for the Assessment indicator.
Although the worksheet constituted summative evaluation, there was no ongoing
assessment throughout the lesson. The vague summary sentences elicited from the
two students yielded no information about the understandings of the rest of the
students. There was no learning objective related to the creation of the dioramas,
and it is doubtful they would tell Miss Johnston much about her students' understandings of key vocabulary and content concepts. Last, her one objective ("The
students will understand how mummies were made") was very general and not
directly measurable. Therefore, the objective was impossible to adequately assess.

FIGURE 9.16 SIOP Evaluation for Miss Johnston: Assessment of Lesson Objectives

4	3	2	①	0	NA
30. Conducts **assessment** of student comprehension and learning of all lesson objectives (e.g., spot checking, group response) throughout the lesson		Conducts **assessment** of student comprehension and learning of some lesson objectives		Conducts no **assessment** of student comprehension and learning of lesson objectives	

Summary

Review and assessment are integrated processes, essential for all learners, but they are critical to the success of English language learners. Effective sheltered teachers carefully plan for periodic review and informal assessment throughout lessons. This informal assessment is authentic, multidimensional, and it includes multiple indicators of students' performance. Effective sheltered teachers also design appropriate evaluation of key vocabulary and content concept objectives at the conclusion of the lesson. Most important, review and assessment guide teaching and re-teaching, inform decision making, lead to supportive feedback, and provide for fair and comprehensive judgments about student performance.

Discussion Questions

1. Many sheltered teachers introduce key vocabulary at the beginning of the lesson, but often neglect to review the new terms systematically throughout the lesson and at its conclusion. How can you ensure that the lesson's key academic vocabulary is reviewed at the end of each lesson? Describe a variety of ways you would review the terms, as well as the mechanisms you could put in place to build a vocabulary review into each lesson.

2. Research has shown that gratuitous compliments to students (e.g., "Good job" or "Keep up the good work") do little to motivate them or assist with their learning. Instead, teachers should give regular, substantive feedback to students on their verbal contributions and on their work. What are some ways to provide constructive, specific feedback to students? Consider class size and English proficiency levels as you answer this question.

3. It is important for teachers to make sure their teaching is "connecting" with their students, particularly ELLs. A well-planned lesson is ineffective if students do not understand the content due to limited language proficiency or unfamiliarity with the background of academic content being taught. Consistent assessment of students' comprehension is critical for effective sheltered lessons. How can teachers check for understanding? How would a teacher know that the students comprehend? Why is ongoing assessment critical when teaching English language learners?

4. One of the features of quality sheltered instruction is that teachers carefully select key content concepts and teach in a way that will ensure students have a good understanding and knowledge of those concepts. What are some ways to conduct a comprehensive review of a lesson's concepts? Why is a final review important?

10 Scoring and Interpretation of the SIOP

The Sheltered Instruction Observation Protocol (SIOP) was designed as an instrument for educators to use in a number of ways. First, we found that school personnel wanted and needed an objective measure of high-quality sheltered lessons, and the SIOP operationalizes a model of effective sheltered instruction. School site administrators use the SIOP as a way to provide clear, concrete feedback to the teachers they observe. The SIOP is also useful to university faculty who teach sheltered instruction strategies, as well as to those faculty who supervise field experience. Although developed as an observational instrument, teachers can use the features of the SIOP as a planning guide (see Appendix B). Finally, the SIOP is a tool for researchers to determine the extent to which sheltered instruction is implemented in a given classroom and then helps to maintain fidelity of implementation.

SIOP Heading

FIGURE 10.1 SIOP Heading

The Sheltered Instruction Observation Protocol (SIOP)
(Echevarria, Vogt, and Short, 2000)

Observer: _____ Teacher: _____

Date: _____ School: _____

Grade: _____ ESL level: _____

Class: _____ Lesson: Multi-day Single-day (*circle one*)

Directions: Circle the number that best reflects what you observe in a sheltered lesson. You may give a score from 0 to 4. Cite under "Comments" specific examples of the behaviors observed.

Total Score: ☐   % Score: ☐   Tape #: _____

The heading on the first page of the SIOP form is fairly self-explanatory (see Figure 10.1). It is intended to provide a context for the lesson being observed. There is space for the observer's name and the date of the observation. Other information, such as the teacher's name, school, grade of the class being observed, ESL level of the students, and the academic content area, is also included. We recognize that an observation at one point in time does not always accurately represent the teacher's implementation of sheltered instruction strategies and techniques. Therefore, there is a place for the observer to indicate if the lesson is part of a multi-day unit, or is a single-day lesson.

In using the SIOP over the past several years, we have found that it is useful to videotape a lesson and analyze it later. Teachers, supervisors, and researchers alike have found this to be an effective way of recording and measuring teachers' growth over time. The heading has a place for the observer to indicate the tape number for a given lesson.

Finally, there is a box for the total score the teacher received on the SIOP. It is most useful to represent a teacher's score as a percent since NA affects a total score number (see next section for an explanation of scoring).

How to Score the SIOP

Scores may be assigned in a number of ways: (1) during the observation itself, as individual features are recognized; (2) after the observation, as the observer reflects on the entire lesson, referring to observational field notes; or (3) after the observation while watching a videotape of the lesson. The third option is often useful so that the teacher and observer are able to share the same point of reference when discussing the lesson.

It is important to stress that not all items on the SIOP will be present in every lesson. However, some items, such as items under Preparation, Comprehensible Input, Interaction, and Review/Assessment, are essential for each lesson. Over the course of time (several lessons, a week), all items should be represented in one's teaching.

Assigning Scores

The observer determines the level of implementation, guided by the scenario descriptions in this book. There are myriad ways that a teacher can implement an item, but the chapters were designed to show a graphic example for each item for scores ranging from 4 to 0. The SIOP provides a 5-point scale as well as space for qualitative data. It is recommended that the observer use the "Comments" section to record examples of the presence or absence of each feature. That way, both the observer and the teacher have specific information, besides a score, to use in their post-lesson discussion. More information may be added to the Comments section during review of the SIOP, documenting the content of the discussion for future reference, which is particularly useful as subsequent lessons are planned.

Naturally, there is an element of subjectivity to interpreting the items and assigning scores. Observers must be consistent in their scoring. For example, one person may think that for Item #3 (Content concepts appropriate for age and educational background level of students) only grade-level materials are appropriate while another observer may feel that the same content found in materials for lower grade levels can be used because of the students' low reading levels or because students have interrupted educational backgrounds. In either case, observers must be consistent in their interpretation and scoring across settings.

We suggest that, to assist in more accurate scoring, the observer ask the teacher for a copy of the lesson plan in advance of observing the class. That way, the observer is better able to score the Preparation section, as well as recognize NA items.

Not Applicable (NA) Category

The Not Applicable (NA) scoring option is important because it distinguishes a feature that is "not applicable" to the observed lesson from a score of "0," which indicates that the feature should have been present but was not. For example, Mr. Leung taught a five-day unit on the solar system. During the first few lessons of the unit, Mr. Leung concentrated on making the rather dense information accessible to his students. He adapted the text to make it understandable for them and provided ample opportunities for students to use strategies. On the final day of the unit, an observer was present. Mr. Leung wrapped up the unit by having the students complete an enjoyable hands-on activity wherein they applied the concepts they had learned. It was obvious that the students had learned the content and were able to use it in the activity. However, because of the nature of that particular lesson, there was no observed adaptation of content (Item #5). Mr. Leung was not penalized by receiving a score of "0" because the lesson did not lend itself to that item and Mr. Leung had covered that item on another day. A score of NA would be correct in this case.

In the case of Mrs. Nash, however, it would be appropriate to score this feature as "0." Mrs. Nash also taught a unit on the solar system. On the first day of the unit, she showed a video about the solar system and had a brief oral discussion following the movie. The next day an observer was present as she read from the text and then had students answer chapter questions. There was no evidence that any of the content had been adapted to the variety of student proficiency levels in her class. In fact, many students appeared to be confused as they tried to answer questions based on readings from the grade-level textbook.

The distinction between a "0" and "NA" is an important one since a score of "0" adversely affects the overall score for the lesson, while an "NA" does not because a percent is to be used.

Calculating Scores

There are 30 items on the SIOP, each with a range of possible scores from "0" to "4," or NA. After scoring each item, the observer then tallies all numeric scores.

The score is written over the total possible score, usually 120 (30 items × a score of "4"). So, an example of a total score would be written, 115/120. Because of the NA, adding the individual scores for a grand total is meaningless. It is more informative to know the total score based on the total possible score.

Let's take a step-by-step look at how a teacher's total score is calculated.

Mr. Leung received a score of "4" on 20 items, a score of "3" on 5 items, a score of "2" on 4 items, and 1 NA. The sum of those scores is 103.

$$
\begin{aligned}
20 \times 4 &= 80 \\
5 \times 3 &= 15 \\
2 \times 4 &= \underline{8} \\
\text{Total score} &= \mathbf{103/116}
\end{aligned}
$$

The score of 116 was derived in this way: If Mr. Leung had received a "4" on each item of the SIOP (a perfect score), he would have had a total score of 116.

$$29 \times 4 = 116$$

The number of items is 29 instead of 30 because one item was not applicable (NA); he was only rated on 29 items.

For the lesson observed, Mr. Leung received a total score of 103/116. The total score can be converted to a percentage, if that form is more useful. Simply divide the numerator by the denominator: 103 ÷ 116. In this case, Mr. Leung implemented the SIOP at a level of 88%. You can see the importance of distinguishing between a score of "0" and NA. For Mr. Leung, a "0" score would have changed his total score from 88% to 85%. Let's see how.

$$
\begin{aligned}
20 \times 4 &= 80 \\
5 \times 3 &= 15 \\
2 \times 4 &= 8 \\
1 \times 0 &= \underline{0} \\
\text{Total score} &= \mathbf{103/120}[1]
\end{aligned}
$$

The step-by-step process for tallying scores is shown in Figure 10.2.

FIGURE 10.2 The Step-by-Step Process for Tallying Scores

1. Add the teacher's scores from all items.
2. Count the number of NAs, multiply by 4, then subtract this number from 120.
3. Divide the number from step 2 into the number from step 1 (the adjusted possible score into the teacher's score).

---

[1]The highest possible score on the SIOP for all 30 items is 120 (30 items × a score of "4"). If Mr. Leung were rated on all 30 items, his total score would be 103/120 or 85%.

Sample Lesson

In this section of the chapter, we will describe an entire science lesson conducted by a sixth-grade teacher and show how she was scored on the SIOP. Ms. Clark received training and has been using the SIOP for lesson planning and delivery for about 16 months. This lesson took place at the end of the first quarter of the school year. The class consisted of beginning ESL students from varying language and country backgrounds. The class has been studying a unit on minerals and visited a local natural history museum. The students have examined rocks in class as well. Ms. Clark provided us with a lesson plan before we conducted the observation.

In the classroom, the desks were arranged in three circular groups. Some students had to turn around to see the board and overhead screen at the front of the room. The class objectives and agenda were written on a whiteboard at the side. Two bulletin boards in the back of the room displayed the students' work for a language arts project and a science project. A Spanish-speaking bilingual aide assisted the teacher and also helped newly arrived Spanish-speaking students. The class period was 45 minutes long.

The teacher began the class by complimenting the students for their performance on a test they had taken on minerals and singled out one student who received the highest "A" in the class. She then asked the students to read the objectives and activities for the day silently while she read them aloud:

> *Objective:* Today we will develop an understanding of what volcanoes are and why they erupt.
>
> - First, I will demonstrate how rocks could move and what happens when they move.
> - Second, you will use a semantic web worksheet to recall what you know about volcanoes.
> - Third, I will use a model to show how a volcano erupts.
> - Fourth, you will make predictions about the story, "Pompeii . . . Buried Alive," and then read pages 4 to 9 silently.
> - Fifth, you will refer to information on page 6 in the book to write on a worksheet the steps that happen before a volcano erupts.
> - Your homework is to draw a volcano and label the parts. The vocabulary words for the day are: melts, blast, mixture, rumbles, straw, pipe shepherd, giant, peddler, crater, lava, magma, magma chamber.

The teacher then demonstrated for the class what happens when rocks move against each other, using two stacks of books. After placing the stacks side by side on a desk, she pushed against one stack so the other stack slid off the desk and scattered onto the floor. She asked the students what happens when one set of rocks moves another set of rocks. The students responded that the rocks break.

The aide distributed semantic web worksheets to the students and asked them to write "Volcano" in the center circle. Then, in the other spaces, they were to write everything they already knew about volcanoes. While the students worked, the teacher and aide circulated to monitor the students' understanding of the task and to see how they were progressing.

After the students filled in their webs, the teacher led them in a discussion of what they had written and wrote some of their comments on the whiteboard:

- Lava melts and explodes
- When it erupts, all that force comes from the middle of the earth
- Volcanoes are formed deep inside the earth
- When a volcano is under water, the lava comes out and makes an island

The teacher repeated that she was going to make a model volcano and asked the class what a "model" is. One student answered that it is an example, not a real volcano. All of the students were watching as the teacher showed them a bottle and explained it would be like the magma chamber that is inside a volcano. She poured a cup of warm water inside the bottle. While it cooled slightly, she showed the class a diagram of the model for the experiment, with the corresponding volcano parts labeled. They discussed each part of the volcano and in doing so emphasized some of the key vocabulary words: crater, magma pipe, lava, magma, magma chamber, basin.

The teacher returned to the model and placed a few drops of liquid dish detergent in the warm water. Next, she picked up an object and asked the students to identify it. One student said it was a measuring spoon. The teacher measured a teaspoon of baking soda and put it into the water and detergent mixture. She asked the students to identify where she was putting it. The students responded, MAGMA CHAMBER. She put in a second teaspoon of baking soda, then held up the bottle for the students to observe, and then they reviewed the ingredients. To speed up the process, she added vinegar to the bottle. She asked them, "When was the last time we used vinegar?" The students said they had used it on the previous day. The "volcano" began to erupt and the teacher displayed the bottle so that the students could see the foam overflowing.

The class reviewed the process and the ingredients for the model volcano. Individual students were called to the front to participate in a second volcano demonstration, each one completing one of the steps to produce another "eruption." The second "lava" flow was a bit larger than the first.

The teacher asked the whole class to think about "What causes a volcano to erupt?" and added, "We used warm water. What will happen to heat in a chamber?" One student answered, "Heat rises." The teacher explained that it was not just the heat that caused the eruption and asked them to think of the other ingredients and what happened when they were mixed. The teacher went on to explain, "The mixture of gases produces carbon monoxide," and wrote "carbon monoxide" and its chemical symbol on the board. She also asked them what they knew about plants and said, "They breathe in carbon monoxide. We breathe out carbon monoxide; we breathe in oxygen." [This part was an error, but the teacher did not realize her mistake in calling carbon dioxide (for plants and humans), carbon monoxide.]

One student wanted to know why rocks come out of volcanoes and another student offered an explanation, "The volcano is inside of a mountain of rocks." The teacher commented that whatever is inside the chamber when it erupts will come out with the lava, and if they had put small bits of material inside their model, those bits also would have come out when it erupted.

The teacher and aide handed out the story books, "Pompeii . . . Buried Alive," to the students, and they began pre-reading activities. The teacher focused their attention on the title and asked them to predict what they thought the book would be about. One student said, "Volcanoes erupting." The teacher asked, "Where do you think it takes place?" Students guessed various places: Nicaragua, Rome, Greece, England. The teacher commented on the togas in the cover's picture. She then directed their attention to the back cover and read the summary aloud, stating the story took place 2000 years ago in Italy. She asked, "Is it a true story?" Some students guessed yes; others no. "How do you know it's true?" They discussed that the term "took place" and the use of a specific time in history meant that it was true. The teacher then asked for a student volunteer to point out Italy on the wall map and the class discussed the location of Italy in southern Europe.

The teacher asked how many of the students came from countries with volcanoes. Students from Ethiopia, El Salvador, and Guatemala said they knew about volcanoes in their countries. One student asked if it had to be a hot country to have a volcano. The teacher asked if they knew where the most recent eruption had occurred. She told them it was Montserrat in the Caribbean and that volcanoes often occur in warm countries but not all are in warm countries. She asked if they knew about a volcano in the United States and told them about Mt. St. Helens in Washington, a state that is cold in winter. She showed them Washington on the map. One student commented on the way precipitation forms and tried to compare it with what happens in the formation of a volcano.

The teacher directed the students to read pages 4 to 9 silently for two minutes. While they were reading, she distributed worksheets with a sequencing exercise to describe what happens before a volcano erupts. The instructions told students to put the sentences in order according to what they read on page 6. They could refer back to the reading.

The teacher began to read the passage aloud slowly about three minutes later, although some students indicated that they had not yet finished reading it silently. As she read, she again displayed the transparency with the model volcano diagram on the overhead and referred to it and to the key vocabulary as she read. She also paused from time to time to ask comprehension questions. Students were able to answer questions orally, using the model and naming the parts of a volcano. They discussed unknown words in the reading, such as peddler, rumbled, and shepherd, as they went along.

As the period drew to a close, the teacher told the students they would complete the sequencing worksheet the next day. She reminded them of the homework—draw a volcano in their journal and label the parts. They were also told to place the webs they had completed in their journals. The teacher then led a brief wrap-up of the lesson, asking questions about a volcano, which students answered.

On the following pages you will see how Ms. Clark was scored on the SIOP items and the Comments that provide evidence for her score (see Figure 10.3).

FIGURE 10.3   Sample Completed SIOP

The Sheltered Instruction Observation Protocol (SIOP)

Observer: _____   Teacher: _____Ms. Clark_____

Date: _____   School: _____

Grade: _____   ESL level: _____6_____

Class: _____   Lesson: Multi-day Single-day (*circle one*)

Directions: Circle the number that best reflects what you observe in a sheltered lesson. You may give a score from 0 to 4. Cite under "Comments" specific examples of the behaviors observed.

Total Score: $^{95}/_{120}$ % Score: 79   Tape #: _____

I. Preparation _____

(4)	3	2	1	0	NA

1. Clearly defined **content objectives** for students   **Content objectives** for students implied   No clearly defined **content objectives**

Comments: Content objectives were written and stated at the beginning of the lesson.

4	(3)	2	1	0	NA

2. Clearly defined **language objec-tives** for students   **Language objectives** for students implied   No clearly defined **language objectives** for students

Comments: Key vocabulary was listed, but the language skills to be targeted were listed and stated as activities and not written as objectives.

4	3	(2)	1	0	NA

3. **Content concepts** appropriate for age and educational background level of students   **Content concepts** somewhat appropri-ate for age and edu-cational background level of students   **Content concepts** inappropriate for age and educational background level of students

Comments: Students appeared to understand the concepts. Several students commented that they had already studied about volcanoes at the elementary level. Therefore, it is unclear why this lesson was being introduced again.

(4)	3	2	1	0	NA

4. **Supplementary materials** used to a high degree, making the lesson clear and meaningful (e.g., graphs, models, visuals)   Some use of **supple-mentary materials**   No use of **supple-mentary materials**

Comments: Good use of supplementary materials to enhance students' understanding of volcanoes such as copies of semantic maps, pull-down maps, a book, Pompeii . . . Buried Alive, *a transparency indicating the parts of a volcano, stacks of books to demonstrate rocks pushing against each other, household items to illustrate a volcanic eruption.*

④	3	2	1	0	NA
5. **Adaptation of content** (e.g., text, assignment) to all levels of student proficiency		Some **adaptation of content** to all levels of student proficiency		No significant **adaptation of content** to all levels of student proficiency	

Comments: All students were given the same text with which to work. There were no specific adaptations made to the text itself to address the varying levels of language proficiency. However, the teacher had prepared a sequencing activity for students to complete where she identified sentences that explained the process of a volcanic eruption and students were required to put the steps in order. In addition, she began reading the text aloud to the students and paused frequently to ask questions and to check for clarification.

④	3	2	1	0	NA
6. **Meaningful activities** that integrate lesson concepts (e.g., surveys, letter writing, simulations, constructing models) with language practice opportunities for reading, writing, listening, and/or speaking		**Meaningful activities** that integrate lesson concepts, but provide little opportunity for language practice with opportunities for reading, writing, listening, and/or speaking		No **meaningful activities** that integrate lesson concepts with language practice	

Comments: There were a lot of meaningful and interesting activities that provided students with language practice (e.g., participation in building the model volcano, discussing information from their semantic maps about volcanoes, and reading authentic text).

II. Instruction

■ 1) Building Background

④	3	2	1	0	NA
7. **Concepts explicitly linked** to students' background experiences		**Concepts loosely linked** to students' background experiences		**Concepts not explicitly linked** to students' background experiences	

Comments: The teacher tapped into students' understanding of volcanoes by asking them to complete a semantic mapping exercise writing everything they knew about volcanoes.

4	3	②	1	0	NA

8. Links explicitly made between past learning and new concepts

Few links made between past learning and new concepts

No links made between past learning and new concepts

Comments: There were few links made between past learning and its connection to new concepts. The teacher initiated the class by reminding the students of the visit to the Museum of Natural History and also reminded them of the rocks they had brought in. However, she did not explain how the visit or the collection of rocks related to that day's lesson about volcanoes.

④	3	2	1	0	NA

9. Key vocabulary emphasized (e.g., introduced, written, repeated, and highlighted for students to see)

Key vocabulary introduced, but not emphasized

Key vocabulary not emphasized

Comments: The key vocabulary words used for this lesson were written on the board, stated to the students at the beginning of the lesson, and reiterated throughout the lesson particularly when the teacher and students constructed the model volcano.

■ **2) Comprehensible Input**

④	3	2	1	0	NA

10. Speech appropriate for students' proficiency level (e.g., slower rate and enunciation, and simple sentence structure for beginners)

Speech sometimes inappropriate for students' proficiency level

Speech inappropriate for students' proficiency level

Comments: The teacher modified her speech throughout the lesson, especially when she read aloud to the students.

④	3	2	1	0	NA

11. Explanation of academic tasks clear

Explanation of academic tasks somewhat clear

Explanation of academic tasks unclear

Comments: The teacher explained tasks well and modeled the demonstrations first before the students participated.

④	3	2	1	0	NA
12. Uses a variety of **techniques** to make content concepts clear (e.g., modeling, visuals, hands-on activities, demonstrations, gestures, body language)		Uses some **techniques** to make content concepts clear		Uses few or no **techniques** to make content concepts clear	

Comments: A variety of techniques were used in this lesson: the use of the OHT with a diagram of a volcano and the labeled parts, brainstorming in the semantic mapping activity, demonstrating a model of a volcanic eruption, and reading about the topic after exploring it orally and visually. Used sequencing steps to check reading comprehension.

■ **3) Strategies**

4	③	2	1	0	NA
13. Provides ample opportunities for students to use **strategies**		Provides students with inadequate opportunities to use **strategies**		No opportunity for students to use **strategies**	

Comments: The teacher used various strategies with students such as accessing prior knowledge and having them make predictions. Students, however, used these strategies with the teacher, not with other students.

④	3	2	1	0	NA
14. Consistent use of **scaffolding** techniques throughout lesson, assisting and supporting student understanding (e.g., think-alouds)		Occasional use of **scaffolding** techniques		No use of **scaffolding** techniques	

Comments: The teacher used various scaffolding techniques throughout the lesson to promote and assess students' comprehension of content concepts by means of questions, visuals, models, graphic organizers, prereading predictions, and demonstrations.

4	③	2	1	0	NA
15. Teacher uses a variety of **question types, including those that promote higher-order thinking skills** (e.g., literal, analytical, and interpretive questions)		Teacher infrequently poses **questions that promote higher-order thinking skills**		Teacher does not pose **questions that promote higher-order thinking skills**	

Comments: Most of the questions for this beginning level consisted of more factual/identification questions. In some cases, more elaborated responses were required of students; for example, "What happens when one set of rocks moves against another?" "Can you think of other places in the world where eruptions have occurred?" "Tell me about volcanoes in your country?" "How do you know this is a true story?"

■ **4) Interaction**

4	③	2	1	0	NA
16. Frequent opportunities for **interaction** and discussion between teacher/student and among students, which encourage elaborated responses about lesson concepts		**Interaction** mostly teacher-dominated with some opportunities for students to talk about or question lesson concepts		**Interaction** primarily teacher-dominated with no opportunities for students to discuss lesson concepts	

Comments: The teacher engaged the students in discussions about volcanoes throughout the class period. The semantic mapping exercise, the demonstration, and the prereading activity were all means that facilitated student interaction. The majority of interactions were teacher-student.

4	3	②	1	0	NA
17. **Grouping configurations** support language and content objectives of the lesson		**Grouping configurations** unevenly support the language and content objectives		**Grouping configurations** do not support the language and content objectives	

Comments: Although students were seated in groups, there was little opportunity for them to interact to practice their language skills. The whole-class setting supported the demonstration about volcanic eruption.

4	③	2	1	0	NA

18. Consistently provides sufficient **wait time for student responses**

Occasionally provides sufficient **wait time for student responses**

Never provides sufficient **wait time for student responses**

Comments: At times there were students who wanted to respond, but were overlooked, perhaps because the period was running out of time. For those students selected to respond, the teacher allowed them time to articulate their thoughts.

④	3	2	1	0	NA

19. Ample opportunities for students to **clarify key concepts in L1** as needed with aide, peer, or L1 text

Some opportunity for students to **clarify key concepts in L1**

No opportunity for students to **clarify key concepts in L1**

Comments: Only a few students could be identified as using their L1 during the lesson and they were seated in the far left corner of the classroom where the bilingual aide assisted them. The other students in the classroom did not seem to need to use their L1 text.

■ **5) Practice/Application**

4	③	2	1	0	NA

20. Provides **hands-on** materials and/or manipulatives for students to practice using new content knowledge

Provides few **hands-on** materials and/or manipulatives for students to practice using new content knowledge

Provides no **hands-on** materials and/or manipulatives for students to practice using new content knowledge

Comments: The lesson involved manipulatives. During the experiment/demonstration for the volcanic eruption, for example, the teacher used materials such as a bottle, liquid detergent, warm water, measuring spoons, baking soda, and vinegar. Only a few students, though, used these materials themselves.

| 4 | (3) | 2 | 1 | 0 | NA |

21. Provides activities for students to **apply content and language knowledge** in the classroom | Provides activities for students to **apply** either **content or language knowledge** in the classroom | | | Provides no activities for students to **apply content or language knowledge** in the classroom |

Comments: For the most part, students applied content and language. More student-student interactions would have been beneficial and provided better opportunities for assessment.

| 4 | (3) | 2 | 1 | 0 | NA |

22. Uses activities that integrate all **language skills** (i.e., reading, writing, listening, and speaking) | Uses activities that integrate some **language skills** | | | Uses activities that apply to only one **language skill** |

Comments: The lesson allowed students an opportunity to use all language skills (some more than others) such as listening, speaking, and reading. Writing was evident mostly in the semantic mapping activity. Some predicting and scanning for information was part of the reading skills practiced.

■ **6) Lesson Delivery**

| 4 | (3) | 2 | 1 | 0 | NA |

23. **Content objectives** clearly supported by lesson delivery | **Content objectives** somewhat supported by lesson delivery | | | **Content objectives** not supported by lesson delivery |

Comments: The demonstration and discussion along with the constant repetition of key vocabulary served to accomplish most of the content objectives for the lesson. While students seemed to indicate an understanding of what volcanoes are, it is not certain that they fully understand what causes them to erupt.

| 4 | 3 | (2) | 1 | 0 | NA |

24. **Language objectives** clearly supported by lesson delivery | **Language objectives** supported somewhat by lesson delivery | | | **Language objectives** not supported by lesson delivery |

Comments: Most of the language objectives were supported by the delivery. Students did not have a chance to complete the sequencing activity based on the reading in order to assess their reading comprehension.

④	3	2	1	0	NA
25. **Students engaged** approximately 90% to 100% of the period		**Students engaged** approximately 70% of the period		**Students engaged** less than 50% of the period	

Comments: Students were on-task throughout the lesson activity.

4	3	②	1	0	NA
26. **Pacing** of the lesson appropriate to the students' ability level		**Pacing** generally appropriate, but at times too fast or too slow		**Pacing** inappropriate to the students' ability level	

Comments: The pacing seemed fine, but was a little rushed at times which prevented students from completing some activities such as the individual silent reading and sequencing activity.

III. Review/Assessment

4	3	②	1	0	NA
27. Comprehensive **review** of key vocabulary		Uneven **review** of key vocabulary		No **review** of key vocabulary	

Comments: Teacher reviewed key vocabulary at the beginning of the lesson and reinforced it throughout. No final review took place at the end of the lesson.

4	③	2	1	0	NA
28. Comprehensive **review** of key content concepts		Uneven **review** of key content concepts		No **review** of key content concepts	

Comments: The key content concepts were reviewed throughout the lesson, but there was no comprehensive review to wrap up the lesson, other than the final question posed to students at the end of the class, "What is a volcano?"

4	③	2	1	0	NA
29. Regularly provides **feedback** to students on their output (e.g., language, content, work)		Inconsistently provides **feedback** to students on their output		Provides no **feedback** to students on their output	

Comments: The teacher gave positive feedback to students' responses in most cases. In some instances, when time was short, she did not always respond to students whose hands were raised. She guided the brainstorming and prereading discussions.

4	3	②	1	0	NA
30. Conducts **assessment** of student comprehension and learning of all lesson objectives (e.g., spot checking, group response) throughout the lesson.		Conducts **assessment** of student comprehension and learning of some lesson objectives		Conducts no **assessment** of student comprehension and learning of lesson objectives	

Comments: Throughout the lesson, the teacher checked students' understanding of some concepts and of the instructional tasks. She monitored the classroom to answer questions and to provide assistance. During the reading activity, however, students were not allotted sufficient time to read individually and the sequencing activity was moved to the following day. Therefore, it is unclear how she was able to assess individual student comprehension before she began reading the text to students.

Using SIOP Scores

Scores can be used "as is" to serve as a starting point for a collaborative discussion between a teacher and a supervisor or among a group of teachers. We have found that videotaping a lesson, rating it, and discussing it with the teacher provides an effective forum for professional growth. We also get valuable information from teachers explaining a student's behavior or why something may not have taken place despite the lesson plan that included it, for example. The discussion may take place between the teacher and the observer, or a group of teachers may meet on a regular basis to provide feedback to one another and assist in refining their teaching.

Scores also can be documented on an SIOP Teacher Rating Form over time to show growth (see Figure 10.4). Using percentages, teachers can see how their

FIGURE 10.4   SIOP Teacher Rating Form

SIOP Teacher Rating Form

Teacher	Observation 1 Score	Observation 2 Score	Observation 3 Score

FIGURE 10.5   Ms. Clark's Scores

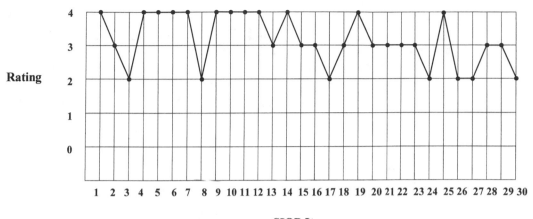

implementation of the SIOP features improves. This type of documentation is also useful for research purposes to document systematic implementation of the SIOP and fidelity of implementation.

Further, plotting scores on a graph, as seen in Figure 10.5, is a very effective way to illustrate strong areas as well as areas that require attention, or areas teachers have highlighted as important for their own growth. If a teacher consistently shows low scores on certain items, that provides the teacher with clear feedback for areas on which to focus.

Finally, while the SIOP is a useful tool for professional development, scores should be used with caution. Many variables impact the success or failure of a given lesson such as time of day, time of year, dynamics between students, and the like. Rather than just doing one observation and scoring of a teacher, several lessons should be rated over time for a fuller picture of the teacher's implementation of sheltered instruction.

Reliability and Validity of the SIOP

After several years of field-testing and refining the SIOP, a study was conducted (Echevarria, Garino & Rueda, 1997) to establish the validity and reliability of the instrument. The findings of the study indicated that the SIOP is a highly reliable and valid measure of sheltered instruction (see Appendix C for a discussion of the study).

Summary

This book has been developed for teachers, supervisors, administrators, teacher trainers, and researchers as a resource for increasing the effectiveness of instruction for English language learners. We have presented a research-based, professional development model of sheltered instruction, operationalized in the SIOP, that can be used as an observation instrument, as well as a lesson planning guide.

The SIOP provides concrete examples of the features of sheltered instruction, and the book has been written as a way to illustrate and elucidate those features by describing how real teachers might actually teach sheltered lessons. The use of vignettes allows readers to "see" what each feature might look like in a classroom setting. The features of the SIOP represent best practice for teaching English language learners.

Discussion Questions

1. The SIOP has a number of uses by different constituencies (e.g., teachers, supervisors, administrators, and researchers). How can you begin using the SIOP? What additional uses might it have for you or other constituencies?
2. Reread the sample lesson on pages 164–175. Would you score this lesson differently from the sample SIOP scores? On what items would you differ? What was the basis of your disagreement?
3. Look at the sample SIOP and change any two scores to NA. What would be the total score and percentage score on the revised and recalculated SIOP?
4. Imagine that you and a supervisor have just watched a videotape of your sheltered lesson. You are discussing the SIOP rating sheet that each of you scored independently. What would be the most collaborative way to approach the discussion of your teaching? What would yield the most useful information for improving your teaching?

The Sheltered Instruction Observation Protocol (SIOP) and Abbreviated SIOP

The Sheltered Instruction Observation Protocol (SIOP)

Observer: _____ Teacher: _____

Date: _____ School: _____

Grade: _____ ESL level: _____

Class: _____ Lesson: Multi-day Single-day (*circle one*)

Directions: Circle the number that best reflects what you observe in a sheltered lesson. You may give a score from 0 to 4. Cite under "Comments" specific examples of the behaviors observed.

Total Score: ☐   % Score: ☐   Tape #: _____

I. Preparation

4	3	2	1	0	NA
1. Clearly defined **content objectives** for students		**Content objectives** for students implied		No clearly defined **content objectives**	

Comments:

4	3	2	1	0	NA
2. Clearly defined **language objectives** for students		**Language objectives** for students implied		No clearly defined **language objectives** for students	

Comments:

The Sheltered Instruction Observation Protocol (SIOP) forms were developed by Jana Echevarria, MaryEllen Vogt, and Deborah Short, through research sponsored in part by the Center for Research on Education, Diversity, & Excellence (CREDE) with a grant from the U.S. Department of Education, Office of Educational Research and Improvement.

4	3	2	1	0	NA

3. **Content concepts** appropriate for age and educational background level of students
Comments:

Content concepts somewhat appropriate for age and educational background level of students

Content concepts inappropriate for age and educational background level of students

4	3	2	1	0	NA

4. **Supplementary materials** used to a high degree, making the lesson clear and meaningful (e.g., graphs, models, visuals)
Comments:

Some use of **supplementary materials**

No use of **supplementary materials**

4	3	2	1	0	NA

5. **Adaptation of content** (e.g., text, assignment) to all levels of student proficiency
Comments:

Some **adaptation of content** to all levels of student proficiency

No significant **adaptation of content** to all levels of student proficiency

4	3	2	1	0	NA

6. **Meaningful activities** that integrate lesson concepts (e.g., surveys, letter writing, simulations, constructing models) with language practice opportunities for reading, writing, listening, and/or speaking
Comments:

Meaningful activities that integrate lesson concepts, but provide little opportunity for language practice

No **meaningful activities** that integrate language practice with opportunities for reading, writing, listening, and/or speaking

II. Instruction _____

Building Background

4	3	2	1	0	NA
7. **Concepts explicitly linked** to students' background experiences *Comments:*		**Concepts loosely linked** to students' background experiences		**Concepts not explicitly linked** to students' background experiences	

4	3	2	1	0	NA
8. **Links explicitly made** between past learning and new concepts *Comments:*		**Few links made** between past learning and new concepts		**No links made** between past learning and new concepts	

4	3	2	1	0	NA
9. **Key vocabulary emphasized** (e.g., introduced, written, repeated, and highlighted for students to see) *Comments:*		**Key vocabulary** introduced, but not emphasized		**Key vocabulary** not emphasized	

Comprehensible Input

4	3	2	1	0	NA
10. **Speech** appropriate for students' proficiency level (e.g., slower rate and enunciation, and simple sentence structure for beginners) *Comments:*		**Speech** sometimes inappropriate for students' proficiency level		**Speech** inappropriate for students' proficiency level	

4	3	2	1	0	NA
11. **Explanation** of academic tasks clear *Comments:*		**Explanation** of academic tasks somewhat clear		**Explanation** of academic tasks unclear	

4	3	2	1	0	NA
12. Uses a variety of **techniques** to make content concepts clear (e.g., modeling, visuals, hands-on activities, demonstrations, gestures, body language) *Comments:*		Uses some **techniques** to make content concepts clear		Uses few or no **techniques** to make content concepts clear	

Strategies

4	3	2	1	0	NA
13. Provides ample opportunities for students to use **strategies** *Comments:*		Provides students with inadequate opportunities to use **strategies**		No opportunity for students to use **strategies**	

4	3	2	1	0	NA
14. Consistent use of **scaffolding** techniques throughout lesson, assisting and supporting student understanding (e.g., think-alouds) *Comments:*		Occasional use of **scaffolding** techniques		No use of **scaffolding** techniques	

	4 3	2 1	0 NA

4   3   2   1   0   NA

15. Teacher uses a variety of **question types, including those that promote higher-order thinking skills** (e.g., literal, analytical, and interpretive questions)
Comments:

Teacher infrequently poses **questions that promote higher-order thinking skills**

Teacher does not pose **questions that promote higher-order thinking skills**

Interaction

4   3   2   1   0   NA

16. Frequent opportunities for **interaction** and discussion between teacher/student and among students, which encourage elaborated responses about lesson concepts
Comments:

Interaction mostly teacher-dominated with some opportunities for students to talk about or question lesson concepts

Interaction primarily teacher-dominated with no opportunities for students to discuss lesson concepts

4   3   2   1   0   NA

17. **Grouping configurations** support language and content objectives of the lesson
Comments:

Grouping configurations unevenly support the language and content objectives

Grouping configurations do not support the language and content objectives

4   3   2   1   0   NA

18. Consistently provides sufficient **wait time for student responses**
Comments:

Occasionally provides sufficient **wait time for student responses**

Never provides sufficient **wait time for student responses**

4	3	2	1	0	NA
19. Ample opportunities for students to **clarify key concepts in L1** as needed with aide, peer, or L1 text *Comments:*		Some opportunity for students to **clarify key concepts in L1**		No opportunity for students to **clarify key concepts in L1**	

Practice/Application

4	3	2	1	0	NA
20. Provides **hands-on** materials and/or manipulatives for students to practice using new content knowledge *Comments:*		Provides few **hands-on** materials and/or manipulatives for students to practice using new content knowledge		Provides no **hands-on** materials and/or manipulatives for students to practice using new content knowledge	

4	3	2	1	0	NA
21. Provides activities for students to **apply content and language knowledge** in the classroom *Comments:*		Provides activities for students to **apply** either **content or language knowledge** in the classroom		Provides no activities for students to **apply content or language knowledge** in the classroom	

4	3	2	1	0	NA
22. Uses activities that integrate all **language skills** (i.e., reading, writing, listening, and speaking) *Comments:*		Uses activities that integrate some **language skills**		Uses activities that apply to only one **language skill**	

Lesson Delivery

4	3	2	1	0	NA
23. **Content objectives** clearly supported by lesson delivery *Comments:*		**Content objectives** somewhat supported by lesson delivery		**Content objectives** not supported by lesson delivery	

4	3	2	1	0	NA
24. **Language objectives** clearly supported by lesson delivery *Comments:*		**Language objectives** supported somewhat by lesson delivery		**Language objectives** not supported by lesson delivery	

4	3	2	1	0	NA
25. **Students engaged** approximately 90% to 100% of the period *Comments:*		**Students engaged** approximately 70% of the period		**Students engaged** less than 50% of the period	

4	3	2	1	0	NA
26. **Pacing** of the lesson appropriate to the students' ability level *Comments:*		**Pacing** generally appropriate, but at times too fast or too slow		**Pacing** inappropriate to the students' ability level	

III. Review/Assessment

4	3	2	1	0	NA
27. Comprehensive **review** of key vocabulary *Comments:*		Uneven **review** of key vocabulary		No **review** of key vocabulary	

4	3	2	1	0	NA
28. Comprehensive **review** of key content concepts *Comments:*		Uneven **review** of key content concepts		No **review** of key content concepts	

4	3	2	1	0	NA
29. Regularly provides **feedback** to students on their output (e.g., language, content, work) *Comments:*		Inconsistently provides **feedback** to students on their output		Provides no **feedback** to students on their output	

4	3	2	1	0	NA
30. Conducts **assessment** of student comprehension and learning of all lesson objectives (e.g., spot checking, group response) throughout the lesson. *Comments:*		Conducts **assessment** of student comprehension and learning of some lesson objectives		Conducts no **assessment** of student comprehension and learning of lesson objectives	

Abbreviated Sheltered Instruction Observation Protocol (SIOP)

Observer: _____   Teacher: _____

Date: _____   School: _____

Grade: _____   ESL level: _____

Class: _____   Lesson: Multi-day Single-day (*circle one*)

Directions: Circle the number that best reflects what you observe in a sheltered lesson. You may give a score from 0 to 4. Cite under "Comments" specific examples of the behaviors observed.

Total Score: ☐   % Score: ☐   Tape #: _____

I. Preparation	Highly Evident 4	3	Somewhat Evident 2	1	Not Evident 0	NA
1. Clearly defined **content objectives** for students	☐	☐	☐	☐	☐	☐
2. Clearly defined **language objectives** for students	☐	☐	☐	☐	☐	☐
3. **Content concepts** appropriate for age and educational background level of students	☐	☐	☐	☐	☐	☐
4. **Supplementary materials** used to a high degree, making the lesson clear and meaningful (e.g., graphs, models, visuals)	☐	☐	☐	☐	☐	☐
5. **Adaptation of content** (e.g., text, assignment) to all levels of student proficiency	☐	☐	☐	☐	☐	☐
6. **Meaningful activities** that integrate lesson concepts (e.g., surveys, letter writing, simulations, constructing models) with language practice opportunities for reading, writing, listening, and/or speaking	☐	☐	☐	☐	☐	☐

Section Comments:

II. Instruction

Building Background	4	3	2	1	0	NA
7. **Concepts explicitly linked** to students' background experiences	❑	❑	❑	❑	❑	❑
8. **Links explicitly made** between past learning and new concepts	❑	❑	❑	❑	❑	❑
9. **Key vocabulary emphasized** (e.g., introduced, written, repeated, and highlighted for students to see)	❑	❑	❑	❑	❑	❑

Section Comments:

Comprehensible Input	4	3	2	1	0	NA
10. **Speech** appropriate for students' proficiency level (e.g., slower rate and enunciation, and simple sentence structure for beginners)	❑	❑	❑	❑	❑	❑
11. **Explanation** of academic tasks clear	❑	❑	❑	❑	❑	❑
12. Uses a variety of **techniques** to make content concepts clear (e.g., modeling, visuals, hands-on activities, demonstrations, gestures, body language)	❑	❑	❑	❑	❑	❑

Section Comments:

Strategies	4	3	2	1	0	NA
13. Provides ample opportunities for students to use **strategies**	❑	❑	❑	❑	❑	❑
14. Consistent use of **scaffolding** techniques throughout lesson, assisting and supporting student understanding (e.g., think-alouds)	❑	❑	❑	❑	❑	❑

	4	3	2	1	0	NA
15. Teacher uses a variety of **question types, including those that promote higher-order thinking skills** (e.g., literal, analytical, and interpretive questions) *Section Comments:*	❑	❑	❑	❑	❑	❑

Interaction	4	3	2	1	0	NA
16. Frequent opportunities for **interaction** and discussion between teacher/student and among students, which encourage elaborated responses about lesson concepts	❑	❑	❑	❑	❑	❑
17. **Grouping configurations** support language and content objectives of the lesson	❑	❑	❑	❑	❑	❑
18. Consistently provides sufficient **wait time for student responses**	❑	❑	❑	❑	❑	❑
19. Ample opportunities for students to **clarify key concepts in L1** as needed with aide, peer, or L1 text *Section Comments:*	❑	❑	❑	❑	❑	❑

Practice/Application	4	3	2	1	0	NA
20. Provides **hands-on** materials and/or manipulatives for students to practice using new content knowledge	❑	❑	❑	❑	❑	❑
21. Provides activities for students to **apply content and language knowledge** in the classroom	❑	❑	❑	❑	❑	❑

	4	3	2	1	0	NA
22. Uses activities that integrate all **language skills** (i.e., reading, writing, listening, and speaking) *Section Comments:*	❑	❑	❑	❑	❑	❑

Lesson Delivery	4	3	2	1	0	NA
23. **Content objectives** clearly supported by lesson delivery	❑	❑	❑	❑	❑	❑
24. **Language objectives** clearly supported by lesson delivery	❑	❑	❑	❑	❑	❑
25. **Students engaged** approximately 90% to 100% of the period	❑	❑	❑	❑	❑	❑
26. **Pacing** of the lesson appropriate to the students' ability level *Section Comments:*	❑	❑	❑	❑	❑	❑

III. Review/Assessment	4	3	2	1	0	NA
27. Comprehensive **review** of key vocabulary	❑	❑	❑	❑	❑	❑
28. Comprehensive **review** of key content concepts	❑	❑	❑	❑	❑	❑
29. Regularly provides **feedback** to students on their output (e.g., language, content, work)	❑	❑	❑	❑	❑	❑
30. Conducts **assessment** of student comprehension and learning of all lesson objectives (e.g., spot checking, group response) throughout the lesson *Section Comments:*	❑	❑	❑	❑	❑	❑

APPENDIX B

SIOP Lesson Planning Guide

This guide was developed as an aid in planning sheltered lessons. The right column can be used for writing notes or as a checklist to ensure attention to each indicator.

■ **Preparation**

1. Clearly defined **content objectives** for students

2. Clearly defined **language objectives** for students

3. **Content concepts** appropriate for age and educational background level of students

4. **Supplementary materials** used to a high degree, making the lesson clear and meaningful (e.g., graphs, models, visuals)

5. **Adaptation of content** (e.g., text, assignment) to all levels of student proficiency

6. **Meaningful activities** that integrate lesson concepts (e.g., surveys, letter writing, simulations, constructing models) with language practice opportunities for reading, writing, listening, and/or speaking

The SIOP Lesson Planning Guide was developed by Jana Echevarria, MaryEllen Vogt, Deborah Short, and Chris Montone, through a research project sponsored by the Center for Research on Education, Diversity, & Excellence (CREDE) with a grant from the U.S. Department of Education, Office of Educational Research and Improvement.

■ Building Background

7. **Concepts explicitly linked** to students' background experiences

8. **Links explicitly made** between past learning and new concepts

9. **Key vocabulary emphasized** (e.g., introduced, written, repeated, and highlighted for students to see)

■ Comprehensible Input

10. **Speech** appropriate for students' proficiency level (e.g., slower rate, enunciation, and simple sentence structure for beginners)

11. **Explanation** of academic tasks clear

12. Uses a variety of **techniques** to make content concepts clear (e.g., modeling, visuals, hands-on activities, demonstrations, gestures, body language)

■ Strategies

13. Provides ample opportunities for students to use **strategies**

14. Consistent use of **scaffolding** techniques throughout lesson, assisting and supporting student understanding (e.g., think-alouds)

15. Teacher uses a variety of **question types, including those that promote higher-order thinking skills** (e.g., literal, analytical, and interpretive questions)

▪ Interaction

16. Frequent opportunities for **interactions** and discussion between teacher/student and among students, which encourage elaborated responses about lesson concepts

17. **Grouping configurations** support language and content objectives of the lesson

18. Consistently provides sufficient **wait time for students' responses**

19. Ample opportunities for students to **clarify key concepts in L1** as needed with aide, peer, or L1 text

▪ Practice/Application

20. Provides **hands-on** materials and/or manipulatives for students to practice using new content knowledge

21. Provides activities for students to **apply content and language knowledge** in the classroom

22. Uses activities that integrate all **language skills** (i.e., reading, writing, listening, and speaking)

▪ Lesson Delivery

23. **Content objectives** clearly supported by lesson delivery

24. **Language objectives** clearly supported by lesson delivery

25. **Students engaged** approximately 90% to 100% of the period

26. **Pacing** of the lesson appropriate to the students' ability level

■ **Review/Assessment**

27. Comprehensive **review** of key vocabulary

28. Comprehensive **review** of key content concepts

29. Regularly provides **feedback** to students on their output (e.g., language, content, work)

30. Conducts **assessment** of student comprehension and learning of all lesson objectives (e.g., spot checking, group response) throughout the lesson.

APPENDIX C

Reliability and Validity Study of the SIOP

The raters were four experts in sheltered instruction (or SDAIE) from three major universities in southern California. Three held doctorates in education while the other was earning a second master's degree (one in education). Their total teaching experience was more than 55 years.

A single-blind design was employed. Three of the videos were judged by the principal investigator to be highly representative of the tenets of SI while the other three were not. The raters observed all six videos (each video was approximately 45 minutes long) and scored the teacher on a 1 (no evidence) to 7 (clearly evident) Likert-type scale on the 31* items that comprised the 8 subscales: Preparation, Building Background, Comprehensible Input, Strategies, Interaction, Practice/Application, Lesson Delivery, and Review/Evaluation. Cronbach's Alpha was calculated for all 8 scales. Because an important decision was going to be made about an individual, Alpha's of .90 or higher were deemed acceptable.

All but one subscale (Comprehensible Input; alpha = .8727) achieved this a priori level of acceptance. The other subscales ranged from .9589 (Preparation) to .9138 (Lesson Delivery). A principle component analysis (PCA) with varimax rotation was then performed on the 31 items to assess the instrument's discriminate validity among the subscales. Three factors were extracted accounting for 98.4% of the variance as indicated by the eigenvalues of the factors that accounted for variances greater than 1.

A discriminant functional analysis (DFA) using the eight subscales as predictors of membership in two groups (performing or nonperforming SI) was used to measure the instrument's concurrent validity (the Principal Investigator's assessment of the videotapes). One discriminant function was calculated, with a chi-square (17) = 24.07, $p < .01$. The univariate tests suggest that the best predictors for distinguishing between SI and non-SI educators are Preparation, Lesson Delivery, Comprehensible Input, Building Background, Strategies, Practice/Application, and Review/Evaluation. Only Interaction failed to discriminate between a SI and non-SI environment. The stability of the classification procedure was checked by a cross-validation run and there was an 81.25% correct classification rate. This indicates a high degree of consistency in the classification scheme.

The preliminary findings of the study on the psychometric properties of the SIOP were that the SIOP was confirmed to be a highly reliable and valid measure

* *Note:* This study used an earlier version of the SIOP.

of SI. Further, the findings suggested that the instrument could be modified by attenuating the factor structure from 8 to 3, and Interaction failed to differentiate between SI and non-SI teachers. Based on these findings, we modified the SIOP to a three-factor structure (Preparation, Instruction, Review/Evaluation) and modified the Interaction items to strengthen their distinction from nonsheltered instruction (e.g., eliminated the item, "Pronunciation and intonation easily understandable"). Further, we changed the scoring to a 5-point scale, using the range 0 to 4.

GLOSSARY

Academic language: Language used in formal contexts for academic subjects. The aspect of language connected with literacy and academic achievement. This includes technical and academic terms (*see* Cognitive/Academic Language Proficiency—CALP).

Additive bilingualism: Rather than neglecting or rejecting students' language and culture, additive bilingualism promotes building on what the child brings to the classroom and adding to it.

Alignment: Match among the ESL and content standards, instruction, curriculum, and assessment.

Alternative assessment: Analysis and reporting of student performances using sources that differ from traditional objective responses such as standardized and norm-referenced tests. Alternative assessments include portfolios, performance-based tasks, checklists, and so forth.

Assessment: The orderly process of gathering, analyzing, interpreting, and reporting student performance, ideally from multiple sources over a period of time.

Basic Interpersonal Communication Skills (BICS): Face-to-face conversational fluency, including mastery of pronunciation, vocabulary, and grammar. English language learners typically acquire conversational language used in everyday activities before they develop more complex, conceptual language proficiency.

Bilingual instruction: School instruction using two languages, generally a native language of the student and a second language. The amount of time that each language is used depends on the type of bilingual program, its specific objectives, and students' level of language proficiency.

Cognitive Academic Language Learning Approach (CALLA): An instructional model developed by Chamot and O'Malley (1987, 1994) for content and language learning that incorporates student development of learning strategies, specifically metacognitive, cognitive, and socio-affective strategies (*see* Learning Strategies).

Cognitive/Academic Language Proficiency (CALP): Language proficiency associated with schooling, and the abstract language abilities required for academic work. A more complex, conceptual, linguistic ability that includes analysis, synthesis and evaluation.

Communicative Competence: The combination of grammatical, discourse, strategic and sociolinguistic competence that allows the recognition and production of fluent and appropriate language in all communicative settings.

Constructivism: A philosophical perspective in which an individual's prior experiences, knowledge, and beliefs influence how understanding is developed and experiences are interpreted. In teaching, the focus is more on how knowledge is constructed rather than on products, with richly contextualized opportunities for students to engage in inquiry and discovery.

Note: The following sources were used for definitions in this glossary: Harris and Hodges, 1995; McLaughlin and Vogt, 1996; and the national ESL Standards (TESOL, 1997).

Content-based ESL: An instructional approach in which content topics are used as the vehicle for second language learning. A system of instruction in which teachers use a variety of instructional techniques as a way of developing second language, content, cognitive, and study skills, often delivered through thematic units.

Content objectives: Statements that identify what students should know and be able to do in particular content areas. They support school district and state content standards and learning outcomes, and they guide teaching and learning in the classroom.

Content standards: Definitions of what students are expected to know and be capable of doing for a given content area. The knowledge and skills that need to be taught in order for students to reach competency. What students are expected to learn and what schools are expected to teach. May be national, state, or local-level standards.

Cross-cultural competence: The ability to understand and follow the cultural rules and norms of more than one system. The ability to respond to the demands of a given situation in a culturally acceptable way.

Culture: The customs, lifestyle, traditions, behavior, attitudes, and artifacts of a given people. Culture also encompasses the ways people organize and interpret the world, and the way events are perceived based on established social norms. A system of standards for understanding the world.

Dialect: The form of a language peculiar to a specific region. Features a variation in vocabulary, grammar, and pronunciation.

Engagement: When students are fully taking part in a lesson, they are said to be engaged. This is a holistic term that encompasses listening, reading, writing, responding, and discussing. The level of students' engagement during a lesson may be assessed to a greater or lesser degree. A low SIOP score for engagement would imply frequent chatting, daydreaming, nonattention, and other off-task behaviors.

English language learners (ELLs):   Children and adults who are learning English as a second or additional language. This term may apply to learners across various levels of proficiency in English. ELLs may also be referred to as non-English speaking (NES), limited English proficient (LEP), and a non-native speaker (NNS).

ESL: English as a second language. Used to refer to programs and classes to teach students English as a second (additional) language.

ESOL: English speakers of other languages. Students whose first language is not English and who do not write, speak, and understand the language as well as their classmates.

Evaluation: Judgments about students' learning made by interpretation and analysis of assessment data; the process of judging achievement, growth, product, processes, or changes in these; judgments of education programs. The processes of assessment and evaluation can be viewed as progressive: first, assessment; then, evaluation.

Formative evaluation: Ongoing collection, analysis, and reporting of information about student performance for purposes of instruction and learning.

Grouping: The division of students into classes for instruction, such as by age, ability, or achievement; or within classes, such as by reading ability, proficiency, language background, or interests.

Holistic score: An integrated analysis of a student's performance based on specified criteria; results in a score on a rubric or rating scale (*see* Rubric and Rating scale).

Home language: The language, or languages, spoken in the student's home by people who live there. Also referred to as first language (L1), primary language, or native language.

Informal assessment: Appraisal of student performance through unstructured observation; characterized as frequent, ongoing, continuous, and involving simple but important techniques such as verbal checks for understanding, teacher-created assessments, and other nonstandardized procedures. This type of assessment provides teachers with immediate feedback.

Inter-rater reliability: Measures of the degree of agreement between two different raters on separate ratings of one assessment indicator using the same scale and criteria.

L1: First language. A widely used abbreviation for the primary, home, or native language.

Language minority: In the United States, a student whose primary language is not English. The individual student's ability to speak English will vary.

Language objectives: Statements that identify what students should know and be able to do while using English (or another language). They support students' language development, often focusing on vocabulary, functional language, questioning, articulating predictions or hypotheses, reading, writing, and so forth.

Language proficiency: An individual's competence in using a language for basic communication and for academic purposes. May be categorized as stages of language acquisition (*see* Stages of language proficiency).

Language competence: An individual's total language ability. The underlying language system as indicated by the individual's language performance.

Limited English Proficient (LEP): A term used to refer to a student with restricted understanding or use of written and spoken English; a learner who is still developing competence in using English.

Mnemonics: From the Greek *mnemon*, meaning "mindful." Mnemonics are devices to jog the memory. For example, steps of a learning strategy are often abbreviated to form an acronym or word that enables the learner to remember the steps. An example of a strategy would be teaching students to use mnemonics to write a complete sentence, such as in the use of PENS (Deshler, Ellis, and Lenz, 1996). The student is taught to Preview ideas, Explore words, Note words in a complete sentence, and See if the sentence is okay (*see* Learning strategy).

Multilingualism: The ability to speak more than two languages; proficiency in more than two languages.

Native language: An individual's first, primary, or home language (L1).

Native English speaker: An individual whose first language is English.

Non-English speaking (NES): Individuals who are in an English-speaking environment (such as U.S. schools) but who have not acquired any English proficiency.

Nonverbal communication: Paralinguistic messages such as intonation, stress, pauses and rate of speech, and nonlinguistic messages such as gestures, facial expressions, and body language that can accompany speech or be conveyed without the aid of speech.

Performance assessment: A measure of educational achievement where students produce a response, create a product, or apply knowledge in ways similar to tasks required in the instructional environment. The performance measures are analyzed and interpreted according to preset criteria.

Performance standards: A performance level stated in terms of specific criteria to be achieved, including ways in which students must demonstrate knowledge and skills; indicators of how well students are meeting a content standard or benchmark.

Portfolio assessment: A type of performance assessment that involves gathering multiple indicators of student progress to support course goals in a dynamic, ongoing process. Portfolios are purposeful collections of student performance that evince students' efforts, progress, and achievement over time.

Primary language: An individual's first, home, or native language (L1).

Pull-out instruction: Students are "pulled-out" from their regular classes for special classes of ESL instruction, remediation, or acceleration.

Rating scale: A way to record student performance on a continuum that indicates the range in which a given skill or competency has been achieved; often a Likert-scale continuum is used.

Realia: Real-life objects and artifacts used to supplement teaching; can provide effective visual scaffolds for English language learners.

Reliability: Statistical consistency in measurements and tests, such as the extent to which two assessments measure student performance in the same way.

Rubrics: Statements that describe indicators of performance, which include scoring criteria, on a continuum; may be described as "developmental" (e.g., emergent, beginning, developing, proficient) or "evaluative" (e.g., exceptional, thorough, adequate, inadequate).

Scaffolding: Adult (e.g., teacher) support for learning and student performance of the tasks through instruction, modeling, questioning, feedback, graphic organizers, and more, across successive engagements. These supports are gradually withdrawn, thus transferring more and more autonomy to the child. Scaffolding activities provide support for learning that can be removed as learners are able to demonstrate strategic behaviors in their own learning activities.

SDAIE (Specially Designed Academic Instruction in English):   The State of California requires that all limited English proficient students receive content instruction in the core curriculum. SDAIE, another term for sheltered instruction, is the instructional methodology used to achieve this. Strategies employed are intended to help English language learners access content information while developing their English language skills (*see* Sheltered instruction).

Self-contained ESL class: A class consisting solely of English speakers of other languages for the purpose of learning English; content may also be taught. An effective alternative to pull-out instruction.

Sheltered instruction (SI):   An approach to teaching that extends the time students have for receiving English language support while they learn content subjects. SI classrooms, which may include a mix of native English speakers and English language learners or only ELLs, integrate language and content while infusing sociocultural awareness. Teachers scaffold instruction to aid student comprehension of content topics and objectives by adjusting their speech and instructional tasks, and by providing appropriate background information and experiences. The ultimate goal is accessibility for ELLs to grade-level content standards and concepts while they continue to improve their English language proficiency (*see* Scaffolding).

Sheltered teachers: Teachers who teach content subject matter to English language learners using sheltered instruction (SI) techniques.

Social language: Basic language proficiency associated with fluency in day-to-day situations, including the classroom (*see* Basic Interpersonal Communication Skills).

Sociolinguistic competence: The degree to which a language is used and understood in a given situation. The use of appropriate comments and responses in conversation (*see* Communicative competence).

Sociocultural competence: The ability to function effectively by following the rules and behavioral expectations held by members of a given social or cultural group.

Stages of language proficiency: (From Krashen and Terrell, 1983, 1984.)

Preproduction: Students at this stage are not ready to produce much language, so they primarily communicate with gestures and actions. They are absorbing the new language and developing receptive vocabulary.

Early production: Students at this level speak using one or two words or short phrases. Their receptive vocabulary is developing; they understand approximately one thousand words. Students can answer "who, what, and where" questions with limited expression.

Speech emergence: Students speak in longer phrases and complete sentences. However, they may experience frustration at not being able to express completely what they know. Although the number of errors they make increases, they can communicate ideas and the quantity of speech they produce increases.

Intermediate fluency: Students may appear to be fluent; they engage in conversation and produce connected narrative. Errors are usually of style or usage. Lessons continue to expand receptive vocabulary, and activities develop higher levels of language use in content areas. Students at this level are able to communicate effectively.

Advanced fluency: Students communicate very effectively, orally and in writing, in social and academic settings.

Standard American English: "That variety of American English in which most educational texts, government, and media publications are written in the United States; English as it is spoken and written by those groups with social, economic, and political power in the United States. Standard American English is a relative concept, varying widely in pronunciation and in idiomatic use but maintaining a fairly uniform grammatical structure" (Harris and Hodges, 1995, p. 241).

Standards-based assessment: Assessment involving the planning, gathering, analyzing, and reporting of a student's performance according to the ESL and/or district content standards.

Strategies: Mental processes and plans that people use to help them comprehend, learn, and retain new information. There are three types of strategies—cognitive, metacognitive, and social/affective—and these are consciously adapted and monitored during reading, writing, and learning.

Subtractive bilingualism: The learning of a new language at the expense of the primary language. Learners often lose their native language and culture because they don't have opportunities to continue learning or using it, or they perceive that language to be of lower status. Loss of the primary language often leads to cultural ambivalence.

Summative evaluation: The final collection, analysis, and reporting of information about student achievement or program effectiveness at the end of a given time frame.

Task: An activity that calls for a response to a question, issue, or problem.

Validity: A statistical measure of an assessment's match between the information collected and its stated purpose; evidence that inferences from evaluation are trustworthy.

Vignette: A short sketch that gives a description of an instructional process drawn from real-life classroom experiences.

REFERENCES

Adamson, H.D. (1990). ESL students' use of academic skills in content courses. *English for Specific Purposes, 9,* 67–87.

Anderson, R.C. (1984). Role of the reader's schema in comprehension, learning, and memory. In R.C. Anderson, J. Osborn, & R.J. Tierney (Eds.), *Learning to read in American schools: Basal readers and content texts.* Hillsdale, NJ: Erlbaum.

Anderson, R.C. (1994). Role of the reader's scheme in comprehension, learning, and memory. In R. Ruddell, M. Ruddell, & H. Singer (Eds.), *Theoretical models and processes of reading* (4th ed.). Newark, DE: International Reading Association.

Applebee, A., & Langer, J. (1983). Instructional scaffolding: Reading and writing as natural language activities. *Language Arts, 60,* 168–175.

August, D., & Hakuta, K. (Eds.). (1997). *Improving schooling for language minority children: A research agenda.* Washington, DC: National Academy Press.

Baker, L. (1997). *Life in the rain forests.* Chicago: World Book.

Baker, L., & Brown, A.L. (1984). Metacognitive skills and reading. In P.D. Pearson (Ed.), *Handbook of reading research.* New York: Longman.

Barnhardt, S. (1997). Effective memory strategies. *NCLRC Language Resource, 1* (6).

Bartolome, L.I. (1994). Beyond the methods fetish: Toward a humanizing pedagogy. *Harvard Educational Review, 64*(2), 173–194.

Baumann, J., Jones, L., & Seifert-Kessell, N. (1993). Using think-alouds to enhance children's comprehension monitoring abilities. *The Reading Teacher, 47*(3), 184–193.

Bear, D.R., Invernizzi, M., Templeton, S., & Johnston, F. (2000). *Words their way: Word study for phonics, vocabulary, and spelling instruction* (2nd ed.). Upper Saddle River, NJ: Merrill-Prentice-Hall.

Bennici, F.J. & Strang, E.W. (1995). *An analysis of language minority and limited English proficent students from NELS 1988.* Report to the Office of Bilingual Education and Minority Languages Affairs. Washington, DC: U.S. Department of Education, August.

Berliner, D.C. (1984). The half-full glass: A review of research on teaching. In P.L. Hosford (Ed.), *Using what we know about teaching* (pp. 51–77). Alexandria, VA: Association for Supervision and Curriculum Development.

Berman, P., McLaughlin, B., Minicucci, C., Nelson, B., & Woodworth, K. (1995). *School reform and student diversity: Case studies of exemplary practices for LEP students.* Washington, DC: National Clearinghouse for Bilingual Education.

Bickel, W.E., & Bickel, D.D. (1986). Effective schools, classrooms and instruction: Implications for special education. *Exceptional Children, 52* (6) 489–500.

Bloom, B., Engelhart, M., Furst, E., Hill, W., & Krathworl, D. (Eds.). (1956). *Taxonomy of educational objectives: The classification of educational goals. Handbook I: Cognitive domain.* New York: David McKay Co.

Bottle biology: An idea book for exploring the world through plastic bottles and other recyclable materials. (1993). Dubuque, IA: Kendall/Hunt Publishing Company.

Bransford, J. (1994). Schema activation and schema acquisition: Comments on Richard C. Anderson's remarks. In R. Ruddell, M. Ruddell, & H. Singer (Eds.), *Theoretical models and processes of reading* (4th ed.). Newark, DE: International Reading Association.

Bruner, J. (1978). The role of dialogue in language acquisition. In A. Sinclair, R. Javella, & W. Levelt (Eds.), *The child's conception of language* (pp. 241–256). New York: Springer-Verlag.

Buehl, D. (1995). *Classroom strategies for interactive learning.* Madison: Wisconsin State Reading Association.

Carrell, P. (1987). Content and formal schemata in ESL reading. *TESOL Quarterly, 21* (3), 461–481.

Cantoni-Harvey, G. (1987). *Content-area language instruction: Approaches and strategies.* Reading, MA: Addison-Wesley.

Chamot, A.U., & O'Malley, J.M. (1987). The cognitive academic language learning approach: A bridge to the mainstream. *TESOL Quarterly, 21*(2), 227–249.

Chamot, A.U., & O'Malley, J.M. (1994). *The CALLA handbook: Implementing the cognitive academic language learning approach.* Reading, MA: Addison-Wesley.

Chiesi, H., Spilich, G., & Voss, J. (1979). Acquisition of domain-related inforination in relation to high- and low-domain knowledge. *Journal of Verbal Learning and Verbal Behavior 18,* 257–274.

Colburn, A., & Echevarria, J. (1999). Meaningful lessons. *The Science Teacher, 66*(2) 36–39.

Collier, V. (1995). *Promoting academic success for ESL students.* Elizabeth, NJ: New Jersey Teachers of English to Speakers of Other Languages–Bilingual Education.

Cooper, J.D., Pikulski, J.J., Au, K., Calderon, M., Comas, J., Lipson, M., Mims, S., Page, S., Valencia, S., & Vogt, M.E. (1999). *Invitations to literacy.* Boston: Houghton Mifflin Company.

Crandall, J.A. (1993). Content-centered learning in the United States. *Annual Review of Applied Linguistics, 13,* 111–126.

Crawford, L.W. (1993). *Language and literacy learning in multicultural classrooms.* Boston: Allyn and Bacon.

Cummins, J. (1981). The role of primary language development in promoting educational success for language minority students. In *Schooling and language minority students: A theoretical framework* (pp. 3–49). Los Angeles: Evaluation, Dissemination, and Assessment Center, California State University, Los Angeles.

Cummins, J. (1994). Knowledge, power and identity in teaching English as a second language. In F. Genesse (Ed.), *Educating second language children: The whole child, the whole curriculum, the whole community* (pp. 33–58). Cambridge: Cambridge University Press.

Cunningham, P.M. (1995). *Phonics they use: Words for reading and writing.* New York: Harper-Collins College Press.

Darling-Hammond, L. (1998). Teacher learning that supports student learning. *Educational Leadership, 55*(5), 6–11.

Darling-Hammond, L., & McLaughlin, M.W. (1995). Policies that support professional development in an era of reform. *Phi Delta Kappan, 76*(8), 597–604.

Dermody, M., & Speaker, R. (1995). Effects of reciprocal strategy training in prediction, clarification, question generation, and summarization on fourth graders' reading comprehension. In K.A. Hinchman, D. Leu, & C.K. Kinzer (Eds.), *Perspectives on literacy research and practice.* Chicago: National Reading Conference.

Deshler, D., Ellis, E. & Lenz, B.K. (1996). *Teaching adolescents with learning disabilities,* 2nd Edition. Denver, CO: Love Publishing Company.

Diaz, D. (1989). *Language across the curriculum and ESL students: Composition research and 'sheltered' course.* (ERIC Document Reproduction Service No. ED326 057).

Dole, J., Duffy, G., Roehler, L. & Pearson, P.D. (199 1). Moving form the old to the new: Research in reading comprehension instruction. *Review of Educational Research, 61,* pp. 239–264.

Echevarria, J. (1995a). Sheltered instruction for students with leaming disabilities who have limited English proficiency. *Intervention in School and Clinic, 30* (5), 302–305.

Echevarria, J. (1995b). Interactive reading instruction: A comparison of proximal and distal effects of instructional conversations: *Exceptional Children, 61* (6) 536–552.

Echevarria, J. (1998). *A model of sheltered instruction for English language learners.* Paper presented at the conference for the Division on Diversity of the Council for Exceptional Children, Washington, D.C.

Echevarria, J., Greene, G., & Goldenberg, C. (1996). *A comparison of sheltered instruction and effective non-sheltered instruction on the achievement of LEP students.* Pilot study.

Echevarria, J. Guarino, A. & Rueda, R. (1997). *The Sheltered Instruction Observation Protocol: Reliability and validily assessment.* Unpublished paper.

Echevarria, J., & Graves, A. (1998). *Sheltered content instruction: Teaching English language learners with diverse abilities.* Needham Heights, MA: Allyn & Bacon.

Erickson, F., & Shultz, J. (1991). Students' experience of the curriculum. In P. W. Jackson (Ed.), *Handbook of research on curriculum.* New York: Macmillan.

Ferrara, S., & McTighe, J. (1992). A process for planning: More thoughtful classroom assessment. In A. Costa, J. Bellanca, & R. Fogarty (Eds.), *If minds matter: A foreword to the future* (Vol. 2). Palatine, IL: Skylight.

Flood, J., Lapp, D., Flood, S., & Nagel, G. (1992). Am I allowed to group? Using flexible patterns for effective instruction. *The Reading Teacher, 45,* 608–616.

Gall, M. (November, 1984). Synthesis of research on teacher's questioning. *Educational Leadership, 40*–47.

Goldenberg, C. (1992–93). Instructional conversations: Promoting comprehension through discussion. *The Reading Teacher, 46* (4), 316–326.

González, J.M., & Darling-Hammond, L. (1997). *New concepts for new challenges: Professional development for teachers of immigrant youth.* McHenry, IL: Delta Systems and CAL.

Goodlad, J. (1984). *A place called school: Prospects for the future.* New York: McGraw-Hill.

Gray, W.S., & Leary, B.E. (1935). *What makes a book readable?* Chicago: The University of Chicago Press.

Green, J. (1998). *Learn about rain forests.* New York: Lorenz Books.

Gunderson, L. (1991). *ESL literacy instruction: A guidebook to theory and practice.* Englewood Cliffs, NJ: Regents/Prentice Hall.

Harris, T.L. & Hodges, R.E. Eds. (1995). *The literacy dictionary: The vocabulary of reading and writing.* Newark, DE: International Reading Association.

Hiebert, E.H. (1983) An examination of ability grouping for reading instruction. *Reading Research Quarterly, 18,* pp. 231–255.

Hunter, M. (1982). *Mastery teaching: Increasing instructional effectiveness in secondary schools, college, and universities.* El Segundo, CA: TIP Publications.

Jimenez, R.T., Garcia, G.E., & Pearson, P.D. (1996). The reading strategies of bilingual Latina/o students who are successful English readers: Opportunities and obstacles. *Reading Research Quarterly, 31*(1), 90–112.

Kauffman, D., Burkart, G., Crandall, J., Johnson, D., Peyton, J., Sheppard, K., & Short, D. (1994). *Content-ESL across the USA.* Washington, DC: ERIC Clearinghouse on Languages and Linguistics.

Keene, E.O., & Zimmerman, S. (1997). *Mosaic of thought: Teaching comprehension in a reader's workshop.* Portsmouth, NH: Heinemann.

Krashen, S. (1985). *The input hypothesis: Issues and implications.* New York: Longman.

Krashen, S. & Terrell, T. (1983). *The natural approach: Language acquisition in the classroom.* Englewood Cliffs, NJ: Alemany/Prentice Hall.

Leinhardt, G. Bickel, W. & Pallay, A. (1982). Unlabeled but still entitled: Toward more effective remediation. *Teachers College Record, 84* (2) 391–422.

Macon, J., Buell, D., & Vogt, M.E. (1991). *Responses to literature: Grades K–8.* Newark, DE: International Reading Association.

Mastropieri, M.A., & Scruggs, T.E. (1994). *Effective instruction for special education.* Austin, TX: ProEd.

McCormick, C.B., & Pressley, M. (1997). *Educational psychology: Learning, instruction, assessment.* New York: Longman.

McDonnell, L.M., & Hill, P. (1993). *Newcomers in American schools: Meeting the educational needs of immigrant youth.* Santa Monica: Rand.

McLaughlin, M., & Kennedy, A. (1993). *A classroom guide to performance-based assessment.* Princeton, NJ: Houghton Mifflin.

McLaughlin, M., & Vogt, M.E. (1996). *Portfolios in teacher education.* Newark, DE: International Reading Association.

Mohan, B.A. (1986). *Language and content.* Reading, MA: Addison-Wesley.

Mohan, B.A. (1990). Integration of language and content. In *Proceedings of the first research symposium on limited English proficient students' issues* (pp. 113–160). Washington, DC: U.S. Department of Education, Office of Bilingual Education and Minority Languages Affairs.

Moss, M., & Puma, M. (1995). *Prospects: The congressionally mandated study of educational growth and opportunity.* (First year report on language minority and limited English proficient students). Washington, DC: U.S. Department of Education.

Mutel, C. F. & Rogers. M.M. (1993). *Tropical rain forests: Our endangered planet.* Minneapolis, MN: The Lerner Publishing Group.

Muth, K.D., & Alvermann, D.E. (1999). *Teaching and learning in the middle grades.* Needham Heights, MA: Allyn & Bacon.

Nagel, G., Vogt, M.E., & Kaye, C. (1998). *Examining levels of thinking in the reflective discourse of teaching portfolios.* Paper presented at the Annual Meeting of the National Reading Conference. Austin, TX.

National Center for Education Statistics (NCES). (1997). *A profile of policies and practices for limited English proficient students: Screening methods, program support, and teacher training* (The 1993–94 Schools and Staffing Survey). Washington, DC: U.S. Department of Education, OERI.

National Commission on Teaching and America's Future (NCTAF). (1996). *What matters most: Teaching for America's future.* New York: Columbia University, Teachers College.

Olsen, R. W-B. (1997). Enrollment, identification, and placement of LEP students increase (again). *TESOL Matters, 7* (4), 6–7.

O'Malley, J.J., & Chamot, A.U. (1990). *Learning strategies in second language acquisition.* Cambridge: Cambridge University Press.

O'Malley, J.M., & Pierce, L.V. (1996). *Authentic assessment for English language learners: Practical approaches for teachers.* Reading, MA: Addison-Wesley.

Palinscar, A.C. & Brown, A.L. (1984). Reciprocal teaching of comprehension-fostering and comprehension monitoring activities, *Cognition and Instruction, 1,* 117–175.

Paris, S.G., Lipson., M.Y. & Wixson, K. (1983). Becoming a strategic reader. *Contemporary Educational Psychology, 8,* 293–316.

Peregoy, S.F., & Boyle, O.F. (1997). *Reading, writing, and learning in ESL: A resource book for K–12 teachers* (2nd ed.). New York: Longman.

Pressley, M. & Woloshyn, V. (Eds.) (1995). *Cognitive strategy instruction that really improves children's academic performance.* Cambridge, MA: Brookline Books.

Pressley, M., Johnson, C., Symons, S., McGoldrick, J.A., & Kurita, J.A. (1989). Strategies that improve children's memory and comprehension of text. *The Elementary School Journal, 90,* 3–32.

Ramirez, J., Yuen, S., Ramey, D., & Pasta, D. (1991). *Executive summary: Final Report: Longitudinal study of structure English immersion strategy, early-exit and late-exit transitional bilingual education programs for language-minority children.* (Contract No. 300087-0156). Submitted to the U.S. Department of Education. San Mateo: Aguirre International.

Readance, J., Bean, T., & Baldwin (1991). *Teaching reading in the content areas.* Dubuque, IA: Kendall Hunt.

Rosenblatt, L.M. (1991). Literacy theory. In J. Flood, J. Jensen, D. Flood, & J. Squire (Eds.), *Handbook of research on teaching the English-language arts.* New York: Macmillan.

Ruddell, M.R. (1997). *Teaching content reading and writing* (2nd ed.). Boston: Allyn & Bacon.

Rummelhart, D.E. (1995). Toward an interactive model of reading. In R.B. Ruddell, M.R. Ruddell, & Singer, H. (Eds.), *Theoretical models and processes of reading.* Newark, DE: International Reading Association.

Saville-Troike, M. (1984). What really matters in second lanuage learning for academic achievement? *TESOL Quarterly, 18,* 117–131.

Sheppard, K. (1995). *Content-ESL across the USA* (Volume I, Technical Report). Washington, DC: National Clearinghouse for Bilingual Education.

Short, D. (1991). *How to integrate language and content instruction: A training manual.* Washington, DC: Center for Applied Linguistics.

Short, D. (1994). Expanding middle-school horizons: Integrating language, culture and social studies. *TESOL Quarterly, 28*(3), 581–608.

Short, D. (1998). Social studies and assessment: Meeting the needs of students learning English. In S. Fradd & O. Lee (Eds.), *Creating Florida's multilingual global work force* (pp. VI-1–12). Tallahassee, FL: Florida Department of Education.

Short, D. (1999). Integrating language and content for effective sheltered instruction programs. In C. Faltis & P.Wolfe (Eds.), *So much to say: Adolescents, bilingualism, and ESL in the secondary school* (pp. 105–137). New York: Teachers College Press.

Sirotnik, K. (1983). What you see is what you get: Consistency, persistency, and mediocrity in classrooms. *Harvard Educational Review, 53,* 16–31.

Stanovich, K.E. (1986). Matthew effects in reading: Some consequences of individual differences in the acquisition of literacy. *Reading Research Quarterly, 21,* 360–406.

Teachers of English to Speakers of Other Languages (TESOL). (1997). *ESL standards for pre-K–12 students.* Alexandria, VA: Author.

Tharp, R., & Gallimore, R. (1988). *Rousing minds to life.* Cambridge: Cambridge University Press.

Tierney, R. & Pearson, P.D. (1994). Learning to learn from text: A framework for improving classroom practice. In R. Ruddell, M. Ruddell, & H. Singer (Eds.), *Theoretical models and processes of reading.* Fourth Edition. Newark, DE: International Reading Association.

Tompkins, G.E. (1997). *Literacy for the 21st century: A balanced approach.* Upper Saddle River, NJ: Merrill-Prentice-Hall.

U.S. Department of Education. (1997). *Excellence and accountability in teaching: A guide to U.S. Department of Education programs and resources.* Washington, DC: Author.

Vacca, R., & Vacca, J.A. (1998). *Content area reading: Literacy and learning across the curriculum* (6th ed.). New York: Longman.

Vogt, M.E. (2000). Content learning for students needing modifications: An issue of access. In M. McLaughlin and M.E. Vogt (Eds.), *Creativity and innovation in the content areas: A resource for intermediate, middle, and high school teachers.* Norwood, MA: Christopher-Gordon Publishers.

Vogt, M.E. (1995). *Jumpstarting: Providing support in advance rather than remediation.* Paper presented at the Annual Conference of the International Reading Association, Anaheim, CA.

Vogt, M.E. (1992). Strategies for leading readers into text: The pre-reading phase of a content lesson. In C. Hedley & D. Feldman (Eds.), *Literacy across the curriculum.* New York: Ablex.

Vogt, M.E., & Verga, M. (1998). Improving comprehension: Developing strategic readers. In C. Cox (Ed.), *Current research in practice.* Los Angeles: Los Angeles County Educational Consortium for the Improvement of Reading.

Vygotsky, L. (1978). *Mind and society: The development of higher psychological processes* (M. Cole, V. John-Steiner, S. Scribner, & E. Souberman, Eds. and trans.). Cambridge, MA: Harvard University Press.

Waggoner, D. (1999). Who are secondary newcomer and linguistically different youth? In C. Faltis & P. Wolfe (Eds.), *So much to say: Adolescents, bilingualism, and ESL in the secondary school* (pp. 13–41). New York: Teachers College Press.

Watson, K., & Young, B. (1986). Discourse for learning in the classroom. *Language Arts, 63*(2), 126–133.

Wong-Fillmore, L., & Valadez, C. (19 8 6). Teaching bilingual learners. In M. C. Wittrock (Ed.), *Handbook of research on teaching* (pp. 648–685). New York: Macmillan.

Zeichner, K. (1993). *Educating teachers for cultural diversity* (NCRTL Special Report). East Lansing, MI: Michigan State University, National Center for Research on Teacher Learning.

INDEX